The Demand for Money

The Demand for Money

Theories, Evidence, and Problems

Fourth Edition

David E. W. Laidler
University of Western Ontario – London

HarperCollins*CollegePublishers*

Acquisitions Editor: John Greenman
Project Editor: David Nickol
Design Supervisor: Mary Archondes
Cover Design: Mary Archondes
Production Administrator: Jeffrey Taub
Compositor: Circle Graphics
Printer and Binder: R. R. Donnelley & Sons Company
Cover Printer: New England Book Components

The Demand for Money: Theories, Evidence, and Problems, Fourth Edition

Library of Congress Cataloging-in-Publication Data

Laidler, David E. W.
    The demand for money : theories, evidence, and problems / David
E. W. Laidler. — 4th ed.
        p.   cm.
    Includes bibliographical references (p.   ) and index.
    ISBN 0-06-501098-1
    1. Demand for money.   2. Demand for money—Mathematical models.
I. Title.
HG226.5.L35   1993   92-11945
332.4'01—dc20   CIP

92 93 94 95   9 8 7 6 5 4 3 2 1

In Memory of
John Alphonse Laidler
January 19, 1899–August 2, 1991

Contents

PART TWO
THEORIES OF THE DEMAND FOR MONEY 39

Preface

The fourth edition of this text is designed to provide an account of the existing literature on the demand for money. It is technically accessible to readers who have completed, or are in the process of completing, an intermediate course in macroeconomic theory, and is often useful to more advanced students. It begins by showing how the demand-for-money function fits into short-run macroeconomic analysis, goes on to discuss alternative theories of the demand for money, and then, after giving an account of data and econometric problems, surveys existing empirical evidence and draws tentative conclusions about theoretical questions raised earlier.

Although the aim, intended readers, and outline remain much the same as in previous editions, the specific ways in which these tasks are undertaken have changed.

MACRO THEORY

In the book's first two editions, macro theory was confined to *IS-LM*. The third edition saw a major change, which is preserved here. Though the fixed price *IS-LM* model is still presented, it is now treated not as an end in itself, but as a necessary prelude to developing the demand side of an aggregate demand and supply framework in which the price level is endogenously determined. I am well aware that many introductory textbooks deploy the aggregate demand curve as a basic tool and confine allegedly more difficult *IS-LM* analysis to appendices. How their authors expect students who are not asked to master *IS-LM* to understand an even more subtle and complex device, for which *IS-LM* provides a logical underpinning, is quite beyond me. Those instructors, and surely there must be many of them, who share my bafflement about this matter will, I hope, find Part One of this book a useful aid in undoing the damage inflicted on their students by such introductory texts.

This edition pays more attention to the idea of rational expectations than its predecessor, in order to bring the analysis as close as possible to the usual content of an up-to-date intermediate macroeconomics course.

THEORIES OF THE DEMAND FOR MONEY

Part Two, dealing with theories of the demand for money, has undergone considerable expansion since the book's first edition. Fisher, Pigou, Keynes, Friedman, Baumol, and Tobin are still here, but I previously added a simple formal model of the precautionary demand for money and in this edition I have introduced accounts of Bennett McCallum's shopping-time model of the demand for money as a means of exchange and Paul Samuelson's overlapping generations approach to the asset demand for money.

DATA AND ECONOMETRICS

In the first two editions of this book, one chapter sufficed to deal with data problems and econometric issues. In the last edition, this treatment was expanded into a new Part Three, containing two chapters, and I have retained this format. I have made many changes of detail in this section of the book to reflect recent developments and have added new material describing the basic properties of co-integration and error-correction modeling, which are now becoming widely used in empirial work on the demand for money.

EMPIRICAL EVIDENCE

Part Four deals with empirical evidence and its implications. The first edition came close to providing a comprehensive survey of the then existing empirical literature on the demand for money, and its bibliography contained all of 47 references. That is about the same number I found necessary to add to this new edition to update it from 1986! I no longer make any claim to comprehensiveness in my coverage. The empirical literature on the demand for money is enormous. I can only express the belief that the selections from it with which I do deal are reasonably representative, and I apologize to the authors of the many useful papers that space limitations make it impossible to discuss.

In selecting material for explicit discussion, I have taken the position that a piece of work does not become less important just because it was done rather a long time ago with now old-fashioned techniques. Where a path-breaking study's results have proved robust over the years and the issues it deals with are currently relevant, I still devote considerable space to it. Thus, work done in the early 1960s on the interest elasticity of demand for money, to which I paid a good deal of attention in 1969, is still discussed in some detail. Where the issues seem to have become less important, or new techniques of investigation have superseded old ones and modified our knowledge, then my revisions have been more extensive. For example, there is less material on the interpretation of lagged dependent variables than in the previous edition, and what remains is there to enable the reader to understand why short-run dynamics have attracted so much attention in the last decade. At the same time, the treatment of those same dynamics has been extended to deal with their error-correction representations.

Most readers of this book are in the United States, and its coverage is therefore tilted somewhat toward work on that economy. Nevertheless, I have tried to give sufficient space to studies of other countries to convince readers that the issues analyzed in the literature on the demand for money have far more than parochial significance.

THE TONE OF THE BOOK

The first edition of this book presented a rather straightforward version of what we would now call a "monetarist" story about the demand for money and its implications; and it did so with considerable confidence. In 1986, I added the word *problems* to the book's subtitle, and I have retained this addition. One thing we have undoubtedly learned over the last two decades is that apparently definitive results, obtained with the very latest in sophisticated econometric techniques, can sometimes be undermined by the accumulation of further evidence. Of course, we should have known that at the outset, but there is nothing like a little firsthand experience to drive the lesson home.

The tone of this edition is intended to be more skeptical than that of the first, without being nihilistic. As the reader will discover, I believe that we have learned some important things about how the monetary sector operates, but I also believe that confidence in the robustness of our empirical knowledge can never be complete. I hope I have succeeded in striking an appropriate balance in dealing with this all-important matter.

ACKNOWLEDGMENTS

Willie J. Belton, Jr., Georgia Institute of Technology; Matthew Hyle, Winona State University; Raymond Lombra, The Pennsylvania State University; Gary Maggs, St. John Fisher College; Helmuth Milde, McGill University; and Patricia C. Mosser, Columbia University, were kind enough to make extensive suggestions about how this book could be revised. Had I taken every piece of advice they offered, the book would have grown inordinately large, but their input was invaluable in helping me organize my revision, and all have left a mark on this version of *The Demand for Money*. Toni Gravelle read and commented extensively on an earlier draft, and he, too, must be given credit for helping to shape the final form of this edition. I do, however, accept sole responsibility for any errors and omissions that the reader discovers in the following pages.

David E. W. Laidler

one

THE MACROECONOMIC FRAMEWORK

chapter *1*

The Role of the Demand Function

ELEMENTS OF SUPPLY AND DEMAND ANALYSIS

We study the demand for any item mainly so that we may make predictions about the consequences of changes in its supply. This statement is as true of money as of anything else, but in the case of money, it is all too easy to lose sight of the simple principle it expresses amid a mass of analytic complications. Let us illustrate this simple principle, with reference to the market for some good, X. Assume that no buyer or seller of X is sufficiently important that he or she alone can influence the price at which X trades. Assume also that expenditure on X is a sufficiently small part of expenditure in the economy as a whole that the market for X may be analyzed as if it operated in isolation from the markets for other goods. In such a market, the decisions of buyers and sellers are independent of one another, and we may characterize the rules according to which those decisions are made in terms of a supply curve and a demand curve, as we do in Figure 1.1. The curves show that the quantity of X supplied per unit of time, per week say, will rise with its price (p_x), and the quantity demanded will decrease.

Since we wish to illustrate the role of the demand function in economic analysis, let us look more closely at this latter relationship. To begin with, it is drawn on an "other things equal" basis. More specifically, elementary consumer theory tells us that, in addition to depending on its own price, the quantity demanded of X will depend

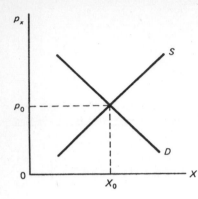

Figure 1.1 The supply and demand for a good X. p_0 is the equilibrium price of the good and X_0 is the equilibrium quantity bought and sold.

on consumers' income and the prices of other goods. Hence our demand curve is drawn for given values of these variables. Moreover, our assumption about the relative unimportance of X as an object of expenditures enables us to treat these variables as influencing the demand for X by their effects on its demand curve, but as not being influenced by happenings in the market for X. They are, in short, *exogenous* variables in our analysis.

Our supply curve tells us the quantities of X that sellers will wish to provide at various prices, and our demand curve tells us the quantities that buyers will wish to purchase. Because exchange is voluntary and because every act of sale is also an act of purchase, for these plans all to be realizable, for the market for X to be in *equilibrium*, the price of X must take a value at which these otherwise independent sets of plans are compatible with one another. That is, the value of this variable is determined at the intersection of the supply and demand curve. The price of X, one of the factors on which the demand for it depends, is thus determined within the model; it is an *endogenous* variable.

Now suppose that the quantity of X that sellers wish to supply at any given price increases by a particular amount, and that, whatever the reason for this, it does not also involve any change in the overall level of income prevailing in the economy or in the price of any other good. The supply curve of X will shift to the right from S_0 to S_1, and the demand curve will remain in place, as is shown in Figure 1.2. Plans that were compatible at the previously existing price no longer are. To restore that compatibility, some variable (or variables) on which the quantity of X demanded depends must change. By assumption, income and the prices of other goods are given, and so in this case it is the endogenous variable, the price of X, that must change, falling, as is shown in Figure 1.2, from p_0 to p_1. Just how much the price of X will change in the face of a given shift in its supply curve will, among other

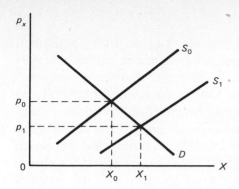

Figure 1.2 The effect of a shift of the supply curve on the price of X. As the supply curve shifts from S_0 to S_1, the equilibrium price of X falls from p_0 to p_1, and equilibrium quantity bought and sold rises from X_0 to X_1.

factors, depend on the sensitivity of the demand for X to its price. If demand is rather sensitive to price, then the demand curve will be relatively shallowly sloped and price will fall relatively little; if it is insensitive, the demand curve will be relatively steeply sloped and price will fall by a relatively large amount. This is illustrated in Figure 1.3(a); in Figure 1.3(b) it is shown that the slope of the supply curve is also a factor affecting the extent to which price falls in the face of a given increase in quantity of X supplied at any price.

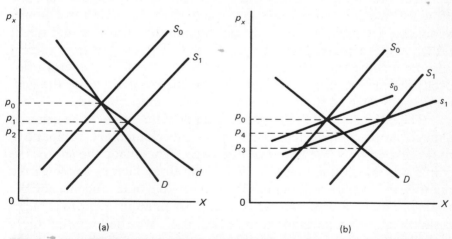

(a)   (b)

Figure 1.3 (a) The more shallowly sloped is the demand curve, the smaller is the effect of a given supply curve shift on the equilibrium price of X. If the demand curve is given by D, then when the supply curve shifts from S_0 to S_1, price falls from p_0 to p_2, but if demand is given by the more shallowly sloped d, the price falls only as far as p_1. (b) The more shallowly sloped is the supply curve of X, the less does its equilibrium price fall when the supply curve shifts to the right. The shift of S_0 to S_1 reduces equilibrium price from p_0 to p_3 but the equal rightward shift of s_0 to s_1 reduces prices only to p_4.

THE CASE OF MONEY

The foregoing analysis could hardly be more elementary, and yet it illustrates all of those fundamental and general characteristics of supply and demand analysis that underlie economists' particular concerns about the nature of the demand-for-money function. First, it shows that, in the face of a shift in the supply function of a particular item, at least one, but of course not necessarily only one, of the variables on which demand depends must change. Second, it shows that the extent to which such a variable (or variables) will change depends on the nature of the relationship between the variable in question and the quantity demanded of the item under analysis. Third, it shows that the outcome of a shift in a supply function, heavily conditioned though it is by the nature of the demand function, does not depend solely on the latter. Other elements (in the foregoing simple case, the slope of the supply function) must also be taken into consideration.

The case of money is a particularly important one for the application of these simple principles for a number of reasons. First, in virtually all contemporary economies, the nature of the supply function of money is such that, by manipulating variables that are directly under their control, the government can, within quite narrow limits, control the quantity of money supplied.[1] By manipulating the quantity of money supplied, the monetary authorities can therefore exert a systematic influence on at least some of the factors on which the quantity of money demanded depends. As we shall see, among the variables that might influence the demand for money are interest rates, the level of real national income (and therefore employment), and the general price level. The importance of the behavior of these variables for the economic well-being of the community is surely quite obvious.

The interaction of the supply and demand for money is, in general, a much more complicated matter than the elementary competitive market experiments we have just discussed. What made the analysis so simple was the assumption that two of the three factors on which the quantity of X demanded could be treated as exogenous. Income and the prices of other goods were held constant, so all adjustment to changes in supply was concentrated on the price of X. We shall see that there might be circumstances in which the consequences of changes in the

---

[1] To say that the authorities can control the money supply if they wish is not to say that they will in fact do so. For example, in an open economy, the government may decide to operate a fixed exchange rate for its currency. It can implement such a policy only by standing ready to buy and sell units of foreign exchange at a fixed price in exchange for domestic money, but if it does that, it clearly cannot control the amount of domestic money it issues.

supply of money impinge on only one of the factors determining demand, but we cannot take it for granted that this is always the case. We must consider the possibility that all of the factors on which the demand for money depends will respond simultaneously to a change in its supply, and hence we must be prepared to analyze their interaction if we are to understand the consequences of a change in the supply of money.

We cannot carry out such analyses with a simple supply and demand apparatus. We need a model of the whole economy rather than of one isolated market. Even with the aid of such a model, we cannot answer all the questions we might like to ask about the consequences of changes in the supply of money on the basis of knowledge of its demand function alone. Other properties of the economy are also important. Just why this is so and what limits it might impose on our knowledge are best discussed in terms of a model that permits us simultaneously to analyze the interaction of the supply and demand for money and the factors that underlie the demand for money. It is to the exposition of such a model that we turn in the next two chapters. In working through that exposition, the reader should try to keep in mind the main purpose of the exercise. First, it is to develop a framework in terms of which we may analyze the interaction of the supply and demand for money with a view to understanding the consequences for the factors that determine the demand for money of shifts in its supply. Second, in the light of that analysis, it is to enable us to formulate questions about the nature of the demand-for-money function, which will enable us better to understand the interaction in question.

chapter *2*

The Demand for Money in a Fixed Price Level Macroeconomic Model

INTRODUCTORY COMMENT

Macroeconomics is controversial. There is no single model upon whose validity all practitioners agree. One area of disagreement of particular importance is the behavior of money wages and money prices. If these are extremely flexible in their response to shocks to the economy, then so will be the general price level. If they are not, then the price level will be slow moving, or "sticky." This matters because the general price level is one of the key variables upon which the demand for money depends. If the price level is flexible, then it is free to move to absorb the consequences of shifts in exogenous factors such as the supply of money, and their effects on other variables, notably real income and employment, will be relatively muted. If the price level is sticky, those consequences will spill over onto real income and employment and cause them to fluctuate relatively more.

This book is not the place to discuss in detail controversies about the extent of price stickiness and its causes. In what follows we shall first construct a macroeconomic model in which the price level is assumed to be rigidly fixed and investigate its properties. Those readers who regard price stickiness as important in the real world may treat the model as dealing with a limiting case of the phenomenon and hence as a device that yields insights into and enables questions to be formulated about how actual economies function. Readers who doubt the empirical relevance of price stickiness will want to treat the model with more skepticism. However, they should not ignore it for the simple reason that once we have developed it, we shall modify it by dropping the price stickiness assumption. To a reader who believes in price flexibility, the properties of a fixed price level macro model may not be empirically interesting in their own right, but it is still necessary to understand them as a stepping-stone to understanding how a macroeconomic model in which the price level is flexible functions.

THE FIXED PRICE MODEL

A macroeconomic model in which the price level is assumed fixed enables us to analyze the determination of two of the three variables upon which the demand for money is commonly thought to depend, namely, the level of real national income and the level of a representative interest rate to which we shall refer as "the rate of interest."[1] If the level of real income is to be able to respond to changes in the level of aggregate demand for goods and services, there must exist in the economy enough productive resources to meet any level of aggregate demand that may arise, and the reader might therefore find it helpful to think of the model economy we are about to analyze as being characterized by significant unemployment.

In our economy, expenditure is made by households, in which case it is called *consumption*, by firms, in which case it is called *investment*, or by the government, in which case it is called *government expenditure*. Conventional assumptions are made about the determinants of these components of expenditure. Consumption is thought of as being an increasing function of disposable income and, since it is for the moment convenient to deal with an economy in which there are no taxes, this means that consumption can be treated simply as a function of income. It is also postulated that the marginal propensity to consume is less than 1. Investment is thought of as being negatively related to the rate of interest, and government expenditure is treated as exogenous, that is, as a variable that may affect, but is not affected by the other variables in the model. This income-expenditure subsystem of our model is in equilibrium when the level of expenditure in the economy, as determined by these functions, is equal to the level of income. In Figure 2.1

---

[1] Because the model we are dealing with here has a fixed price level, it is unnecessary to deal with the distinction between the nominal interest rate and the real interest rate, the latter being the nominal rate adjusted to account for the effects over time of inflation on the purchasing power of the capital value of bonds. With a fixed price level, there can be no inflation to make adjustments for.

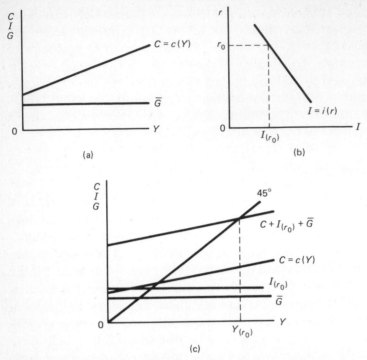

Figure 2.1 The simple geometry of income determination. C is consumption, I is investment, G is government expenditure, Y is income, and r is the rate of interest; c and i denote functional relationships; the bar over G indicates that it is an exogenous variable.

the reader will find the system set out in familiar geometric terms. (*Note:* In the figure labels, many variables carry subscripts in parentheses. This notation indicates that the variable carrying the subscript takes the value it does given that the variable in the subscript takes the value mentioned in the subscript. For example, in Figure 2.1, $Y_{(r_0)}$ indicates the value income takes given that the rate of interest takes the value r_0.)

Figure 2.1(a) shows the consumption function $C = c(Y)$ and the exogenous level of government expenditure $\overline{G}$; the investment function $I = i(r)$ is plotted in Figure 2.1(b). If it is assumed that the rate of interest is fixed at level r_0, the level of investment will be determined at $I_{(r_0)}$. In Figure 2.1(c), this level of investment is added to consumption and government expenditure to produce the curve $C + I_{(r_0)} + \overline{G}$, which gives the relationship implicit in the model between the level of aggregate expenditure and the level of income. The 45° line plots all the points at which aggregate expenditure measured on the vertical axis can be equal to income measured on the horizontal axis. The aggregate expenditure curve crosses this line at the only point at which expenditure as determined by the functional relationships involved in the model is equal to the level of income. $Y_{(r_0)}$ is then the equilibrium level of income, but only so long as the rate of interest remains at r_0. If it takes some other value, so will the level of investment, and the equilibrium level of income will be different.

Implicit in the foregoing analysis is a relationship between the value of the rate of interest and the equilibrium level of income, and it is easy enough to make this relationship explicit. Figure 2.2(a) shows the relationship between investment and the rate of interest. Figure 2.2(b) shows various relationships between aggregate expenditure and income, each based on the same consumption function and level of government expenditure, but each assuming that the rate of interest takes a different value: r_1 is a lower interest rate than r_0, and r_2 is lower still. The lower the rate of interest, the higher the level of investment, as Figure 2.2(a) tells us, and the higher the level of investment, the higher the level of aggregate expenditure. Thus, in Figure 2.2(b), $C + I_{(r_2)} + \bar{G}$, lies above $C + I_{(r_1)} + \bar{G}$, which in turn lies above $C + I_{(r_0)} + \bar{G}$. Corresponding to each of these aggregate expenditure curves is an equilibrium level of income. As can readily be seen, the

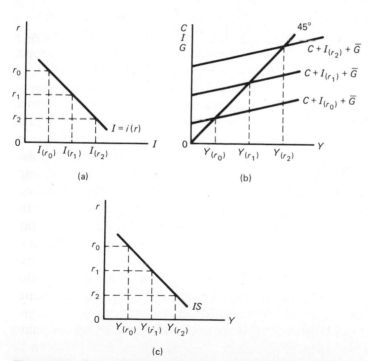

(a)

(b)

(c)

Figure 2.2   The equilibrium relationship between the rate of interest and the level of income implicit in the model of the real-goods market.

lower the level of the rate of interest, the higher this level of income. This relationship between the rate of interest and the equilibrium level of income is plotted as the curve *IS* in Figure 2.2(c). (*IS* refers to the fact that in a model without government expenditure, any point along this curve is one at which investment is equal to saving. It is now general to use this label for any curve showing real-goods market equilibrium.)

The income-expenditure system portrayed in Figure 2.2(c) can tell us what the equilibrium level of income is if we know the rate of interest or, for that matter, what the rate of interest is if we know the equilibrium level of income. The clue to completing our model, so that income and the interest rate are both determinate, lies in the fact that people not only make decisions about current flows of goods and services, about how much to consume, about how much to invest, and so on, but also about stocks, about how to hold their wealth. As we shall now see, it is at this point that the demand-for-money function appears on the scene.

There are many ways of holding wealth.[2] An individual can own consumer durable goods, corporate equities, bonds, and so forth, but for present purposes it is sufficient to assume that only two types of assets are available—money and bonds. The problem facing individuals as far as holding their wealth is concerned is how to allocate it between money and bonds. If we take the level of wealth as given, then if money is not held, bonds must be, and the problem reduces to that of how much money to hold. The bulk of this book is devoted to examining various hypotheses about what variables are involved in this decision, but for the moment we merely assert a commonly held simple hypothesis about the determinants of the demand for money, already alluded to above, and see how it can be fitted into our model.

Because money is a universally acceptable means of exchange, it is usual to argue that the demand for it increases with real income. Moreover, because bond holding is the alternative to money holding, interest income is forgone by holding money. The higher the rate of interest, the higher is the opportunity cost of holding money, and so, it is argued, the lower is the demand for money. As to the supply side of the money market, it is usual to assume as a first approximation that the quantity of money supplied is completely under the control of monetary authorities whose behavior may be treated as exogenous to the model. As with any supply and demand problem, we have equilibrium when the supply and demand for money are equal.

Figure 2.3 deals with all this in geometric terms. We measure

---

[2] Here we are referring only to what is nowadays called *nonhuman* wealth. The relevance of a more inclusive concept of wealth that encompasses human wealth to the analysis of the demand for money is discussed on pages 57–59.

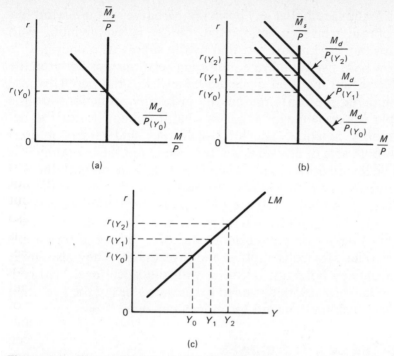

Figure 2.3   The equilibrium relationship between the rate of interest and the level of income implicit in the model of the money market. M is the quantity of money and P is the price level, so that M/P is the quantity of money measured in units of constant purchasing power. The subscripts s and d stand for supplied and demanded, and the bar over M_s indicates that it is an exogenous variable.

money in units of constant purchasing power and denote its quantity M/P. This detail is of no significance so long as we hold P, the general price level, constant, but it becomes important when we relax this assumption. In Figure 2.3(a) we graph the demand for money as a function of the rate of interest at the level of income Y_0. With a given money supply and price level, we have equilibrium when the rate of interest is equal to r_{Y_0}. Note, however, that this is an equilibrium value only so long as the level of income is at Y_0, as Figure 2.3(b) shows clearly enough. Here Y_2 is a higher level of income than Y_1, which in turn is higher than Y_0. Since the demand for money at any rate of interest increases when the level of income rises, the whole curve relating the demand for money to the rate of interest shifts to the right as income increases. With a given money supply, this involves the equilibrium interest rate's rising. As far as equilibrium between the supply and demand for money is concerned, there is thus implicit in the model a positive relationship between the level of income and the rate of interest. This is plotted in Figure 2.3(c) and labeled, as is customary, *LM*.

(*LM* refers to the fact that at any point on this curve, "liquidity prefer-ence," a phrase which in this simple model is synonymous with "demand for money," is just satisfied by the supply of money.)

We now have two different equilibrium relationships between the rate of interest and the level of income. However, the people whose decisions underlie the consumption and investment functions are the same people whose behavior vis-à-vis wealth holding yields the de-mand-for-money function. The level of income and rate of interest involved in both sets of decisions are the same, and the economy as a whole can be in equilibrium only when their values lie on both the *LM* curve and the *IS* curve. Obviously, this can occur only where the two curves intersect. In Figure 2.4, the two curves are plotted against the same axes, and the equilibrium level of income is given at Y_e with the rate of interest having an equilibrium value of r_e. These in turn imply equilibrium values for consumption and investment. They also imply equilibrium money holdings, because, with the price level held con-stant, our model has now determined for us the values of the two other variables on which the demand for money depends.

SHIFTS OF THE *LM* AND *IS* CURVES

If the demand for money depends on the price level, real income, and the interest rate, and if we hold the first of these constant, then it follows that if equilibrium between the supply and demand for money is to be maintained, a change in the quantity of money supplied must cause the latter two determinants of the demand for money to change in some combination or other. The *IS-LM* system we have just developed en-ables us to make more precise statements about this matter. Figure 2.5 is essentially the same as Figure 2.3. In panel (a) we show the demand for money as a function of the rate of interest at two (rather than three,

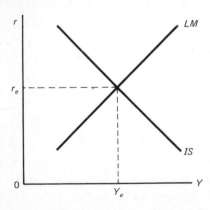

Figure 2.4 The determination in the complete model of the equilibrium levels of the interest rate and of income.

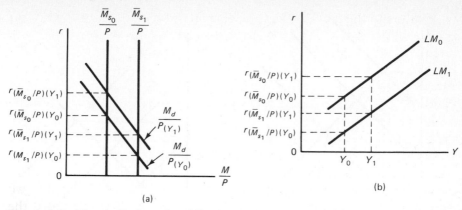

Figure 2.5 The derivation of a shift of the LM curve caused by an increase in the money supply.

in order to maintain geometric clarity) different levels of real income. We then consider what would happen if the supply of money were to be increased from $\overline{M}_{s_0}$ to $\overline{M}_{s_1}$. It is clear from panel (a) that, for any level of income, the rate of interest would have to fall in order to maintain equilibrium between the supply and demand for money. This in turn implies that the LM curve, which, in the initial situation, is at LM_0, shifts to the right to LM_1, as in panel (b). By similar reasoning, it can be shown that a decrease in the money supply will shift the LM curve to the left. If, in Figure 2.6(a), we superimpose such shifts of the LM on a given IS curve, we may deduce how a change in the quantity of money will affect the level of income and the value of the interest rate. Clearly, the precise amounts by which a change in the money supply will affect interest and output will depend on two sets of factors. First they will depend on the distance the LM curve shifts and on its slope; the distance and the slope, in turn, depend on the demand-for-money function. Second, they will depend on the slope of the IS curve, which is determined by the properties of the consumption and investment functions.

We shall return to some of these matters in more detail in a while, but for now note that, as Figure 2.6(b) shows, just as we need to know about the properties of the IS curve if we are to be able to make statements about the consequences of a shift of the LM curve, so if we are to say anything about the effects of a shift of the IS curve, we must know about the properties of the LM curve. Thus, knowledge of the nature of the demand-for-money function is necessary to make predictions not only about the consequences of a change in the supply of money, but also about the consequences of any factor that causes the

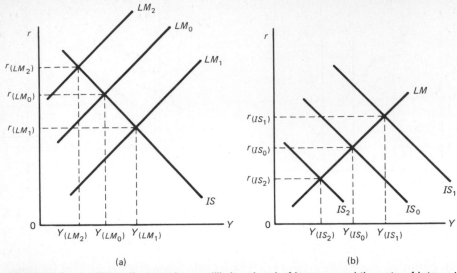

(a)   (b)

Figure 2.6 (a) The effect on the equilibrium level of income and the rate of interest of shifting the *LM* curve. The shift from LM_0 to LM_1 is the result of an increase in the money supply and that from LM_0 to LM_2 of a decrease. (b) The effects on income and the interest rate of shifts of the *IS* curve to the right (from IS_0 to IS_1) and to the left (from IS_0 to IS_2).

IS curve to shift. A glance back at Figure 2.2 will be helpful at this stage, since it is there that the derivation of this curve is shown.

Recall that the negative relationship between the rate of interest and the level of income embodied in the *IS* curve arises because investment is a component of aggregate expenditure and because it increases as the rate of interest falls. Every point on the *IS* curve involves a given rate of interest generating a certain level of aggregate expenditure. Three factors can cause the *IS* curve to shift. If, as in Figure 2.7(a), the relationship between the rate of interest and the level of investment shifts to the right, this implies a higher level of aggregate expenditure at any level of the rate of interest, as shown in Figure 2.7(b), so that the *IS* curve shifts to the right, as shown in Figure 2.7(c). A similar argument follows in reverse. If the level of government expenditure increases, the level of aggregate expenditure increases for any given level of the rate of interest, so that the *IS* curve again shifts to the right. Figure 2.8 shows this. A cut in government expenditure has the opposite effect.

The third factor, namely, a shift in the relationship between consumption and income, needs looking at with a little care, since it is by shifting the consumption function that taxes have their main macroeconomic effect on the economy. Recall that consumption depends on disposable income, and consider Figure 2.9(a) in which taxes are ini-

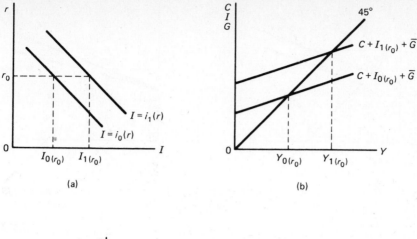

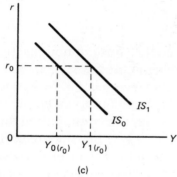

Figure 2.7 The derivation of a shift of the IS curve caused by a shift of the investment function.

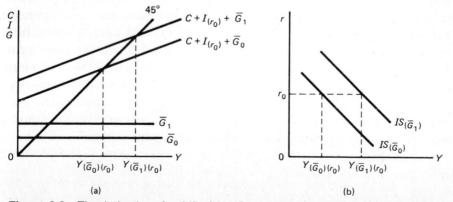

Figure 2.8 The derivation of a shift of the IS curve (b) caused by a change in the level of government expenditure (a). $\bar{G}_1 > \bar{G}_0$.

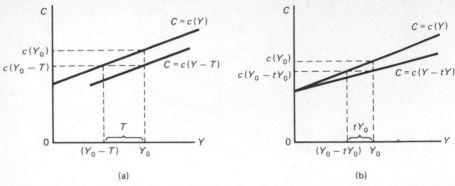

Figure 2.9   The effect on the consumption function of introducing (a) a fixed level of taxation T and (b) proportional taxation at the rate t. Note that a change in taxes is equal to an opposite change in disposable income, so that the effect of such a change on consumption at a given level of national income is to reduce it by the marginal propensity to consume times the change in taxes.

tially assumed to be zero so that the consumption function is first given by $C = c(Y)$. If a tax of a fixed amount T is levied, the level of income Y_0 will correspond to a disposable income of $Y_0 - T$, and consumption will now be equal to $c(Y_0 - T)$. A similar argument holds for any level of income. In the presence of a tax, the consumption function must be shifted to the right to $C = c(Y - T)$ by the amount of the tax in order that it will still enable us to determine the level of consumption given the level of before-tax income. This is equivalent to shifting the consumption function downward by an amount equal to the marginal propensity to consume times the amount of the tax, as should be clear from an inspection of Figure 2.9(a).[3]

In general, an increase in taxes shifts the consumption function downward and a cut in taxes shifts it up, shifting the aggregate expenditure curve in the same direction and by the same amount. Thus, an increase in taxes shifts the *IS* curve to the left, and a cut in taxes shifts it to the right. Although we have here discussed cuts in the *amount* of taxes, the same conclusions follow for alterations in tax *rates*. A change in a tax rate can be converted into a change in the amount of taxes paid by multiplying the change in the rate by the level of income. The only analytic difference here is that the shift in the consumption function is no longer a parallel one. This is shown in Figure 2.9(b).

The implications of the preceding discussion are of considerable

---

[3] The reader who wishes to understand what is going on should try to prove that an equal increase in government expenditure and taxes will shift the *IS* curve to the right by the amount of the increase in government expenditure, that is, that the balanced-budget multiplier is equal to 1.

importance. Shifts in the investment function, which many economists would argue are both frequent and difficult to predict in the real world, influence real income and interest rates (in our fixed price level model) by causing the *IS* curve to shift. Governments implement their fiscal policies through changing their levels of expenditure and taxes, and changes in these factors also affect real income and the interest rate by shifting the *IS* curve. In turn, the manner in which the consequences of *IS* curve shifts are divided between the level of income and the interest rate depends on the slope of the *LM* curve. Thus, if we wish to say anything precise about the extent to which fluctuations in investment will lead to fluctuations in real income and, therefore, employment, or about the extent to which fiscal policy can be used to iron out such fluctuations, knowledge of the nature of the demand-for-money function is required, just as much as it is required if we are to say anything about the consequences of monetary policy.

ALTERNATIVE ASSUMPTIONS ABOUT THE RELATIONSHIP BETWEEN THE INTEREST RATE AND THE DEMAND FOR MONEY

It has been assumed throughout this chapter that the demand for money is stably and negatively related to the rate of interest. This is a key assumption in the derivation of the upward-sloping *LM* curve on which so many of our conclusions rest. Some economists have suggested, however, that the demand for money is likely to be so insensitive to the rate of interest as to make it a reasonable approximation to treat it as not related to that variable at all. Other economists have suggested that when the interest rate is very low relative to its normal level, the demand for money is so sensitive to the interest rate as to make it worthwhile to treat the relationship as one of infinite elasticity, a so-called *liquidity trap*.

The theoretical bases of these suggestions are taken up in Part II of this book, but it is worthwhile now to look at the effects that these different postulates have on the behavior of our model. Figure 2.10 depicts demand functions for money drawn on various assumptions concerning the role of the interest rate. Panel (a) depicts the usual case in which the relationship between the demand for money and the interest rate is assumed to be negative. Panel (b) assumes there is no relationship between the demand for money and the rate of interest, but the higher the level of income, the greater is the quantity of money demanded. In this case, the demand function becomes a series of vertical lines, those further to the right being associated with higher income levels. Panel (c) assumes that at r^*, the demand for money

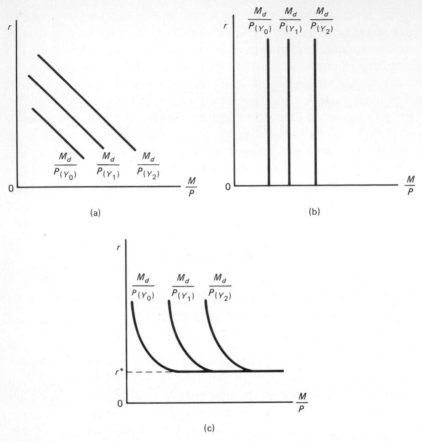

Figure 2.10 Demand-for-money functions drawn on different assumptions about the relationship between the demand for money and the rate of interest: $Y_2 > Y_1 > Y_0$.

becomes completely elastic with respect to the rate of interest. At interest rates greater than r^*, the demand for money increases with income, but the curves drawn for different levels of income all converge and become perfectly elastic at r^*, because at this interest rate level, increases in the level of income are not capable of causing an already unlimited demand for money to increase further.

Let us now look at the implications of these hypotheses about the demand for money for the shape of the LM curve. The proposition that the demand for money is insensitive to the rate of interest implies that the LM curve is a vertical line, as shown in Figure 2.11(b). An equilibrium in which the demand for money is equal to a given money supply can occur at one, and only one, level of income if the demand for money is a continuously increasing function of that variable and depends on no other. The opposite proposition about the relationship between the

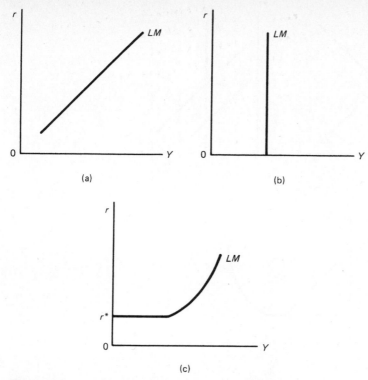

Figure 2.11 *LM* curves derived from the demand-for-money functions portrayed in Figure 2.10.

demand for money and the rate of interest, namely, that the relationship can be one of infinite rather than zero elasticity of demand, produces an analogously opposite implication for the *LM* curve. Though it is positively sloped above r^*, it becomes horizontal at that level of the interest rate. This is shown in Figure 2.11(c). Figure 2.11(a) reproduces the *LM* curve used earlier.

   Given the *LM* curves that they imply, we can investigate the consequences for the behavior of the complete model of these various assumptions about the relationship between the demand for money and the rate of interest. Figure 2.12 deals with the effects of shifting the *IS* curve. The results differ quite dramatically depending on what form the *LM* curve is assumed to take. Panel (a) presents results based on an upward-sloping *LM* curve, which show that the level of income and the interest rate rise and fall together as the *IS* curve shifts. Panel (b) shows the results of no relationship between the demand for money and the rate of interest. The only effect of shifting the *IS* curve in this case is to raise and lower the rate of interest. Panel (c) shows that in the case

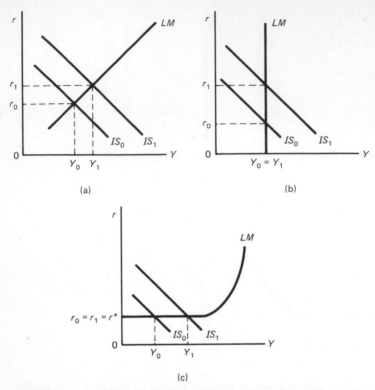

Figure 2.12   The effects of shifting the *IS* curve given different forms of the *LM* curve.

of a horizontal *LM* curve, all the effects of shifting the *IS* curve fall on the level of income and none on the rate of interest.

   Figure 2.13 deals with the consequences of shifting the *LM* curve. Panel (a) shows the upward-sloping *LM* curve case for purposes of comparison. Panel (b) shows that when the demand for money is completely interest-inelastic, shifts of the *LM* curve influence both the level of income and the rate of interest. For a given shift of the *LM* curve to the right, the changes in both variables are greater than when there is zero interest elasticity of demand for money, but the resulting level of income depends only on the location of the new *LM* curve and not on any property of the *IS* curve. Panel (c) shows that when the demand for money is perfectly interest-elastic, so long as one is operating in the region of the *LM* curve where the rate of interest is down at r^*, shifts in the curve alter neither the rate of interest nor the level of income, implying that in such circumstances changes in the quantity of money have no discernible effects on any of the variables that concern us here. These last two results may be restated in terms of the simple principles

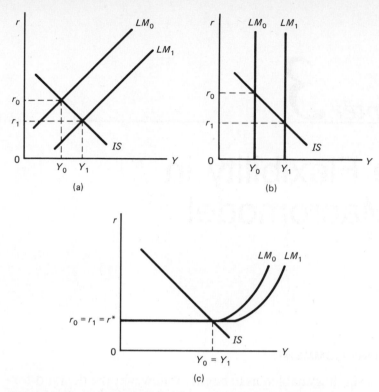

Figure 2.13   The effects of shifting *LM* curves of different forms.

of supply and demand analysis developed in the previous chapter. The first result amounts to saying that if we remove the interest rate as a determinant of the demand for money and hold the price level constant, then real income is the only variable left to adjust when it becomes necessary to adapt the quantity of money demanded to a change in its supply. The second result simply confirms that if, at a particular level of the interest rate, people are willing to hold an indefinitely large quantity of money, then, when the quantity of money supplied increases, there is no need for any variable to adjust in order to get it willingly held.

chapter *3*

Price Flexibility in the Macromodel

INTRODUCTORY COMMENT

Our analysis so far has enabled us to begin to show why the demand-for-money function is an important relationship. It has also enabled us to say something about specific aspects of the relationship, notably those involving the rate of interest, which might be worth particularly close investigation. However, all of our results have come from a model in which the price level is held constant; and not only is the price level an important endogenous, and far from constant, variable in the real world, but it is also, as we have already asserted, an important determinant of the demand for money. By treating this variable as an exogenous constant, we have considerably simplified our analysis of the interaction of the supply and demand for money, but there can be no guarantee that in simplifying our analysis, we have not also rendered it misleading. The only way to assuage our doubts about this issue is to relax our assumption of a constant price level and see how this step changes the nature of our model.

NOMINAL MONEY AND REAL MONEY

If we are to deal with a flexible price level, it is important first of all to distinguish between *nominal money*, measured in units of current purchasing power, and *real money*, measured in units of constant purchasing power. As we shall show later, economic theory leads to the prediction that the demand for nominal money is proportional to the price level; and this in turn means that the demand for real money is independent of the price level, varying only with real income and the interest rate. A glance back at Figures 2.3, 2.5, and 2.10 will confirm that our analysis of the interaction of the supply and demand for money does in fact deal with money measured in real terms. When the price level is held constant, any change in the supply of nominal money is also a change in the quantity of real money, and so this just-mentioned property of our analysis did not need to be stressed earlier. It does now, because the supply of money the monetary authorities can control in any actual economy is the nominal supply. Given the *nominal* money supply, what the *real* quantity of money will be depends on the *price level*. For a given nominal quantity of money, the lower the price level, the proportionately higher will be the quantity of real money and vice versa. The effects on our *IS-LM* model of decreasing (increasing) the price level by a given proportional amount while holding the quantity of nominal money constant are identical to those of increasing (decreasing) the quantity of nominal money by an equal proportion while holding the price level constant. This must be the case because, as we have seen, the variable measured on the horizontal axis of our demand for money diagram (for example, Figure 2.3) is M/P, nominal money divided by the price level or, equivalently, real money.

THE AGGREGATE DEMAND CURVE

Our *IS-LM* model has implications about the interrelationship of the price level and the level of real income. For a given *IS* curve (with all that the phrase implies about the constancy of government expenditures and taxes, not to mention stability of the consumption and investment functions), a given nominal money supply M_{s_0}, and a given price level P_0, we have in Figure 3.1(a) an equilibrium level of real income Y_0. If the price level were to fall successively from P_0 to P_1 to P_2, the *LM* curve would shift rightward from LM_0 to LM_1 to LM_2 and the level of real income would increase from Y_0 to Y_1 to Y_2. We plot in Figure 3.1(b) all pairs of real income and price level values generated in a manner exactly analogous to that in which we constructed our original *IS* and *LM* curves (see Figures 2.2 and 2.3, respectively) in order to create what is usually called an *aggregate demand curve*.

This label can be misleading. To begin with, the curve *AD* in Figure 3.1(b) is not a behavior relationship of the type we called a demand curve when carrying out the analysis embodied in Figures 1.1–1.3.

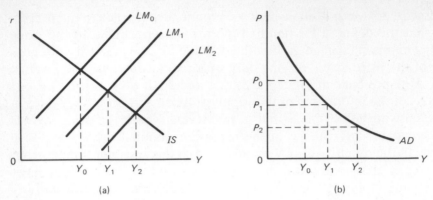

Figure 3.1 (a) For a given level of the nominal money supply M_{so}, the lower the price level, the further to the right does the *LM* curve lie and the higher is the equilibrium level of income. LM_0, LM_1, and LM_2 are associated with successively lower price levels P_0, P_1, and P_2. (b) The curve *AD* ("aggregate demand") makes explicit the relationship between the price level and the level of real income implicit in panel (a).

Rather it is a locus line that embodies the interaction of a number of behavior relationships as they determine (on certain assumptions about what is to be held constant, which we have already specified) those combinations of real income and price level that are compatible with equilibrium in our *IS-LM* system. Second, and more subtly, it is not even the case that the relationships embodied in that *IS-LM* system deal only with the demand side of the economy. Recall that in deriving the *IS* curve, which underlies the curve labeled *AD*, we assumed that, at every point on it, aggregate demand in the economy, the sum of consumption, investment, and government expenditure, was satisfied by aggregate supply. That is the meaning of deriving points on the *IS* curve from the intersection of the curves labeled $C + I + G$ with the 45° line as we did in Figure 2.2. Be that as it may, the term *aggregate demand curve* is well established, and misleading though it is, we label the curve whose properties we are about to discuss *AD*.

Consider an economy characterized by the conventionally sloped *IS* and *LM* curves portrayed in Figure 3.1(a). In this economy, for a given *LM* curve, anything that shifts the *IS* curve to the right (left) will increase (decrease) the level of income compatible with equilibrium. It will therefore shift the *AD* curve to the right (left). Also, an increase (decrease) in the nominal money supply requires a proportionally higher (lower) price level in order to maintain a given equilibrium level of real income. Hence, an increase (decrease) in the nominal money supply shifts the *AD* curve upward (downward) by a proportional

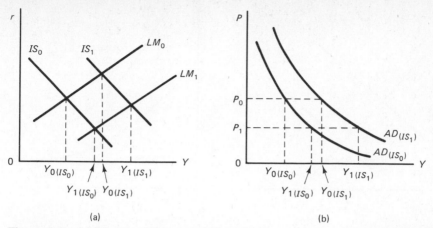

Figure 3.2 (a) The two *LM* curves LM_0 and LM_1 are drawn on the assumption that the nominal quantity of money is constant, but the price level P_0 underlying the former is higher than P_1 underlying the latter. The further to the right is the *IS* curve, the higher is the equilibrium level of income associated with a given *LM* curve. (b) The relationships between real income and the price level implicit in panel (a) are here made explicit. As the *IS* curve is shifted to the right, a higher level of income is associated with any given price level, so the curve *AD* also shifts to the right.

amount. These matters are illustrated in Figures 3.2(a) and (b) and 3.3(a) and (b), respectively. (*Note:* The seemingly arbitrary distinction between rightward and upward shifts implicit here is not in fact arbitrary, for reasons that will soon be apparent.)

Earlier we discussed how the properties of the *IS-LM* system are affected by special assumptions concerning the sensitivity of the demand for money to the rate of interest, and it should not surprise anyone to learn that these assumptions also have implications for the *AD* curve. First, if the demand for money is independent of the rate of interest, shifts in the *IS* curve do not change the level of real income; nor do such shifts move the *AD* curve whose location in this case is determined solely by the interaction of the supply and demand for money. Second, if, in addition to being independent of the rate of interest, the demand for real balances is proportional to real income,

$$\frac{M_d}{P} = kY \tag{3.1}$$

then a simple rearrangement of this expression combined with the requirement that the supply and demand for money be equal to one another yields

$$\overline{M}_s = M_d = kPY \tag{3.2}$$

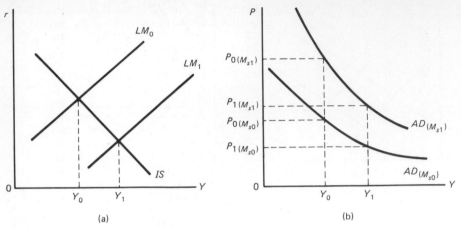

Figure 3.3   (a) The curve LM_0 is drawn first on the assumption that the money supply is M_{so} and the price level $P_{0(M_{so})}$ and the curve LM_1 on the assumption that the money supply is M_{so} but the price level is at a lower level $P_{1(M_{so})}$. For a given IS curve, the AD curve implied by these LM curves is drawn as $AD_{(M_{so})}$ in panel (b). Now suppose that the nominal money supply is at some higher level M_{s1}. There is a price level $P_{0(M_{s1})}$ which exceeds $P_{0(M_{so})}$ by the same proportion in which M_{s1} exceeds M_{so}, and if it rules, LM_0 is the relevant LM curve. Thus, with this new quantity of money, Y_0 is still the equilibrium level of real income when this new higher price level rules. An exactly parallel argument holds with respect to LM curve LM_1. (b) The relationships between prices and real income implicit in panel (a) is here made explicit. Specifically, at each level of real income the equilibrium price level is proportionately higher the higher is the nominal money supply.

so that

$$PY = \frac{1}{k}\overline{M}_s \qquad (3.3)$$

The term PY, however, is simply another name for the value of national income measured in units of current purchasing power, or nominal income. In this case, nominal income is determined solely by the supply of money. If the product of P and Y is a constant, then the curve linking them is a rectangular hyperbola, as in Figure 3.4.

   If we make the polar opposite assumption about the relationship between the demand for money and the rate of interest, namely, that at some low but positive level of the interest rate it becomes one of perfect elasticity, then the aggregate demand curve is downward sloping at "high" values of the price level, which correspond, for a given nominal money supply, to "low" quantities of real money, but becomes vertical at that level of real income (call it Y^*) corresponding to the sum of consumption, investment, and government expenditure generated at

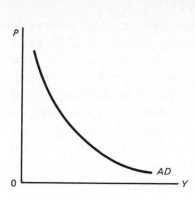

Figure 3.4 The *AD* curve is a rectangular hyperbola if the demand for real money balances is independent of the rate of interest and proportional to real income. Because, in this case, shifts of the *IS* curve do not change real income, they do not shift the *AD* curve. Shifts in the nominal money supply do shift the *AD* curve up in proportion, and because it is a property of the rectangular hyperbola that the product of the variable measured on the vertical axis and that on the horizontal is a constant, this implies that money income varies in proportion to the nominal money supply.

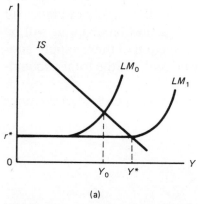

(a)

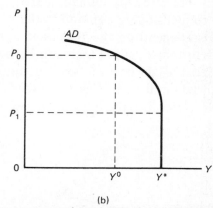

(b)

Figure 3.5 (a) With a given quantity of nominal money, the lower the price level, the further to the right does the *LM* curve lie, but with a liquidity trap at r^* the level of income cannot exceed Y^*. Thus, as the price level falls from P_0 to P_1, the level of income increases from Y_0 to Y^* but only to this latter level. (b) The relationship between the price level and real income for a given nominal quantity of money implicit in panel (a) is here made explicit. At Y^* the *AD* curve becomes vertical.

r^*, the value of the interest rate at which the demand for money becomes perfectly interest-elastic. Such an *AD* curve is shown in Figure 3.5. Y^*, along with the whole *AD* curve, may be shifted rightward by any factor that shifts the underlying *IS* curve rightward, but it cannot be moved by a change in the nominal money supply, which will affect the *AD* curve only at levels of income below Y^*, shifting it, as I have remarked above, upward.[1]

----

[1] The reader who is unsure of the relationship between the *IS-LM* apparatus and the *AD* curve will find it instructive to derive these results explicitly.

THE LONG-RUN AGGREGATE SUPPLY CURVE

By itself, an AD curve, no matter what its precise form, does not enable us to say anything about the consequences for real income and the price level of changes in the supply of money. To close the system, we need a complementary relationship, an *aggregate supply curve*, and we shall first derive the *long-run* version of this curve. The meaning of the adjective will emerge in the course of our discussion. Consider an economy in which the stock of capital is constant, or at least growing so slowly that it may be treated as if constant. In this economy, output will vary with labor input. With capital being constant, the relationship will display diminishing returns to labor, as shown in Figure 3.6(a). Suppose now that perfect competition reigns throughout this economy. In that case, the demand curve for labor will be given by its marginal product's being equated to the real wage, and the supply of labor will also depend on the real wage. The real wage and labor input will be determined, as in Figure 3.6(b), by the intersection of these supply-and-demand curves for labor, and output may be read off the total-product-of-labor curve in Figure 3.6(a).[2]

Because the level of output in question is independent of the price

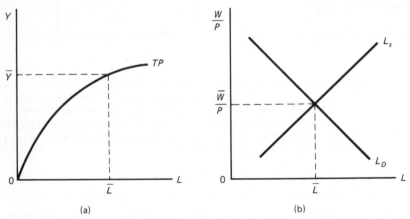

(a)   (b)

Figure 3.6 (a) *TP* is the total product curve of labor, drawn on the assumption that the capital stock is fixed. (b) L_D is the demand for labor as a function of the real wage and is the marginal product curve corresponding to the total product curve displayed in panel (a). L_s is a supply curve of labor. On the assumption of complete money wage and price flexibility, the supply and demand for labor determine equilibrium in the labor market at $(\overline{W}/P)\overline{L}$. With employment given at $\overline{L}$ we may read the equilibrium level of output $\overline{Y}$ off the vertical axis of panel (a).

[2] The reader who is unsure about the relationships between total product, marginal product, and the demand for a factor of production should consult an intermediate microeconomics book on these issues. See, for example, Laidler and Estrin (1989).

level, it may be represented, in the price level output space in which the curve *AD* has been drawn, as the vertical line *AS*. As has been re-marked, this label is rather misleading. In order for the marginal-product-of-labor curve to be the demand curve for labor, we need to assume perfect competition, and a perfectly competitive economy is one in which, among other things, each firm can sell as much of its output as it chooses at the going price. Thus, the curve *AS* in Figure 3.7 is derived on the assumption that the level of aggregate demand for output in the economy is such as to enable sellers' plans to be satisfied. The key to ensuring that this condition is fulfilled is that the price level is free to move in order to equilibrate the aggregate demand for output with its aggregate supply. Thus, an *AD-AS* framework with a vertical *AS* curve, such as is drawn in Figure 3.7, enables us to investigate the properties of a macroeconomic system in which the price level is per-fectly flexible instead of being fixed (as in Chapter 2).

Be that as it may, in Figure 3.7, the curves *AD* and *AS* are used to determine the levels of real income and prices. This vertical *AS* curve case is of particular interest to students of the demand for money because in it the level of real income in the economy is determined by factors that are quite independent of the demand supply of money. Moreover, if we change the nominal money supply while holding all the factors underpinning both the *AS* curve and the *IS* curve constant, the requirement that, in equilibrium, the level of real income not change must also involve the rate of interest in remaining constant. The rate of interest must take the value at which, given the consumption function and given the level of government expenditure, investment is just such as to ensure that the aggregate demand for goods and services equals the quantity produced. In this case, then, two of the three factors determining the demand for money are pinned down and only the

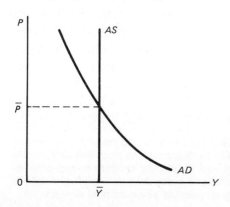

Figure 3.7 The determination of the equilibrium levels of real income and the price level by the interaction of the *AD* and *AS* curves. In the wage-price flexi-bility case, the curve *AS* is vertical at $\bar{Y}$ and the curve *AD* determines only the price level.

general price level moves to restore equilibrium between the demand and supply of money; and so, regardless of the precise nature of the demand for money–real income relationship, or the demand for money–interest rate relationship (provided that this is not one of perfect elasticity), we may make an unambiguous prediction about the consequences of a change in the nominal money supply.[3] It will change the price level in equal proportion and will leave the values of all real variables, including the real quantity of money, unchanged. This case is known as that of *neutral money*.

No one regards the vertical *AS* curve case as relevant at all times and places, but it might describe, in a rough-and-ready way, the situation toward which an economy not continually subject to disturbances might converge over time. After all, so long as money wages and prices are to some degree flexible, and so long as market forces tend to push them down when the level of output is below that given by *AS*, which is, after all, the level of output determined by equilibrium in the labor market (of Figure 3.6), and up when aggregate demand in the economy exceeds that level, that is how the economy will move. Moreover, in the case of an economy subject to continuous shocks, the type of equilibrium described in Figure 3.7 might characterize the average value of output (and of other underlying real variables) about which the actual values of output and such will fluctuate over time. If we think in these terms, however, we must also remember that, with ongoing capital accumulation and population growth, the *AS* curve will move to the right with the passage of time.

AGGREGATE SUPPLY IN THE SHORT RUN

The preceding paragraph amounts to arguing that the assumption of perfect price flexibility is as much a limiting case as that of complete price rigidity. Though money wages and prices are not immutable, they may not be flexible enough to keep the labor market in the equilibrium described in Figure 3.6 and hence the economy on a long-run *AS* curve portrayed in Figure 3.7 at each and every moment. There is much debate among economists as to why this is the case and what its conse-

---

[3] Of course, we here rule out the case in which, because of a liquidity trap, the *AD* curve becomes vertical at a level of output lower than that determined by the *AS* curve. In this case, there would be no equilibrium in the macroeconomic system we are describing and prices would fall forever. Only if the *IS* curve was subject to a "wealth effect," which caused the consumption function to shift up as the price level fell, would falling prices shift the *AD* curve to the right and eventually produce an equilibrium between *AS* and *AD*. Whether or not such a case is more than an analytical curiosity depends on whether or not the liquidity trap notion has any empirical content.

quences are for the behavior of output, employment, and prices over time as the economy responds to shocks. At one time it was thought that a mechanism such as we shall now describe was sufficient to capture the forces at work here, but it is now universally agreed that the mechanism deals with only part of the story at best. Nevertheless, it is worth a little attention.

Suppose we were to begin with an economy in full equilibrium on a long-run AS curve such as we have portrayed in Figure 3.7, and then suppose that some factor, say, a cut in the nominal money supply or a shift of the investment function, were to cause the AD curve to shift downward and to the left, as in Figure 3.8. Then suppose it were plausible to argue that initially prices remained at their previous equilibrium value of $\bar{P}_0$. If they did, we would in effect be dealing with the fixed price version of our macromodel, which we described in detail in the previous chapter. In that model, of course, with prices fixed, output changes to maintain the system in equilibrium when factors influencing aggregate demand change. We may capture this idea in Figure 3.8 by drawing what we may call a "short-run" aggregate supply curve, as, in the form of a horizontal line at the initial equilibrium level of prices $\bar{P}_0$. The initial response of the economy to our posited shift in aggregate demand is then for output to fall from $\bar{Y}$ to Y_1, with the price level remaining constant. However, as time passes, provided that there is some degree of price flexibility in the system, the price level will begin to fall. As it does, the price level and output will move back along the new AD curve (as the LM curve underlying it shifts to the right) until output returns to $\bar{Y}$ at a new, lower long-run equilibrium price level $\bar{P}_1$.

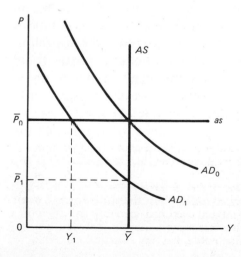

Figure 3.8 If prices are rigid in the short run, then the economy will respond to a shift of the AD curve from AD_0 to AD_1 by moving along the short-run horizontal as curve till output falls to Y_1. Subsequently, as the price level falls, the economy will move toward a new long-run equilibrium at P_1 and the original level of output.

The problem with the foregoing analysis is that it is just too simple and mechanical. The rational expectations hypothesis of J. F. Muth (1961), and Robert E. Lucas (1973, 1976) tells us that, in making decisions, economic agents will make full use of all relevant information at their disposal. Applied to the problem under analysis here, the hypothesis suggests that prices might initially remain constant in the face of an exogenous shock if the shock arises totally unexpectedly and its effects on the economy are not discerned until after it has begun to cause output to shift. Shocks that fit this description sometimes might possibly arise in the real world. However, if the shift of the AD curve is the result of some kind of policy change, the change might well have been debated and preannounced. In that case, one might expect that some economic agents would have understood its significance and would have prepared to meet it with price changes as soon as it occurred. Then the economy's initial response would involve a mixture of output and price responses. Indeed, in the limiting case in which all agents expected the change in question, understood its consequences, and acted on that information, the economy would move immediately to a new long-run equilibrium at $\overline{P}_1 \overline{Y}$ with no output response at all. The implication of arguments such as these is that it is unlikely that one can generalize in any way about the economy's short-run response to shifts of AD. That response will depend on the source of the shift, the extent to which it is expected to occur, and the extent to which agents in the economy are free to respond to it by altering prices. Thus, the horizontal short-run *as* curve is at best a special case, sometimes relevant and sometimes not.

The same kind of considerations would apply to our simple analysis of the time path that prices and output take after initial shock. Why should the price level fall smoothly until the new long-run equilibrium is reached? Might not the very fact of falling prices set up expectations of further price falls, which will in turn cause the rate of price fall to speed up? After a shift in AD, the economy is obviously not at its old equilibrium. Might agents not devote some time and trouble to investigating the source of the shock in order better to design their response to it, and will this not affect the subsequent time path of prices and output? In addition to all of this, is it not artificial to assume that the economy is in equilibrium at full employment and at a given price level when the curve AD shifts? Suppose, instead, that the economy is in the midst of an ongoing inflation. How would it then respond to a fall in investment? Perhaps, instead of prices falling in absolute terms, their rate of increase would simply slow down relative to past trends.

To discuss the hows and whys of these matters any further would take us deeply into the subject matter of contemporary macroeconomic debates. Some of the issues involved in these debates will turn up later in this book, but there is not space here to treat them in any detail. This is a book about the demand for money, not a general treatise on macroeconomic theory, and for our present purposes the last few paragraphs yield all the lessons we require.[4] To begin with, we have seen that it is only in the long run that we need consider nothing but the relationship between the demand for money and the price level when we try to deduce conclusions about the effects of changes in the supply of money on the economy; we have also seen that the "long run" is not so much a well-defined period of time, but rather one that varies with the speed with which agents can gather, process, and act upon information. So long as there is any degree of price level stickiness in the economy, no matter what its source, factors that cause the *AD* curve to shift, not the least any changes in the money supply, will have consequences for real income and interest rates as well as the price level—or indeed instead of the price level in the extreme case of short-run price rigidity. Thus, in general we need to know about all aspects of the demand-for-money function if we are even to begin to understand the way in which the macroeconomy responds to money supply changes and such, and the simple fixed price level model set out in the preceding chapter yields important, if incomplete, insights into what is and is not of particular relevance here.

Equally important is the negative lesson that emerges from the foregoing discussion. Knowledge of the nature of the demand-for-money function is necessary for understanding the way in which the macroeconomy responds to changes in exogenous factors, not the least the supply of money, but it is not sufficient. As we have argued, the time path that the price level and real income are likely to trace in response to any factor's shifting the *AD* curve is going to depend on the state of the economy when the shock occurs, the extent to which its occurrence comes as a surprise to economic agents, and the speed with which the agents are able to learn more about it and respond to that knowledge after the shock has taken place. These matters do not have much to do with the demand-for-money function, but they will nevertheless influ-

[4] The reader who wishes to investigate these issues would do well to consult a modern macroeconomics text such as Parkin and Bade (1984) or Barro (1984). I have given my own account of them, albeit at a more advanced level, in Laidler (1982, Chapters 3 and 4).

ence the way in which the arguments of that function interact over time in response to exogenous shocks. The only general conclusion we can draw from the above discussion is that the interaction is likely to differ from time to time and from place to place.

QUESTIONS ABOUT THE DEMAND FOR MONEY

We are now in a position to pull together the main conclusions that may be drawn from the analysis set out in this and the preceding chapter. Let it be emphasized, though, that these conclusions are tentative and not all of them will emerge unaltered from the closer study of the theories and empirical evidence on the demand for money to which the rest of this book is devoted. One conclusion that will not change is that the significance of the demand for money stems from the fact that the variables that seem to determine it are important in their own right. Real income, interest rates, and the general price level (and other factors we shall discuss later) have a vital bearing on the economic well-being of any community. Because, in the case of money, as with anything else, one or more of the variables affecting demand must change to accommodate variations in supply, the nature of the demand-for-money function is of particular interest if we wish to understand the impacts of monetary policy on the economy.

We cannot get answers to all the questions we might want to ask by looking at the demand-for-money function alone. For example, in an earlier section of this chapter we have seen that, if wages and prices are sufficiently flexible to keep the economy in equilibrium at full employment, then the effects of variations in the money supply will be concentrated on the general price level. The relevance of this result turns upon characteristics of the labor market, rather than of the demand-for-money function. It does, nevertheless, suggest that knowledge of the demand-for-money function is likely to be of particular importance to anyone wishing to understand the phenomenon of inflation, and particularly inflation that persists for a sufficiently long period for the assumption that other factors affecting the demand for money are independent of the behavior of the supply of money to be sustainable (at least in a rough-and-ready way.) In this context, then, our analysis suggests that we should ask questions about the theoretical basis and empirical support for the proposition that the demand for nominal money is proportional to the general price level. We should also query the tentative suggestion that, with price and wage flexibility, all factors affecting the demand for real money are indeed determined independently of the supply of nominal money. When we do so, we shall discover that this is one instance in which our simple analysis is a little too simple.[5]

The long-run behavior of the price level is only one area for which knowledge of the demand-for-money function is important. If, over short periods, wages and prices are sufficiently sticky, the fixed price *IS-LM* model developed earlier is of some relevance to understanding the effects not only of money supply changes, but also of factors shifting the *IS* curve, such as fiscal policy and fluctuations in private-sector investment. In this context, the role of the rate of interest in the demand-for-money function was of particular importance. If the demand for money is very sensitive to changes in the interest rate, then very small changes—in the limit zero—in its value are sufficient to absorb changes in the supply of money. In this case, money supply changes will have little effect on real income, but real income will be particularly sensitive to disturbances emanating from the markets for goods and services as opposed to those for assets. If, on the other hand, the demand for money is insensitive to the rate of interest, we get an exactly contrary set of conclusions. Clearly, then, the theory underlying the demand for money–rate of interest relationship and empirical evidence relevant to it are worth a good deal of attention. They will get that attention in the pages that follow.

Quite apart from such specific issues, we must consider the general question of the stability over time of the demand-for-money function. If the relationship between the demand for money and the factors affecting it shifts around unpredictably, we lose our ability to derive results about the consequences of changes in the quantity of money for the variables that concern us, and we must face the possibility that shifts in the demand-for-money function themselves are an independent source of disturbance to the macroeconomy. The theoretical reasons why we ought (or ought not) to expect the demand-for-money function to remain stable over time are therefore worth attention, as is the empirical evidence on the extent to which it does or does not, in fact, remain stable. As we shall see, one of the questions we shall have to consider here is whether any observed shifts in the function are the result of genuinely random and hence unpredictable factors or are the

---

[5] As we shall discover, the analysis underlying the relationship between the demand for money and the rate of interest also has important implications for the way in which the demand for money interacts with the inflation rate in an economy where prices are rising systematically over time.

result of changes in some variable or variables we ought to have included in the function but omitted through faulty theorizing.

The foregoing discussion by no means exhausts the list of problems with which the rest of this book deals, but it does indicate some of the key issues that arise in analyzing the role of the demand-for-money function in a macroeconomic context and some of the reasons why economists regard understanding the demand-for-money function to be well worth the effort. Let us now turn to a discussion of various theories about the demand for money which yield competing hypotheses about the nature of the function, leaving until Part IV the assessment of the available empirical evidence on these matters.

two

THEORIES OF THE DEMAND FOR MONEY

chapter *4*

A Brief Overview

METHODOLOGICAL CONSIDERATIONS

The statement that the demand for money measured in real terms depends on the level of real national income and the rate of interest is a particular hypothesis about the nature of the demand function for money. The issues raised in the final section of Chapter 3 amount to asking how good a hypothesis it is. At first sight, this seems to be a question to be answered by immediate reference to empirical evidence, for it is reasonable to suppose that one could ask how much of the variation in the quantity of money demanded in any particular economy can be explained by variations in these variables. This can, of course, be done, but before embarking upon such an empirical study, one should ask in advance what conclusions could be drawn from its results.

If it were to turn out that all the variation in the demand for money could be explained by the variables in question, it might be concluded that the theory was a perfect one. At the other extreme, if these variables turned out to explain none of the variation, the theory might be judged perfectly useless.[1] Neither of these outcomes is likely; more

---

[1] But "all the variation" implies that one has all the relevant evidence. Since such evidence is continually being generated, one never has all of it, and the notion of a theory's being completely verified by the evidence is totally irrelevant to scientific procedure. Even if a theory is found that explains all available evidence perfectly, there is always the possibility that new evidence, incompatible with that theory, may turn up.

probably the theory will turn out to explain 50% or 90% of the variation in the demand for money, and whether a theory that can explain 90% of the variation in the demand for money is good or bad is not a question that can be sensibly answered. It all depends on how one defines *good* and *bad*. Provided there is no difference between two theories in terms of scope, logical simplicity, or consistency with other economic models and such, one can say that a theory that explains 90% of the variation in the demand for money is *better* than one that explains 50%. If there are several alternative theories, one can pick the best of them on the basis of a criterion such as this, for so long as it also satisfies the other criteria mentioned, a theory is "good" if it passes empirical tests better than some other theory and "bad" if it does not. In short, to learn about economic theory by referring to empirical evidence, we need not one but several hypotheses that can be put to the test simultaneously. Only in this way can useful theoretical ideas be sorted out from misleading ones.

The lesson here for the problem of the demand for money is that it is not possible to learn much about the empirical relevance of the proposition that the demand for real money depends stably and predictably on the level of real income and the rate of interest until the predictions that follow from this proposition are compared with those that follow from different hypotheses about the variables on which the demand for money depends. As we shall see in the next few chapters, there is no shortage of alternative theories and much of what we know about the empirical nature of the demand-for-money function has been learned from tests that sought to compare the performance of competing hypotheses. It is useful, then, to go over the various theories in some detail before considering any empirical evidence.

ALTERNATIVE THEORETICAL APPROACHES

It may strike the reader as strange that one should talk about the theory of the demand for money at all. This is not the economist's usual approach to such problems. Textbooks of microeconomics do not contain chapters with titles like "The Theory of the Demand for Refrigerators," but rather present a generalized analytic framework in terms of which the demand for any good can be treated. Though a substantial body of literature does deal with the demand for money as merely a special case of the general theory of demand, the demand for money is often treated as a case apart, needing separate analysis, and plausible reasons for doing this are not hard to find. The usual approach to demand theory is to postulate that consumers receive satisfaction from the consumption of various goods, and that from this satisfaction, usually called *utility*, the market demand for goods and services derives. In the case of durable goods, there is an intermediate step, for the demand for a *stock* of durable goods is derived from the utility the consumer receives from the *flow* of services they provide. Usually, the nature of the utility function involved is dismissed as the business of psychology, and apart from some very general assumption about its nature involving the principle of the diminishing marginal rate of substitution between goods in consumption, it is not investigated by economists.

Now, money does not seem to fit well into this framework. It is not physically consumed, nor does it, like other consumer durable goods, seem to yield a flow of services that give psychological satisfaction. It does not keep food fresh as does a refrigerator or provide entertainment as does a television set. Stocks and bonds are in the same category, but they yield their owners a cash income that may be spent on consumption goods, and money does not always do this. In some economies, interest income is to be had from some assets also used as money, but the desire to hold cash cannot be explained by this fact. There are many instances of money's yielding no interest and being held nevertheless. It may look, then, as if utility theory cannot be used as a direct explanation of why money is held, so that the demand for it must be treated as a special case. Two peculiar and interrelated characteristics of money are usually emphasized in theories that set it apart from other goods. The first is that money is acceptable as a means of exchange for goods and services; the second is that its market value is, if not always stable, then at least generally highly predictable, over short time periods at least.

These two characteristics are usually collectively called *liquidity* and are not the exclusive property of money. Other assets also possess them in varying degrees. In some cases, it may be possible to convince the seller of a good to accept some other item in exchange for it; furthermore, the prices of some assets are quite predictable and fluctuate little. Thus, sellers of new automobiles are willing to accept used vehicles as trade-ins, and the existence of a well-developed used-car market makes the trade-in price of a particular vehicle at a particular time relatively easy to predict. However, unlike such assets as used cars, money is *universally* acceptable as a means of exchange, and its value in terms of goods in general is usually more predictable than that of other assets. Money is the most liquid of assets, and it is argued that this characteristic leads to its being demanded for two reasons.

When transactions are undertaken, it is usually necessary to have money on hand with which to make payments. However, this fact alone is not a sufficient explanation of why money is held.[2] In a perfectly frictionless world, individuals would buy an income-earning asset the moment they received a payment, selling it again only the very moment they required money to make a payment on their own account. They would thus never hold money. However, the world is not frictionless; purchases and sales of assets take time and trouble and hence are not costless. Also, it is far from sure that an income-earning asset can be sold at any particular moment at the price for which it was bought. An element of uncertainty is involved, and though gains are to be made by holding such assets, so are losses. Costs and losses alike can be avoided by bridging the gap between the receipt of payments and the making of expenditures by holding money rather than other assets.

Closely related to this argument is the consideration that individual agents cannot be completely certain about when it is that they will be involved in acts of buying and selling goods and services. Thus, they can never be quite sure that current receipts will match current planned expenditures at every moment. Again, this would not matter in a perfectly frictionless world but, where it is costly to exchange income-earning assets for money, it pays individuals to keep money on hand in order to acquire extra flexibility for market activities. Because of the costs involved in buying and selling income-earning assets, because the price of such assets can be uncertain, because the timing of some market transactions is uncertain, and because money is readily acceptable in any transaction, money comes to be held. Notions such as these form the basis of a great deal of theorizing about the demand for money.

In the last few paragraphs we have argued that money does indeed perform important services for its owners, even if such services are not of the kind that yield psychological satisfaction. Since, however, it is not usually necessary to investigate the nature of the psychological satisfaction that arises from the consumption of other goods in order to analyze the demand for them, it can well be argued that the psychological overtones with which utility theory is invested are irrelevant. If one adopts such a view, it becomes sufficient to postulate that money yields services to its owner and then to analyze the determinants of the demand for money in the same way one would for any other good. Whether this is a sensible approach or not is better judged by the

---

[2] The requirement that payments be made in money at the time goods are purchased is an institutional arrangement sometimes referred to as a "cash in advance constraint." Such a constraint was introduced into modern monetary theory by Robert Clower (1967) and has been the basis of much theoretical work on the role of money in general equilibrium analysis. Clower's work, however, was not aimed at generating a theory of the demand for money.

predictive power of the theory that emerges from it than by philosophical discussions of its underlying assumptions.

CONCLUDING COMMENT

Theories of the demand for money based on an application of the general theory of demand are not logically incompatible with the notion that the demand for money in fact arises from its usefulness in making transactions or with the proposition that it is an excellent hedge against the risks inherent in holding other assets. Nor are the latter two approaches contradictory to one another. In principle they are complementary. However, theories that stress the importance of transactions lead us to emphasize the importance of variables in the demand-for-money function that differ from those indicated by theories that stress the uncertainty involved in holding other assets. An approach that deliberately avoids any analysis of motivation and simply applies generalized notions about the determination of the demand for any good to the demand for money leads to a yet different, but for obvious reasons less tightly specified, model.

These various models could be regarded as leading us toward one general theory of the demand for money, and Gilbert (1953) argued that all theories of the demand for money rest on considerations having to do with uncertainty and the passage of time; but it is methodologically convenient to treat them as alternatives and then to ask how much of the variation in the demand for money is to be explained solely by the factors that each particular hypothesis suggests are important. If it is the case that no one set of variables dominates the demand-for-money function, one will find this out from experiments, but if a particular set of variables does dominate the scene, that will also be discovered from such a procedure, and information of this character would be of particular interest. The more one can explain with fewer variables, the simpler and hence more manageable and easy to understand will be the theory that emerges from such work. As a matter of method, then, rather than as a matter of strict logic, the theories presented in subsequent chapters are stated so that their differences rather than their similarities are emphasized. They are presented as alternatives and their complementary characteristics are downplayed. In this way, we make it easier to state clearly the issues that have been dealt with in empirical work.

chapter 5

The Classics, Keynes, and the Modern Quantity Theory

IRVING FISHER'S VERSION OF THE CLASSICAL QUANTITY THEORY

Historians of economic thought trace the development of modern monetary theory back to the mid-eighteenth century or even earlier, and the so-called classical version of the *quantity theory of money* retains considerable relevance even today. It is therefore convenient to begin our exposition of theories of the demand for money with a brief account of that theory as it stood at the beginning of this century. The then dominant version of the quantity theory stressed not the demand for money, but the concept of the transactions velocity of circulation of money, the rate at which it passes from hand to hand. Irving Fisher (1911) gave a definitive statement of this approach to monetary economics in his book *The Purchasing Power of Money*.

Fisher's analysis begins with a simple identity. Every transaction has both a buyer and a seller. Hence, for the aggregate economy, the value of sales must equal the value of receipts. Now, the value of sales must be equal to the number of transactions conducted over any time period multiplied by the average price at which they take place. The value of purchases must be equal to the amount of money in circulation in the economy times the average number of times it changes hands over the same time period. Hence, where M_s is the quantity of money, V_T is the number of times it turns over (its transactions velocity of circulation), P is the price level, and T is the volume of transactions, one can write, as an identity

$$M_s V_T \equiv PT \tag{5.1}$$

Nothing follows from an identity except another identity, but it can be used as a classificatory device in the process of theory building; one can consider the four variables listed above and ask what determines their values. In broad outline, Fisher's answers were as follows. M_s, the quantity of money, is determined independently of any of the three other variables and at any time can be taken as given. T, the volume of transactions, can also be taken as determined independently of the other variables in the identity. In an economy that has its only long-run equilibrium at full-employment levels of income—and Fisher in company with nearly all his contemporaries held this view—it seems reasonable to assume that there is a certain stable ratio of the volume of transactions to the level of output.[1] Fisher also treated V_T as independent of the other variables in the identity, although he did not regard it as being immutable over time. These considerations permit our identity, the *equation of exchange*, to be transformed into a version of the *quantity theory of money*, a theory of the determination of the price level, which can be written

$$\overline{M}_s \overline{V}_T = P\overline{T} \tag{5.2}$$

with the bars over V_T, T, and M_s signifying that they are determined independently of the other variables. More specifically, if we hold $\overline{V}_T$ and $\overline{T}$ constant by assumption and treat M_s as an exogenous variable, we arrive at the conclusion that the equilibrium price level moves in strict proportion to the quantity of money.

Though not stated as such by Fisher, the foregoing argument is equivalent to the following analysis cast in supply and demand terms. The demand for nominal money depends on the current value of the transactions to be conducted in the economy and is equal to a constant fraction of those transactions. Furthermore, the supply of nominal money is exogenously given, and in equilibrium the demand for money must be equal to its supply. This can be written

$$M_d = k_T P\overline{T} \tag{5.3}$$

$$M_d = \overline{M}_s \tag{5.4}$$

---

[1] Though Fisher and his contemporaries did not use the analytic device explicitly, it is not misleading to think of them as analyzing an economy that was usually fluctuating around an equilibrium on the vertical AS curve discussed in Chapter 3 (pages 30–32).

These two equations combine to yield

$$M_s \frac{1}{k_T} = \overline{M}_s \overline{V}_T = P\overline{T} \tag{5.5}$$

where

$$\overline{V}_T \equiv \frac{1}{k_T} \tag{5.6}$$

Whether one puts this approach in terms of velocity or in terms of a demand function linking money balances to the volume of transactions in an economy, one still has to ask the question what determines the equilibrium value of velocity (or its inverse, the money-transactions ratio). When the matter is posed this way, theorizing about the demand for money inevitably begins to concentrate on the nature of the institutional arrangements surrounding the transactions-making process. To give one example, it appears that an economy in which the use of credit cards is widespread would require less money to carry on a given volume of business than one in which all payments must be made directly in cash. For similar reasons, the practices of businesses with regard to granting one another trade credit attracts attention. On another level, the quality of communications in an economy appears important. Being able to transmit funds by telephone or telegraph should lead to a smaller requirement for money than having to send all messages by mail. One could list such examples as these almost without end, but enough has been said already to give the reader the flavor of this approach to the theory of the demand for money.

Now factors such as credit practices, communications, and so on, though they can certainly change over time, do not alter rapidly. If one thinks of them as being the principal determinants of the demand for money in an economy, it can be argued that over short time periods there is little scope for variation in the amount of money demanded relative to the volume of transactions being conducted. One would thus expect the equilibrium value of the velocity of circulation to be stable over short periods and would expect changes in velocity over longer periods to be rather slow and drawn out, responding to gradual institutional changes.

It is also tempting to look at the relationship between the volume of transactions and the level of national income in this way, depending as it does on such matters as the number of stages goods go through between the raw material and the final-product stage and the number of independent firms involved. Though vertical integration of industries can certainly take place and cut down on the volume of transactions associated with any given level of output, it is not likely to be a rapid process. Similarly, the proportion of national income actually involved in market transactions can change over time as economic units become more and more specialized and hence interdependent, producing less and less for their own consumption and more and more for the market. Again, however, a change such as this is not likely to be a rapid one and can perhaps be ignored for short-run purposes. As we shall see, however, such long-run changes in transactions of technology can be rather important to understanding the behavior of velocity over long time periods.[2]

When it comes to short-run behavior, it is sometimes argued that classical monetary economics predicts constancy in the ratio of money holdings to national income. If V_T is an institutionally determined constant and the ratio of transactions to national income is also given, then this certainly follows. In terms of the fixed price macro model of Chapter 2, we would then have a state of affairs in which the level of real income depends solely upon the quantity of money; in terms of the flexible price model of Chapter 3, the quantity of money would determine the level of nominal income, independently of its division between real income and price level components. This hypothesis is an interesting one, and we shall discuss empirical evidence relevant to it in due course. However, it is not really accurate to treat it as an implication of the classical version of the quantity theory.

Exponents of that theory certainly held V_T constant in the course of theoretical arguments in order to draw out its logical implications, as we did in connection with Equation (5.2) above, and they also argued that as an empirical matter, its *equilibrium* value would be stable, at least over time periods brief enough for institutional change to be negligible. However, they also left open the possibility that, in the short run, velocity might fluctuate around this equilibrium value. The reasons why such short-run fluctuations in velocity were possible emerge most clearly from the version of the quantity theory developed by Alfred Marshall and Arthur C. Pigou at the University of Cambridge, which received a definitive exposition in Pigou (1917).

THE CAMBRIDGE APPROACH TO THE CLASSICAL QUANTITY THEORY

The Cambridge economists did not ask, as Fisher did, what determines the amount of money an economy needs to carry out a given volume of transactions, but rather what determines the amount of money an

---

[2] This whole line of reasoning, however, abstracts from the large and rapid fluctuations that can take place in the volume of transactions conducted in financial markets. For a discussion of long-run effects, see pages 169–170.

individual agent would wish to hold given that the desire to conduct transactions makes money holding attractive at all. Their approach drew attention to the choice-making behavior of individuals where constraints and opportunity costs are the central factors interacting with agents' "tastes." In the Cambridge approach, the principal determinant of people's taste for money holding is the fact that it is a convenient asset to have, being universally acceptable in exchange for goods and services. The more transactions an individual has to undertake, the more cash he or she will want to hold. To this extent the approach is similar to Fisher's. The emphasis, however, is on *want* rather than *have* to hold; and this difference of emphasis is important.

An individual agent cannot hold all the money he or she wants, if only because the stock of cash balances cannot exceed total wealth, the constraint on money holding. Moreover, even if it were possible for people to have all their wealth in the form of money, it is far from clear that this would be what they would desire. There are alternative ways of holding assets, and many of them offer advantages relative to money. Stocks and bonds yield an interest income that money does not; if, against a given institutional background, the more money held, the less is the convenience to be gained from holding yet more of it, then after a point it will prove preferable to sacrifice some of this convenience in order to have some interest income. Moreover, stock and bond holding brings with it a chance for making capital gains (or losses), as indeed does more money holding in times of a fluctuating price level, and agents ought to take such matters into account before deciding how much of their wealth to allocate to money balances.

All this is to say that in addition to depending on the volume of transactions individuals may be planning to conduct and the nature of the markets in which they operate, the demand for money also varies with the level of wealth and with the opportunity cost of holding money, the income forgone by not holding other assets. Moreover, in the Cambridge approach, the demand for money measured in nominal terms varies exactly in proportion to the price level. The convenience of holding money derives from its usefulness in carrying out the transactions necessary to obtain goods and services. If prices of the goods and services were to increase by a certain proportion, the quantity of money an individual would have to hold to achieve the same convenience as before would have to increase by the same proportion.

When formalizing their model, the Cambridge economists, particularly Pigou, chose to simplify it by assuming that for an individual the level of wealth, the volume of transactions, and the level of income— over short periods at least—move in stable proportions to one another.

They then argued that, *other things being equal*, the demand for money in nominal terms is proportional to the nominal level of income for each individual and hence for the aggregate economy as well. Thus, they wrote the demand equation for money:

$$M_d = kPY \tag{5.7}$$

which, combined with an equilibrium condition for the money market,

$$M_d = \overline{M}_s \tag{5.4}$$

yields

$$\overline{M}_s \frac{1}{k} = \overline{M}_s V = PY \tag{5.8}$$

This looks similar to Equation (5.5), but V represents not the *transactions* velocity of circulation of money, referred to above as V_T, but rather its *income* velocity—not the number of times a unit of money physically turns over, but rather its rate of circulation relative to the rate of production of real income.

Equation (5.7) is a demand-for-money function devoid of a rate of interest term, and from the point of view of the formal properties of a macroeconomic model, it yields the implications sketched out above (pages 27–29). However, although this is the way in which Cambridge economists wrote down their version of the quantity theory, they qualified it with an *other things being equal* clause. They did not explicitly include such variables as the rate of interest in the formal algebraic expression of their ideas about the demand for money, but their verbal expositions contain many suggestions about the potential importance of that and other variables. They left it to their successors, notably John Hicks (1935) and John Maynard Keynes (1930, 1936), to develop these suggestions.

KEYNESIAN THEORY

Keynes's development of the Cambridge approach to the problem of the demand for money now forms the basis of the treatment of the subject in macroeconomics textbooks.[3] He analyzed with more care than his

---

[3] The distinction between the Cambridge approach and the work of Keynes is a somewhat arbitrary one. Keynes was a Cambridge economist and *A Tract on Monetary Reform* (Keynes, 1923) is completely within the tradition of Marshall and Pigou. What we are here calling the Keynesian approach to the theory of the demand for money was well developed in *A Treatise on Money* (Keynes, 1930), but it is only in *The General Theory of Employment, Interest, and Money* (Keynes, 1936) that its full macroeconomic implications are worked out.

predecessors the motives that lead people to hold money and was more precise on the nature of the convenience to be had from its possession. The peculiar characteristic of money as an asset emphasized by Fisher and the Cambridge school was that money, alone among assets, is universally acceptable as a means of exchange. Keynes also listed the "transactions motive" as an important, but by no means the only, factor underlying the demand for money. He postulated that the level of transactions conducted by an individual, and also by the aggregate of individuals, bears a stable relationship to the level of income and hence that the "transactions demand" for money depends on the level of income.

Keynes confined the use of the term *transactions motive* to describing the necessity of holding cash to bridge the gap between receipts and planned regular payments. He suggested that people also find it prudent to hold some cash in case they are not able to realize other assets quickly enough to be of use to them for those classes of payments that cannot be considered regular and planned, such as paying unexpected bills, making purchases at unexpectedly favorable prices, and meeting sudden emergencies caused perhaps by accidents or ill health. This he called the *precautionary motive* for holding money and suggested that the demand for money arising from it also depends, by and large, on the level of income.

Keynes himself did not regard the demand for money arising from the transactions motive and the precautionary motive as being in any sense technically fixed in its relationship to the level of income. He was quite clear that the convenience to be had from holding cash for these purposes can be traded off against the return from holding other assets and made the transactions and precautionary demands for money functions of the rate of interest. However, he did not stress the role of the rate of interest in this part of his analysis, and many of his popularizers ignored it altogether, not because the rate of interest is not important in Keynes's analysis, but because its chief importance is to be found in the role it plays in determining the *speculative demand* for money.[4] Marshall and Pigou had suggested that uncertainty about the future was a factor influencing the demand for money. Keynes's analysis of the speculative motive represents an attempt to formalize one aspect of this suggestion and to draw conclusions from it. Rather than talk of uncer-

---

[4] The distinction between the demand for transactions and precautionary balances, determined chiefly by the level of income, and that for speculative balances, determined by the rate of interest, is often referred to as the distinction between the demand for *active* and *idle* balances. Since all money is at each moment being held by someone, this terminology is not too helpful empirically, and we do not use it in this book.

tainty in general, the field is narrowed to uncertainty about one economic variable—the future level of the rate of interest—in the following manner.

A bond is an asset that carries with it the promise to pay its owner a certain income per annum, fixed in money terms, and the decision to buy a bond is a decision to buy a claim to such a future stream of income. How much any individual agent is willing to pay for a bond, hence the market value of that bond, depends critically on the rate of interest because prospective purchasers will wish to earn at least the going rate of interest on that portion of wealth being held in the form of bonds. Thus, if the rate of interest is 5%, that individual will be willing to pay up to, but no more than, $100 for a bond that offers an income of $5 per annum in perpetuity. If the rate of interest is 10%, however, no one will be willing to pay more than $50 for the same bond.

It follows, then, from the very nature of bonds that changes in the rate of interest involve changes in their price; a rise in the interest rate means that their market value falls, and a fall in the interest rate means that it rises. Changes in the rate of interest thus involve capital gains and losses for bond holders. However, these same changes in the rate of interest do not involve any change in the value of money. If we consider the choice between holding money and bonds, it should be clear that, in addition to offering the attraction of an interest income—which money does not always offer—bonds, when the rate of interest is expected to fall, also offer to their owners the possibility of making capital gains. In such circumstances, they are particularly attractive to hold; but when the rate of interest is expected to rise, the situation is the opposite, for then bond holders face capital losses. It follows that when the rate of interest is expected to fall, the demand for money is relatively low, since people hold bonds in anticipation of capital gains; when it is expected to rise, the demand for money is greater, as people seek to avoid capital losses on holding bonds. This is all well and good, but the theory as stated thus far lacks a variable to tell us when the rate of interest is expected to change and in what direction. Keynes's solution to this problem was to consider the current level of the rate of interest.

He argued that, at any time, there is a value, or perhaps a range of values, of the rate of interest that can be regarded as *normal*, so that when the rate is above this normal range, there is a tendency for people to expect it to fall, and, when it is below this range, to expect it to rise. In this view, any individual agent at any particular moment either expects the rate to fall, in which case the agent anticipates capital gains as well as interest income from holding bonds and will definitely hold bonds, or he or she expects the rate to rise and anticipates capital losses on bonds. So long as these expected capital losses are not enough to offset the interest income from bond holding, the agent will continue to keep all available wealth in bonds.[5] However, if the capital losses in question are expected to be large enough more than to offset interest earnings, the agent will hold nothing but money. There is a third possibility, namely, that expected capital losses just offset interest earnings so that the overall anticipated yield from bond holding is zero. In the special case where bonds are perpetuities, so that capital value changes are inversely proportional to changes in the rate of interest, this occurs when the expected rate of change in the rate of interest is equal to the current level of the rate of interest; in such circumstances, the agent is indifferent as to what proportion of wealth is held in money.

For an individual agent with given and precise expectations about the future value of the interest rate, the speculative demand for money is a discontinuous function of its current level. There is a given value of the current rate above which the expected yield on bond holding is positive, below which it is negative, and at which it is zero. These yields in turn involve (1) a zero speculative demand for money, (2) a speculative demand for money equal to the individual's available wealth, and (3) any demand for money between these two extremes. For the aggregate economy, however, it is postulated that, given the normal range of the interest rate, different people have different expectations about its rate of change toward their own precise estimate of its future value. The lower the current rate, the more rapidly people will expect it to rise, hence the more individuals will want to hold all their resources in money; by similar reasoning, the higher the rate, the smaller the aggregate demand for speculative balances. Provided that the money and bond holdings of each agent are insignificant relative to the totals for the economy, and provided that there is some diversity of opinion about the expected rate of change of the rate of interest at any moment, the aggregate speculative demand-for-money function becomes a smooth and negative function of the current level of the rate of interest.

THE KEYNESIAN DEMAND-FOR-MONEY FUNCTION

The simplest form of the total Keynesian demand-for-money function makes transactions and precautionary balances functions of the level of income and speculative balances a function of the current rate of interest and the level of wealth, the latter variable being included because

---

[5] The adjective *available* should remind the reader that some of the individual's wealth will be devoted to holding transactions and precautionary balances.

the foregoing argument about the speculative demand for money is cast in terms of the proportion of its total assets the economy will seek to hold in cash. Moreover, these two relationships are thought of as being additive. We obtain, then, as the demand function for money, with W representing real wealth,

$$M_d = [kY + l(r)W]P \qquad (5.9)$$

The first term within the brackets represents transactions and precautionary balances, and the second term represents speculative balances.[6] If we confine the analysis to short periods of time over which the level of wealth does not vary, this variable can simply be ignored, and we are left with an equation for the demand for money similar to that used in Chapters 2 and 3.

The equation is similar, but not identical, for the parts of Keynes's analysis of particular interest for the behavior of the macromodel developed there concern the speculative demand for money and suggest that it cannot be treated as a simple, stable, approximately linear, negative relationship with respect to the rate of interest. Let us look at this more closely. For the individual the choice is to hold wealth either in money or bonds, depending on what is expected to happen to the rate of interest; smoothness in the aggregate relationship between the demand for money and the rate of interest arises from the fact that different individuals have different expectations about the future rate of change of the rate of interest at given levels of this variable. The lower the rate of interest, the more rapidly it will be expected to rise and the more people will hold money rather than bonds.

It is a short step from this to argue that at some low level of the rate of interest, everyone in the economy will expect the rate to rise rapidly enough to make them either unwilling to hold bonds, preferring

---

[6] The parentheses around the term r in this equation indicate that l denotes a functional relationship rather than a linear parameter. The relationship in question is, of course, to be regarded as a negative one, but, as we shall see below, the whole point of Keynes's analysis of the speculative demand for money is to suggest that the relationship between the speculative demand for money and the rate of interest cannot be treated as well approximated by a stable, linear relationship. The fact that the whole expression is multiplied by P, the price level, indicates that this theory, like the preceding ones, is a theory of the demand for real money. It therefore implies that, other things being equal, the demand for nominal money is proportional to the price level. Note, however, that the "other things being equal" here include the level of real wealth. A change in the price level can cause this to change if people hold some of their wealth in instruments denominated in nominal terms. Thus, to say that the demand for nominal balances is proportional to the price level is not the same as saying that a change in the price level will lead to a proportional change in the demand for nominal balances. This is true only if everything else is left unaffected by the change in the price level.

money instead, or indifferent between bonds and money. At this point, the demand for money in the aggregate becomes perfectly elastic with respect to the rate of interest. The rate of interest can fall no further, and any increases in the quantity of money will simply be absorbed without any fall in interest rates. This is the doctrine of the *liquidity trap*, which argues that the interest elasticity of the demand for money can, at low levels of the rate of interest, take the value infinity. As we saw in Part I, this hypothesis implies that when such circumstances arise, monetary policy is quite without effect, fiscal policy being the only means of economic control. Even though Keynes himself was skeptical about its practical significance, it is clearly a doctrine to be compared carefully with the empirical evidence.

Although the liquidity trap doctrine is the most striking of the implications to be derived from Keynes's work on the subject of the demand for money, it is not the only one that is important in the context of the model described in Part I of this book. His analysis of the speculative demand for money rests on the proposition that at any moment there is a value, or range of values, of the rate of interest that people regard as normal. Nothing in the analysis suggests that this normal range of the rate of interest is constant over time, but the amount of money demanded for speculative purposes depends on the current level of the rate of interest relative to this normal level. This model implies, then, that the relationship between the demand for money and the rate of interest is likely to be unstable over time, shifting around as what is regarded as a normal range for the rate of interest changes. If this hypothesis is true, then all of the conclusions drawn in Part I, which hinged on stability of the relationship between the demand for real money, real income, and the interest rate, are misleading. Obviously, this hypothesis about the demand-for-money function is well worth investigating.

FRIEDMAN'S MODERN QUANTITY THEORY

Keynes's work on the demand for money represents a development of one line of the earlier Cambridge theory, inasmuch as it is based on a much closer analysis of the motives that prompt people to hold money than appears in the work of Marshall and Pigou. However, the view that the demand for money should be treated not as a special matter, but as a particular application of the general theory of demand is never far in the background in the Cambridge tradition. A body of theory, often referred to as the *modern quantity theory*, which receives its most comprehensive statement in the work of Milton Friedman (1956), brings this aspect of Marshall and Pigou's work to the forefront and makes the general theory of demand the explicit starting point of the analysis.[7] Friedman's work in the demand for money draws attention away from the motives that prompt the holding of money and—taking for granted the fact that people do hold money—carefully analyzes the factors that determine *how much* money people want to hold under various circumstances. He thus treats money in exactly the same way economists would treat any durable good, were they asked to construct a model of the demand for it. In doing so, he formulates a demand function whose form is dictated by the ultimate aim of testing its predictions against empirical evidence.

Friedman begins by postulating that money, like any other asset, yields a flow of services to the agent who holds it. Apart from noting that these services derive from the fact that money is a "temporary abode of purchasing power," there is no detailed analysis of the motives that are satisfied by the services. All that Friedman says about them is that the more money held, the less valuable relative to the services of other assets those flowing from money become. This is but a particular application of the general principle of the diminishing marginal rate of substitution between goods in consumption. As with any other application of demand theory to a special case, the bulk of Friedman's effort is put into closely analyzing the nature of the budget constraint and picking out relevant variables to measure the opportunity cost of holding money. That wealth is the appropriate constraint on asset holding and, therefore, on the demand for money should go without saying, as it should that the rates of return to be earned by holding assets other than money are the relevant opportunity costs. This much is evident from the work of Marshall and Pigou, but they do not provide a careful working out of the specific definition of wealth to be used in analyzing the demand for money on an empirical level or a precise listing of the relevant alternative rates of return to be considered. It is here that Friedman's key contributions lie. Let us take up the wealth concept first.

One role played by the budget constraint in demand theory is to define the maximum amount that can be bought of whatever good is being studied, or, in the case of an asset, the maximum amount of it that can be held. If an individual agent were to dispose of all assets, durable goods, bonds, and the like, he or she could certainly acquire and hold

[7] The emphasis here should perhaps be on "modern" rather than "quantity" theory, because, as some commentators, for example, Patinkin (1969), have suggested, Friedman's analysis of the demand for money is in some respects an extension of that of Keynes. However, Friedman's empirical views are, as we shall see, very different from those of Keynes, no matter what the similarities of their theoretical ideas.

money instead, and this stock of assets is what we usually would refer to as the agent's wealth. However, in a world in which there are no restrictions on what can be bought or sold, wealth thus defined does not impose a maximum bound on the amount of money an agent can hold. If the agent has labor income, there is no reason why a claim to this income stream cannot be sold and the proceeds devoted to money holding as well. Bonds are nothing more than a claim to future interest income and stocks a claim to the future income from some piece of capital equipment. There is not that much *economic* difference between trade in these assets and trade in future labor income, and this suggests that the concept of wealth should include the present value of labor income or, as it has come to be called, *human wealth*. Analytic precision certainly suggests that this is a sensible course to take. There are, however, practical arguments that suggest that, as far as empirical analysis is concerned, there is an important distinction to be made between human and nonhuman wealth.

Nonhuman wealth can be bought and sold, and there can be substitution almost without limit within this class of wealth. In the absence of slavery, the scope for substitution between human and nonhuman wealth in the portfolio is limited. There is some scope; an individual is always at liberty to sell nonhuman assets and spend the proceeds on further education to improve his or her earning power or, conversely, to neglect education and accumulate nonhuman wealth instead. However, the possibilities for such substitution between human and nonhuman wealth are limited, and the question arises in the context of the demand for money whether or not nonhuman wealth alone is a better measure of the constraint on the holding of it than is total wealth. Friedman's theoretical approach is to postulate that an inclusive definition of wealth should be employed, but that, in recognition of the problems raised by the lack of a market in human wealth, the ratio of human to nonhuman wealth should also be considered a subsidiary variable in the demand-for-money function. No one to my knowledge has made use of this variable in an empirical study, though in recognition of the problem that caused Friedman to suggest its use, some economists have preferred to employ a narrower, more conventional nonhuman definition of wealth. As we shall see, nothing of fundamental importance seems to hinge on this matter.

The opportunity cost of holding money is the income to be earned from holding bonds, equity (in the sense of durable goods yielding a service income to their owners as well as corporate stock), and human wealth, if it is included in the constraint. The principle of the diminishing marginal rate of substitution between money and other assets ensures that if the return on any of these other assets rises, the demand for money will fall. The return on these other assets has two components. First, the interest (or service) income yielded by them must be considered, but so also must the way in which their market prices are expected to vary, for a forgone capital gain (or loss) is every bit as much a part of the opportunity cost of holding money as is forgone interest. As explained earlier, the price of income-earning assets varies inversely with the market rate of interest, so that the expected percentage rate of change of this rate of interest can be used to measure the expected percentage rate of capital gain and loss from holding other assets. The percentage rate of change of the rate of interest is, of course, opposite in sign to the rate of capital gain (or loss) it is here being used to measure. It must be subtracted from the rate of interest itself to obtain the expected yield on the relevant asset, this yield being what is forgone if money rather than the asset in question is held.[8]

Though we have talked about rates of return on various assets as separate variables, it should be obvious that a change in one rate of return will lead to a change in all the others. If the rate of return on bonds rises, for example, they will become more attractive to hold, so that people will try to exchange other assets, such as equities, for them, thus bidding up the price of bonds and bidding down the price of equities, continuing to do so until the rates of return on various assets are brought back into an equilibrium relationship. If the rates of return on various assets move together, we can greatly simplify the demand-for-money function by picking one representative rate and letting it stand for all the others in the function. Which rate fulfills this role best is an empirical matter, but for the moment let us simply call it "the rate of interest" and include it, as well as its rate of change, in the demand function for money, leaving the question of finding its empirical analog until later.

If the rate of return on holding money were constant, we could leave matters here, but if the price level can vary, this is not the case. If the price level rises, the real value of money holdings, denominated as they are in nominal terms, falls, and vice versa. Rising or falling price levels provide a return to money holding, which in the former case is negative and in the latter case positive. The expected percentage rate of change of the price level must then be interpreted as an expected own rate of return to money holding. Other things being equal, the higher the expected rate of return to holding money, the more of it will be held,

---

[8] This is, of course, the same variable that underlies the Keynesian speculative demand for money, but this does not make Friedman's views the same as Keynes's. The essentially Keynesian step is to relate the expected rate of change of the interest rate to its current level, and Friedman does not do this.

and the lower it is, the less will be held. Thus the expected rate of inflation is a potentially important variable in the demand-for-money function. Since money is held for the services it provides its owners, and since these services arise from its being an "abode of purchasing power," it follows that the demand function for money we have been discussing is one that determines the demand for money measured in units of constant purchasing power, for real money balances. If we wish to convert it into a demand function for nominal balances, it must be multiplied through by the price level.

A FORMAL STATEMENT OF FRIEDMAN'S MODEL

Friedman's model of the demand for money can be written as follows, where M_d is the demand for money in nominal terms, r is the rate of interest, W is wealth, h is the ratio of human to nonhuman wealth, P is the price level, and all time derivatives denote expected rates of change:

$$M_d = f\left(W, r - \frac{1}{r}\frac{dr}{dt}, \frac{1}{P}\frac{dP}{dt}, h\right)P \qquad (5.10)$$

with the following restrictions being put on the relationships between the variables in question.

$$\frac{\delta M_d}{\delta[r - (1/r)(dr/dt)]} < 0 \qquad (5.11)$$

or, other things being equal, the higher the yield on other assets, the smaller the demand for money.

$$\frac{\delta M_d}{\delta[(1/P)(dP/dt)]} < 0 \qquad (5.12)$$

or, other things being equal, the higher the rate of change of prices, the smaller the demand for money.

$$\frac{\delta M_d}{\delta P} = f\left(W, r - \frac{1}{r}\frac{dr}{dt}, \frac{1}{P}\frac{dP}{dt}, h\right) \qquad (5.13)$$

or, other things being equal, the higher the level of prices, the proportionately higher the demand for money. So long as money is a "normal" as opposed to an inferior good, we also have

$$\frac{\delta M_d}{\delta W} > 0 \qquad (5.14)$$

or, other things being equal, the higher the level of wealth, the greater the demand for money.[9]

This theory identifies certain variables as being potentially important determinants of the demand for money and also (with the exception of h) specifies the sign of the relationship which the demand for money can be expected to bear toward them. It does not, however, say anything about how large or important any of these relationships are, leaving these matters open to empirical investigation. One cannot say more about this approach to the problem of the demand for money without reference to empirical evidence. We do not expect conventional demand theory to tell us much about the relative importance of various factors affecting the demand for other consumer durables, and there is no reason why it should tell us more about the demand for money.

In light of the analytic method Friedman adopts, theory has done its job if it states the problem in such a way as to sort out what empirical questions can usefully be asked. Once this has been done, it remains to carry out the empirical work that will enable one to find out whether the relationships between the demand for money and the variables listed above are important and whether or not they are stable over time. Since wealth—possibly defined in a novel way—rather than income appears in this particular function, and since the rate of interest is but one of several other variables, not least the expected rate of inflation, listed as being of potential importance, this model, worked out as it is from the first principles of demand theory, suggests that the demand-for-money function used in the model presented in Chapters 2 and 3 may be quite a poor approximation of reality. The answers to the empirical questions posed by this approach, then, are clearly worth having.

---

[9] The variable h is not discussed here, not only because it is not used in any of the empirical work we shall describe, but also because it is far from clear from Friedman's analysis what sign its derivative should take.

chapter **6**

The Demand for Money as a Means of Exchange

INTRODUCTORY COMMENT

The models described in the preceding chapter were, on the whole, developed in order to serve as components of a macroeconomic model much like that set out in the first part of this book. They are, particularly the so-called quantity theory equations both classical and modern, more concerned with questions about what determines how much money agents in aggregate will want to hold than with analyzing the motives underlying that choice. But, as we noted earlier, money does seem to be a rather special object of choice, and it may well be that explicit analysis of its peculiar characteristics will lead to extra insights into the nature of its demand function.

Money's most obvious distinguishing characteristic is that it is the economy's means of exchange, and Keynes's transactions and precautionary motives for holding money derive from this fact. A good deal of subsequent work on the demand for money has followed up this lead, and in this chapter we shall discuss theories of the demand for money that emphasize money's means-of-exchange role. We defer until the next chapter discussion of models of the demand for money as an asset, a pure store of value, which are more in the tradition of Keynes's analysis of the speculative demand for money.

THE BAUMOL-TOBIN MODEL OF THE TRANSACTIONS DEMAND FOR MONEY

Theoretical work on the transactions demand for money by both Baumol (1952) and Tobin (1956) seeks to draw more precise implications about the variables that determine this segment of the demand for money than Keynes's analysis did.[1] To obtain precise conclusions from a model, one must usually make precise assumptions. Those we make here yield the simplest version of Baumol's model. This model enables us to illustrate the most important insights of this body of work without leading us into the mathematical complexities that more elaborate versions of the approach produce.

Let us consider an individual agent, be it a firm or a household, who receives an income payment once per time period, say, per month.[2] Suppose also, for the sake of simplicity, that the whole of the agent's receipts are spent at a constant rate over the period. Then, at every moment except the final instant at the end of the month when the last item of expenditure is made, the agent will hold some assets, the as yet unspent portion of the month's income. How will the agent hold these assets, given that interest-yielding bonds can be owned as well as cash and that there is a fixed cost involved in exchanging bonds for cash?

Clearly, the agent will try to arrange things so as to minimize costs over the period. This problem can be solved in the following way. Let T be the real value of the agent's income, which is also equal to the real value of the volume of transactions carried out; r the rate of interest per period, which is assumed constant over the period; b the real cost of turning bonds into cash (what Baumol calls the "brokerage fee"); and K the real value of bonds turned into cash every time such a transfer takes place. The costs incurred by the agent have two components. First, every time bonds are sold, a brokerage fee is paid. Since all income is spent and bonds are sold in equal lots of size K, the outlay in brokerage fees is equal to $b(T/K)$. At the same time, if money is held instead of bonds, interest is forgone, and this, too, must be treated as a cost. Since expenditure is a constant flow, the agent's average money

[1] Baumol and Tobin worked independently on this problem, coming to similar conclusions about it. Of the two, Baumol took a slightly simpler approach, and it is his analysis that is followed here. A geometric exposition of the model can be found in Johnson (1963).

[2] The actual time period involved is of little importance, for it follows from the analysis presented below that the level of cash balances demanded for a given level of income per annum is independent of the frequency of payment except in certain very special cases. See footnote 3, page 64.

holding over the period is $K/2$, that is, half the amount of his receipts from a sale of bonds. The average money holding over the period multiplied by the rate of interest per period gives the opportunity cost of holding money.

The total cost of making transactions, where γ is the cost, can then be written

$$\gamma = b\frac{T}{K} + r\frac{K}{2} \qquad (6.1)$$

To find the value of K that minimizes this cost, we need only take the derivative of Equation (6.1) with respect to K, set it equal to zero, and solve for K. This gives

$$\frac{\delta\gamma}{\delta K} = \frac{-bT}{K^2} + \frac{r}{2} = 0 \qquad (6.2)$$

so that

$$K = \sqrt{\frac{2bT}{r}} \qquad (6.3)$$

Since, as noted above, money holdings over the period have an average value of $K/2$, the demand-for-money equation that emerges from this analysis is

$$\frac{M_d}{P} = \frac{K}{2} = \frac{1}{2}\sqrt{\frac{2bT}{r}} \qquad (6.4)$$

That is, the demand for transactions balances measured in real terms is proportional to the square root of the volume of transactions and inversely proportional to the square root of the rate of interest.[3] This can be rewritten as

$$M_d = \frac{1}{2}\sqrt{\frac{2bT}{r}}P = \alpha b^{0.5}T^{0.5}r^{-0.5}P \qquad (6.5)$$

[3] Some readers may note that this is but a particular application of a well-known general approach to the problem of inventory management. It should be noted that it follows from Equation (6.4) that a lengthening of the income period, which involves an increase in T for a given level of annual income, will involve an equiproportional increase in r, leaving the demand for money unchanged. Also, note that if the size of b is sufficiently great that the agent never finds that it pays to hold bonds, and if the payment period then lengthens, the agent's money holding will vary. The reader may also note that, although Equation (6.4) looks like a continuous function, there is in fact a problem of interpretation here. It is derived from a model that assumes that the size of the average cash withdrawal times the number of withdrawals is exactly equal to T, the volume of transactions. This assumption puts discrete limits on the value K can take. For example, the maximum value K can take is to be equal to T. If we set r equal to zero in Equation (6.4) and solve for K, we would think that a withdrawal of infinite size might result. I am indebted to Alvin Marty for drawing my attention to this problem.

where

$$\alpha \equiv \frac{1}{2}\sqrt{2}$$

Note that if one substitutes zero for b in Equation (6.4), the expression will clearly reduce to zero. Without the brokerage fee, it would pay to synchronize bond sales perfectly with purchases of goods, so that money would not be held except at the instant at which it passes through the hands of the person selling bonds and buying goods. The brokerage fee is then the vital variable here, and it is important to interpret it carefully. To think of its analog in the real world as being literally a fee charged by a bond dealer for selling assets for a client is misleading, for this puts too narrow an interpretation on what it represents. The role it plays in the model is that of any cost involved in selling income-earning assets; this could just as well be a time-and-trouble cost as anything else. To put matters simply, if it takes time and causes wear and tear to one's shoes to walk around the corner to a savings bank to obtain cash for a deposit there, one is incurring a brokerage fee in doing so just as much as if one were paying someone to sell government bonds in an organized securities market. This example underlies frequent references the reader may encounter in the monetary economics literature to the "shoe-leather costs" of transacting. When the brokerage-fee concept is interpreted in this general way, suspicions that it is unrealistic to treat its value as being independent of the value of the transfer made, rather than being related to its size, should diminish. In any case, if we add a component to the brokerage fee that varies with the size of the cash withdrawal so that each withdrawal involves a cost of $b + cK$, this will simply add a term $cK(T/K) = cT$ to Equation (6.1) and will have no effect on the optimal size of K.

The brokerage fee is not necessarily the same for all individuals or constant over time for any one individual. It arises from the time taken to transform income-earning assets into cash, and its value will vary with the value of time to the individual concerned. Time not spent on financial transactions can be spent earning income, and so the wage rate of the individual is a determinant of the brokerage fee involved in financial transactions. The higher the wage rate, the more it costs the individual to spend a given amount of time transforming income-earning assets into cash. This is a point of some importance because it suggests that if this theory of the demand for money is of empirical relevance, we ought to find that the level of wage rates has an influence on the quantity of money demanded in addition to that of the volume of transactions (or of the level of income standing as a proxy for the volume of transactions).[4]

Income payments in the real world are usually made in terms of cash rather than bonds, and there may be costs involved in acquiring bonds in exchange for money at the beginning of each period. So long as this cost does not vary with the size of the bond purchase, it does not affect anything. Where g is the fixed cost of acquiring bonds in exchange for cash, Equation (6.1) becomes

$$\gamma = b\frac{T}{K} + r\frac{K}{2} + g \qquad (6.6)$$

Since g does not vary with the size or frequency of cash withdrawals, the optimal values of these variables are independent of it, except in the case where the cost of acquiring bonds is so high as to persuade the individual to keep all assets in cash if cash is initially received. Usually, however, even when modified in this way, the model continues to predict that the demand for money will increase in less than proportion to the volume of transactions, that is, that there are economies of scale in money holding for the individual.[5]

This prediction has two potentially important implications for macroeconomics. The first is that for the aggregate economy the de-

[4] The relationship between the brokerage fee and the level of wages developed here was not set out by Baumol and Tobin in their original articles. We are applying an insight developed by Thomas Saving (1971) in the context of an analysis of the precautionary demand for money. Joel Fried (1973) and Edi Karni (1974), drawing on a suggestion of Barro and Santomero (1972), independently applied the idea to the transactions demand for money.

[5] The reader should note that in the aggregate it is impossible for everyone to receive one income payment per period and spend it continuously. Somebody must be acquiring continuous receipts and making lump-sum expenditures once per period. It is easy to show that, provided there is a brokerage fee for the exchange of cash for bonds, this type of individual's demand for money will also be proportional to the square root of the volume of transactions and inversely proportional to the rate of interest per period. This point is analyzed by Baumol (1952). Of course, once individuals are in a position to choose their own pattern of payments and receipts, it is far from clear that their activities will result in a simple reciprocal pattern of continuous outflows matched by lump-sum inflows. Certain theoretical aspects of this problem are investigated by Clower and Howitt (1978).

The reader should also note that to add a variable component to the brokerage fee adds a term in the level of transactions to the resulting demand-for-money function and, as Brunner and Meltzer (1967) have shown, the individual's elasticity of demand for money with respect to the volume of transactions ceases to be a constant 0.5 in this case, but becomes a variable that approaches a lower limit of 0.5 as the volume of transactions becomes small and an upper limit of 1.0 as it becomes large. How large the volume of transactions has to become before the economies of scale in money holding that this model predicts become unimportant is an empirical question, and in any event much effort has been put into seeking empirical evidence of such economies.

mand for money depends on the distribution of income as well as on its level. If we assume, as we have before, that the volume of transactions conducted in an economy is in a fixed ratio to the level of national income, it will be apparent that the more a given amount of income is concentrated in a few hands, the lower will be the demand for money for a given level of aggregate income. Economies of scale in money holding accrue to the individual agent, so that one agent carrying out a given volume of transactions will hold less cash than two agents carrying out half that volume each. If the distribution of income varies, so will the demand for money.

The second noteworthy implication of there being economies of scale in money holding is that, with a given distribution of income, any increase or decrease in the supply of money will have a greater short-run effect on the level of real income than it would if the demand for money were proportional to the level of income. At a given interest rate and price level, a doubling of the quantity of money in the proportional case requires a doubling of the level of real income to absorb it. Under the simple square-root rule, a quadrupling of real income is needed. In the long run, however, holding real transaction volume and the real value of the brokerage fee constant, the price level will move in proportion to the money supply, as in other models. Both the nominal value of transactions and the nominal value of the brokerage fee vary in proportion to the price level, producing a proportional relationship between the demand for money and the price level, as shown in Equation (6.5).

THE PRECAUTIONARY MOTIVE

The Baumol-Tobin model of the demand for money assumes that the pattern of income receipts and expenditures is given and known with perfect certainty. Suppose, though, that there was uncertainty about the timing of cash inflows and outflows. Several economists have developed models of the precautionary demand for money to deal with issues that arise in this context. The following represents an attempt to present the key features of this analysis in as simple a form as possible.[6]

---

[6] The genesis of this line of work in recent literature is to be found in Patinkin (1965, Chapter 5). Much of the subsequent literature is surveyed by Orr (1970), but the reader's attention is also directed to papers by Whalen (1966), Gray and Parkin (1973), and Goldman (1974). Note, however, that the basic work on these matters was that of Edgeworth (1888). Although worked out independently by the author in an attempt to simplify the model of Gray and Parkin (1973), the following analysis is similar in all its essentials to that of Weinrobe (1972).

Consider an individual whose income matches expenditure, not on a period-by-period, let us say month-by-month, basis, but on average over a number of months. In any particular month, there may arise an excess or a shortfall of income over expenditure. If there is an excess, it is added to wealth, but a shortfall must be made good within the month by decreasing wealth. The individual can hold wealth in the form of money or in terms of interest-earning bonds and decides at the beginning of the month how to allocate wealth holding over the month between bonds and money. In doing so, the agent bears in mind that money can be used to meet any shortfall of income from expenditure without cost, but if bonds have to be sold during the month to obtain cash, a lump-sum brokerage fee whose size is independent of the value of the bonds sold is incurred.[7]

Clearly, a key ingredient in this decision must be an estimate of the frequency with which cash shortfalls of particular sizes are likely to occur, and it is assumed that the individual has knowledge of this. The agent does not know in which month shortfalls of any particular size will occur, but does know the proportion of months in which they will occur or, to put the same matter another way, the agent knows the probability distribution of such shortfalls. Figure 6.1 shows one form such a distribution could take. It portrays a normal distribution. The horizontal axis measures the difference between cash outflows and inflows in any month, and the vertical axis measures the proportion of months in which, on average, a discrepancy between expenditure and outlays of a particular size will occur.

Our normal distribution is drawn symmetrically about zero, and the following assumptions are implicit in its shape. First, equality between expenditure and receipts occurs more frequently than any specific positive or negative discrepancy. Second, the larger the size of a particular discrepancy, the less frequently it occurs. Third, an excess of expenditure over receipts of any given size occurs just as frequently as an excess of receipts over expenditure of the same amount; such discrepancies cancel out on the average, and our initial assumption of long-run equality between expenditure and receipts is thus satisfied. Nothing crucial hinges on the precise shape we have assumed for this distribution, although it is important that at some stage the frequency

---

[7] This assumption of a lump-sum brokerage fee is made partly to maintain an affinity between this analysis and that of the transactions motive carried out above, but it also makes a crucial contribution to the simplicity of the argument set out here. The relationship between the probability distribution of discrepancies between payments and receipts and the demand-for-money function becomes considerably more complex if a component is introduced into the brokerage fee whose size varies with the magnitude of a bond sale. We take this point up again below.

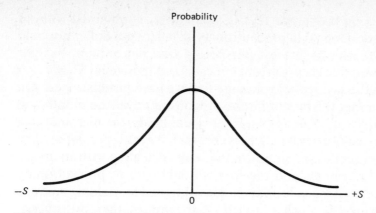

Figure 6.1 The probability distribution of the shortfall (S) of receipts from expenditure.

with which a particular discrepancy arises falls with the size of the discrepancy in question. It will now be shown that, given our assumptions, a demand-for-money function can be derived directly from the segment of the curve that lies to the right of zero in Figure 6.1.

Consider an agent who enters each month holding an amount of money equal to M (in dollars). In those months in which income falls short of expenditure by less than M, the agent has no need to sell bonds and incur a brokerage fee, but in all other months, he or she will incur such a fee. The proportion of months in which a brokerage fee is incurred times the brokerage fee gives the agent's average monthly outlay for such costs. Where $C(M)$ is the average brokerage-fee outlay associated with holding M of precautionary balances, and $p(S > M)$ is the proportion of months in which, or the probability that, the shortfall of income below expenditure will exceed M, we can write, where b is the brokerage fee,

$$C(M) = p(S > M)b \qquad (6.7)$$

Now suppose that the agent adds $1 to money holdings,

$$C(M + I) = p(S > M + 1)b \qquad (6.8)$$

Clearly, the amount that adding $1 to money holdings saves in brokerage fees is obtained by subtracting the second expression from the first,

$$C(M) - C(M + 1) = p(M + 1 > S > M)b \qquad (6.9)$$

Or, in words, adding an extra dollar to money holdings saves an individual, on average per month, the brokerage fee times the proportion of months in which the amount of cash needed to make good an excess of expenditure over income falls between M and $M + 1$.

This saving in brokerage fees is not, however, obtained without cost. An extra dollar held in precautionary balances is a dollar not held in bonds. If the rate of interest per period (*not* per annum, but per month in this example) is r (percent), it costs our individual $\$1 \times r = r$ cents to obtain the savings in brokerage fees we have just discussed. On the assumption that the rate of interest is constant over the month and independent of the number of bonds the agent holds, the marginal cost of adding to precautionary balances is constant at r cents per dollar. The individual agent seeking to minimize the costs of dealing with an uncertain pattern of payments and receipts will add cash to precautionary balances until the saving in brokerage fees obtained by yielding an extra dollar falls to a level at which it just offsets the interest thereby forgone.

Figure 6.2 puts the above reasoning in geometric terms. On the vertical axis we measure both the marginal cost per dollar, in terms of interest forgone, of adding an extra dollar to precautionary balances and the marginal saving in brokerage fees obtained by so doing. Given a constant rate of interest, the marginal cost curve is simply the horizontal line r, and the curve relating marginal savings in brokerage fees to the amount of cash held is derived from the right-hand segment of the probability distribution drawn in Figure 6.1.

As we have seen, to find the saving obtained by adding the $(M + 1)$th dollar to money holdings, we multiply the probability of having a shortfall of receipts from outlays of just $M + 1$ dollars by the brokerage fee, and similarly for any other value of money holdings. Thus, the curve labeled D in Figure 6.2 is simply the right-hand side of the probability distribution depicted in Figure 6.1 with the probability variable on the vertical axis multiplied by the constant brokerage fee b. The point at which this curve crosses the horizontal line r gives us the level of precautionary balances at which the marginal benefits obtained in terms of saved brokerage fees just equal the marginal costs incurred.

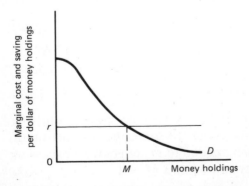

Figure 6.2 The demand curve for precautionary balances.

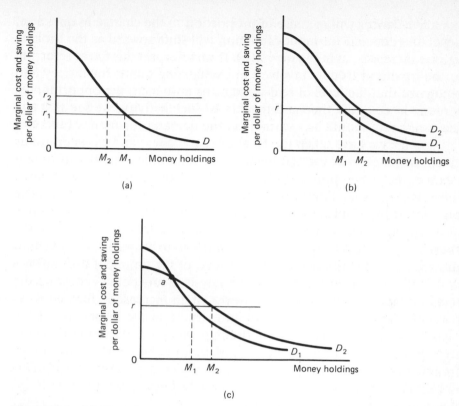

Figure 6.3 (a) The effect of an increase in the interest rate on the precautionary demand for money. (b) The effect of an increase in the brokerage fee on the precautionary demand for money. (c) The effect of an increase in income and expenditure on the precautionary demand for money.

Hence it tells us what quantity of precautionary balances will be held. In short, the curve D is the demand curve for precautionary balances.[8]

We are now in a position to see what factors this analysis of the precautionary motive suggests we should find influencing the quantity of money demanded. Their effects are depicted in Figure 6.3. Consider the rate of interest. An increase in the rate of interest increases the marginal cost of holding money from r_1 to r_2 and causes a shift along the demand-for-money function from M_1 to M_2, as depicted in Figure 6.3(a). The demand for money also varies with the brokerage fee. If this increases, the marginal savings from holding any given level of precau-

---

[8] It should now be clear to the reader why it was remarked above that, although nothing critical hinges on the normality of the probability distribution portrayed in Figure 6.1, it is important that at some point, as we move to the right, it begins to slope downward.

tionary balances will increase in proportion to the change in question, hence the demand-for-money function will shift upward as the brokerage fee increases, as in Figure 6.3(b). If we interpret this fee as referring to the time and trouble involved in exchanging bonds for money and recognize that the level of real-wage rates influences the opportunities forgone in devoting time and trouble to such activity, we see that the real-wage rate should be a variable in the demand-for-money function.

So far we have taken the level of real income and expenditure as given. In general, we can assume that the higher the overall level of real income and expenditure, the greater the chance that the shortfall of receipts over expenditure will exceed any given value in any period. The precise extent of this tendency cannot be deduced unless we are much more specific than we have been about the nature of the processes that cause the patterns of cash inflows and outflows to be uncertain and about the nature of the interdependence, if any, of the timing of cash inflows and outflows. To carry out such an analysis in any detail is beyond the technical scope of this book.[9] However, if an increase in income is, as it usually will be, associated with an increase in the dispersion of the distribution of the discrepancy between payments and receipts depicted in Figure 6.1, it will result in the pivoting of the demand-for-money function about some point such as a, as depicted in Figure 6.3(c). This is because, if the probability of relatively large discrepancies is in-

[9] The following example gives the outline of such analysis. Suppose the individual's monthly volume of expenditures is a random variable described by a normal distribution and that monthly receipts can be characterized by a similar distribution. Then, provided that in any month the values of receipts and expenditures are independent of one another, the mean of the distribution of the difference between expenditures and receipts is simply the difference between the mean of the two separate distributions. Given our assumption that, on average, expenditures and receipts balance, this difference will be zero. The variance of the distribution of expenditures minus receipts is the sum of the variances of the two independent distributions, and its standard deviation is the square root of this variance. Now suppose that the individual's volume of transactions doubles in such a way that, after this doubling, we can treat the new distribution of expenditures as if it were the result of adding together two independent distributions of expenditures with equal means and variances. Make an exactly similar assumption about the way in which the distribution of receipts changes, and then the new distribution of the difference between expenditures and receipts will have a zero mean and a variance twice that of the original distribution. But this implies that when the volume of expenditures and receipts doubles in this way, the standard deviation of the distribution will increase in proportion to the square root of 2. Hence we have derived the result that, other things being equal, the level of precautionary balances that will result in a given probability of having to make a cash withdrawal will vary in proportion to the square root of the volume of transactions. This result will hold only if there is strict independence of the distributions of payments and receipts. Any tendency for payments and receipts to be inversely correlated month by month will reduce the extent of such economies of scale in money holding, and a tendency toward a positive correlation between them will accentuate it.

creased, it must be at the expense of the probability that relatively small discrepancies will fall. The sum of the probabilities attached to all possible discrepancies must always, by definition, equal unity.

This argument about the effect of an increase in the average volume of payments and receipts on the demand-for-money function implies that the lower is the rate of interest, and hence the higher are money holdings initially, the greater will be the positive effect on the demand for precautionary balances associated with an increase in income and expenditure. At very high interest rates, above a in Figure 6.3(c), the demand for money will actually fall as income and expenditure increase. This rather odd result—for which, it should be added at once, there is no empirical support—begins to vanish from the analysis when a variable component, depending on the size of the cash withdrawal, is added to the brokerage fee. A formal analysis of the reason for this is far beyond the technical scope of this book. Suffice it to say that it arises from the fact that as the dispersion of the distribution we are discussing increases, the implied increase in the probability of making a large, *hence expensive*, withdrawal increases. The effect of larger withdrawals' being more expensive is to give an extra incentive to increase money holding, an incentive that is absent from the fixed brokerage fee model in which the cost of all withdrawals, regardless of size, is the same.

It should also be pointed out that the precautionary demand for money model suggests that there might exist a basic interdependence— an *externality*, to put it in the technical language of microeconomics— among individuals' money holdings. The chances of any one individual's encountering a cash shortfall depend, among other things, on the abilities of others to make their payments promptly when these come due; and this in turn depends upon the size of their own money holdings. Thus, when, for example, the rate of interest falls, each agent will wish to hold more cash, but this tendency will be partly offset because every other agent is simultaneously increasing money holdings. As a result, the interest elasticity of demand for money of the aggregate economy will be smaller than one would be led to expect from an analysis of the individual acting in isolation. This implication of the precautionary demand model has not been tested empirically, and indeed it is hard, if not impossible, to do so in an economy in which the opportunity cost of holding money always changes simultaneously for all agents; but it has significance for the analysis of the effects on economic welfare of inflation. This matter, which is beyond the scope of this book, is discussed in more detail by Laidler (1990, Chapter 3).

Finally, note that, like every other theory of the demand for money we have discussed and shall discuss, this is a theory of the demand for real balances. It implies that the demand for nominal balances varies in proportion to the price level. If the average price at which each transaction takes place were to double, this would amount to no more than doubling the size of the units in terms of which payments, receipts, and the brokerage fee are measured and would thus result in a doubling of the nominal quantity of money demanded.

SHOPPING TIME AND THE DEMAND FOR MONEY

The two models of the demand for money we have discussed so far in this chapter, though they pay attention to money's means-of-exchange role in the economy, do not focus on that role explicitly. They take it for granted that, in order to buy goods and services, agents must offer money in return, but they explain the holding of money, not in terms of this factor, but in terms of the costs of converting into money income-earning assets that cannot be used in transactions. Some economists, notably Bennett McCallum (1989, Chapter 3), McCallum and Goodfriend (1987), and Kevin Dowd (1990), have found this rather disconcerting and suggest that we analyze the demand for money by taking explicit and direct account of its role as a means of exchange in markets for goods and services.

Trade by barter, they note, is hopelessly inefficient and time consuming. Trade with money runs much more smoothly and hence generates large savings of what may be called *shopping time*. Such savings are valuable, because time not spent shopping can be devoted to utility-yielding leisure or to paid employment. The formal models in which this appealing idea is developed are beyond the technical scope of this book (the interested reader can find versions of them in the foregoing references), but an intuitive account of them enables us to derive the insights that they yield about the demand-for-money function.[10]

Consider an individual agent who derives utility, now and into the future, from the consumption of goods and leisure. Make the following assumptions: that the economy which that agent inhabits provides him or her with a stream of "unearned" income (by way of transfers from the government, perhaps), opportunities to earn further income by selling labor services, and opportunities to rearrange consumption over time by participating in a capital market where bonds (claims on future goods) may be bought and sold; that the agent can obtain consumption

[10] The argument below follows McCallum and Goodfriend (1987). Dowd abstracts from intertemporal choice, but his simpler analysis permits the Baumol-Tobin square root rule to be derived as a special case of his model.

goods in exchange for income only by spending time shopping for them; that the technology of shopping is such that the more consumption goods are bought, the more time must be spent doing so, and that the more real money is carried on shopping expeditions, the less time is needed to acquire a given quantity of consumption goods; that the purchasing power of money is subject to erosion by expected inflation; and that, at the time we encounter our agent, he or she is holding a certain quantity of bonds and money inherited from past activities. This agent will seek to maximize the utility derived from consumption and leisure subject to the constraints imposed by the conditions we have just described. The outcome of this maximization process will be equations determining current and future demands for consumption, leisure, bond holding, and money holding, not to mention labor supply, as functions of the exogenous variables that enter the above-mentioned constraints.

Of this array of equations, the one relating current money holding to inherited assets, to expected unearned income, and to current and expected future wage rates, interest rates, and inflation rates will correspond to what we usually mean when we speak of the agent's demand-for-money function. At first sight, such a relationship seems utterly unlike anything we have encountered so far in this book, but a moment's reflection will reveal this is not really so. The value of inherited assets and the expected stream of future unearned income might be crudely summarized into a single variable that we could call nonhuman wealth. We might also, in a rough-and-ready way, summarize the extent of the agent's ability to earn future labor income in a concept that could be labeled human wealth. We have here not so much a new and strange demand-for-money function, but something akin to a carefully derived and precisely formulated version of Friedman's equation. The greater precision of the shopping time model, however, yields important insights into the nature of the demand for money that were left obscure in Friedman's analysis.

In particular, this model draws attention to the fact that decisions about current money holding are not taken in isolation, but are part of a utility-maximizing strategy that governs future plans as well as current behavior. Anything that will affect future plans is likely, therefore, to affect current money holdings, too. For example, this period's demand for money is sensitive not just to the current values of such variables as, say, inflation or the interest rate, but also to the values they are expected to take in future periods. Furthermore, the shopping time model also implies that money holdings and current expenditures on goods, that is, the current volume of market transactions, are simultaneously chosen as part of the agent's maximizing strategy. McCallum and Goodfriend's (1987) model also yields what they call a "portfolio balance" equation in which real money appears on the left-hand side and real income and the rate of interest appear on the right-hand side. This relationship, however, does not imply that real income determines the demand for money. It arises because both variables are simultaneously influenced by deeper underlying forces.

As the reader will note, the shopping time model does not generate predictions about the demand for money that are strikingly different from those we have already encountered in this and the preceding chapter. It is important, nevertheless, because it demonstrates that a rather general approach to modeling the demand for money, such as that of Friedman, which provided the starting point for a great deal of empirical work, has roots in money's means-of-exchange role in the economy. Also, in drawing attention to the potential relationship between money holdings and consumption expenditure that arises from their being simultaneously chosen variables, it opens up the possibility of interpreting a certain body of evidence, which we shall discuss below (pages 180–181), as being consistent with a means of exchange approach to modeling the demand for money.

CONCLUDING COMMENT

The models we have discussed in this chapter are a small, but, it is to be hoped, representative subset of those that seek to derive the demand-for-money function from explicit consideration of money's role as a means of exchange. Among other things, the analysis of shopping time helps us understand why money is used as a means of exchange in the first place, the Baumol-Tobin model tells us how its use in regular and completely foreseen transactions might lead to the holding of a stock of money, and the precautionary demand model shows us how less regular and harder to predict transactions come into the picture. These models are theoretically interesting in their own right, but it is empirical predictions that matter from the point of view of this book; and questions about economies of scale in money holding and about the role of the wage rate as an argument in the demand-for-money function are put firmly on the empirical research agenda by these models.

chapter 7

The Demand for Money as an Asset

INTRODUCTORY COMMENT

As we saw in Chapter 5, Keynes's main contribution to the theory of the demand for money was his analysis of the so-called speculative motive, but this motive has nothing whatsoever to do with money's means-of-exchange role in the economy. Rather it originates in the fact that the price of money, unlike that of bonds, does not vary with the rate of interest, so that money is an asset that protects its holder from risks associated with fluctuations in the rate of interest. Moreover, when we first introduced the idea of the demand-for-money function into the macro-economic analysis presented in Part I of this book, we did not refer to its means-of-exchange role either. Money was there treated as one way of holding wealth. Perhaps, then, despite the obvious fact that in the real world money is indeed a means of exchange, it is possible to analyze the demand for it fruitfully without referring to this characteristic. We cannot be sure one way or the other until we have tried and discovered where such a treatment leads us. In this chapter, therefore, we shall explore the properties of a sample of models that ignore money's means-of-exchange role and treat it as an asset pure and simple.

INTEREST RATE RISK AND THE DEMAND FOR MONEY

One of the best known models of the demand for money as an asset is James Tobin's (1958). This model builds on Keynes's idea that money holding provides a hedge against interest rate fluctuations, but it offers a much more sophisticated analysis of the individual choice involved here than did Keynes's work. In Keynes's analysis the individual agent was poised, as it were, on a knife edge, holding nothing but money, nothing but bonds, or being indifferent between the two, depending upon expectations about the interest rate. However, even quite casual observation shows that people hold diversified portfolios, a mixture of assets. If agents really did behave as if they were certain about the future, they would hold only the asset they expected to yield the highest return. The holding of diversified portfolios thus needs explaining. The theory described—though it is here confined to dealing with the problem of diversification between money and bonds—is capable of quite general application to this problem.[1]

The key to the analysis is a relatively simple proposition about agents' tastes: they treat wealth as a "good," something that adds to utility, and risk as a "bad," something that reduces the satisfaction derived from wealth. To give a concrete example, it is postulated that an agent prefers, say, $100 offered with certainty to a fifty-fifty chance of receiving either $50 or $150. In both cases, the expected gain is $100. In the first case, the sum is guaranteed; in the second, if the offer is accepted many times, on half the occasions $50 will be forthcoming and on the other half $150, making $100 on average. However, in the second case, there is a risk attached to the outcome, and the risk is thought of as reducing the desirability of this alternative. If the risk were larger, if say the possible sums were $25 and $175, the alternative would be even less desirable.[2]

Now let us see how this quite simple and appealing notion can be applied to the demand for money. Consider an agent who receives

---

[1] The analysis that follows is not a straight exposition of Tobin's article. In particular, it differs in making utility a function of expected wealth and risk rather than a function of the expected rate of return on a portfolio and risk. The latter procedure involves an assumption that the composition of a portfolio is independent of its size, that the wealth elasticity of the demand for money and bonds is unity. This assumption rules out the theoretically interesting possibility of a perverse relationship between the demand for money and the rate of interest dealt with below. Tobin's original paper is not altogether clear on this matter, and I am indebted to Peter Diamond for first drawing my attention to some of the problems involved.

[2] The notion of a trade-off between risk and return in fact follows from the assumption that the marginal utility of wealth falls as wealth increases. Consider the accompanying diagram, where wealth (W) is measured on the horizontal axis and utility (U) is measured cardinally on the vertical axis. $100 with certainty yields a utility of $U(100)$, while a fifty-fifty chance of $150 or $50 yields a fifty-fifty chance of $U(150)$ or $U(50)$, and the average utility expected here is obviously less than $U(100)$ because $50 in excess of $100 represents less of a gain than $50 subtracted from $100 represents a loss. This is because the marginal utility of wealth is diminishing. Clearly, a similar argument would show that a fifty-fifty chance of $25 or $175 would yield even less utility. This analysis becomes more complex as continuous distributions are attached to potential outcomes of situations but, provided the distributions in question are normal, it is

income once per period and who saves. That agent must have some way of holding savings between periods, so let the assets available be money and bonds. If we assume the price level to be constant, there is no question of money's either earning a return for or imposing any risk on the person who holds it. However, since bonds pay interest and are subject to fluctuations in price, they yield income—albeit an uncertain one. This income has two components: the interest payments accruing to the bond holder, an amount we take as certain, and capital gains and losses, which must be predicted. For the sake of simplicity, in the analysis that follows we assume that the agent assesses the probabilities of making capital gains and losses on bonds in such a way as to make the expected value of such gains and losses zero, so that the expected value of the yield on holding bonds becomes just equal to the market rate of interest.[3] However, there is a risk attached to the return to be had from bonds, which can be measured by the standard deviation, a common measure of dispersion, of the probability distribution in terms of which the individual describes expectations about the future price of bonds.[4]

Now the problem confronting the agent at the end of a period is to allocate savings, whose amount it is assumed has already been decided, between bonds and money so as to maximize the utility the agent expects to derive from them. Holding more bonds increases the ex-

---

possible to treat utility as a function of expected wealth and the standard deviation of the distribution about this expected value, the latter variable measuring risk.

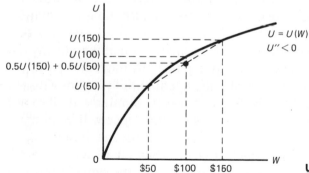

Utility as a function of wealth.

[3] This assumption is not a necessary one. One may have a positive or negative expected value of capital gains and losses without basically altering the analysis. However, to take this approach complicates things, for the slope of the budget constraint in the figures that follow is no longer given by the interest rate in such a case, but rather by the interest rate plus the expected rate of capital gain. Unless one can relate the latter variable to the interest rate, perhaps in the way Keynes did, the relationship between the demand for money and the interest rate produced by this theory becomes obscure.

[4] The use of the standard deviation of this distribution is not arbitrary, but is in fact dictated by the utility theory that underlies this model. On this matter, the skeptic can consult Tobin (1958).

pected interest income to be earned on savings and this increases the wealth he or she expects to have in the next period. To this extent it tends to increase utility. However, it also increases the dispersion of the possible values wealth will take in the next period.[5] Since risk reduces the agent's utility, the introduction of extra bonds into the portfolio involves trading off extra expected wealth in the next period against extra risk. A diagram or two will help to make this clear and will enable us to carry the analysis further.

In Figure 7.1, expected wealth in the next period w is measured on the vertical axis and risk on the horizontal axis. The curves I_0, I_1, and so on, are *indifference curves* whose interpretation is familiar. Each curve represents a locus of combinations of expected wealth and risk among which the agent is indifferent. Each curve slopes upward to the right as a result of the assumption that expected wealth is a "good" and risk is a "bad." It follows from this assumption that if wealth is increased, the individual will be better off unless risk is also increased to restore the same level of satisfaction as ruled before. For the same reason, the indifference curves are to be interpreted as reflecting higher levels of utility as one moves upward and to the left. More wealth with no extra risk attached or less risk with no compensating decrease in wealth makes the agent better off. The curves are convex downward, because it is posited that the more wealth owned, the less some extra wealth will mean to the agent and hence the smaller the increase in risk he or she will be willing to bear to increase expected wealth further.

The line $w_0 - w_0(1 + r)$ is the budget constraint, the line that shows the combinations of risk and expected wealth the individual can actually choose among in arranging the portfolio. If all wealth is held in the form of money, no return will be earned, but neither will any risk be faced. Hence the budget constraint passes through the point w_0, which measures the amount of wealth the agent initially begins with and ends up with if it is all held in the form of money. Similarly, if all wealth is held in bonds, expected wealth in this circumstance will be equal to $w_0(1 + r)$, where r is the rate of interest and σ_0 is the maximum risk the wealth holder can bear, that which is faced when all assets are held in the form of bonds. If all bonds are assumed to be the same in terms of the interest they offer and the risk that holding them carries with it, any point along $w_0 - w_0(1 + r)$ is available to the wealth holder; money and

[5] In the model discussed here, holding more bonds means bearing more risk. It is not difficult to think of a model in which it is money that is the risky asset. For example, if the bonds in question are redeemable at a given value in real terms in the next period, and if the price level in the next period is uncertain, it is money holding that involves risk. However, in a model such as this, an individual will still hold a diversified portfolio and the demand for money will still vary with the rate of interest. Matthews (1963) deals with several aspects of this type of problem.

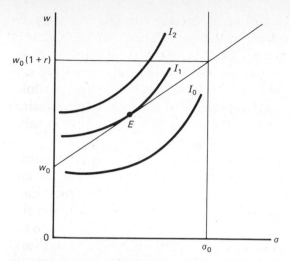

Figure 7.1 The individual agent's choice of how to allocate wealth between money and bonds involves trading off expected wealth against risk.

bonds can be mixed in the portfolio, and the more bonds the agent holds, the proportionately more return he or she can expect to earn, while the risk taken also increases in proportion to the bond content of the portfolio.

Now the wealth-holding agent's problem is to obtain the maximum amount of utility from his or her portfolio, given the rate of interest and given the riskiness attached to holding bonds. The aim is to reach the highest indifference curve available, and this is clearly at the point E where the budget constraint is just tangent to indifference curve I_1. At this point the agent will be holding a portfolio consisting partly of money and partly of bonds. This analysis then succeeds in explaining asset diversification in portfolios, but its use extends beyond this because one can use it to derive a relationship between the market rate of interest and the demand for money.

THE DEMAND FOR MONEY–INTEREST RATE RELATIONSHIP

Consider Figure 7.2, which is essentially the same as Figure 7.1. If the market rate of interest is r_1 rather than r_0, and the riskiness of bonds is the same, the slope of the budget constraint obviously is steeper. Instead of being in equilibrium at E_0, the wealth holder will settle at E_1, which in Figure 7.2 is to the right of and above E_0. Thus, the holder will be earning more return and bearing more risk. However, though the rate of interest is different in the two situations, the riskiness of bonds

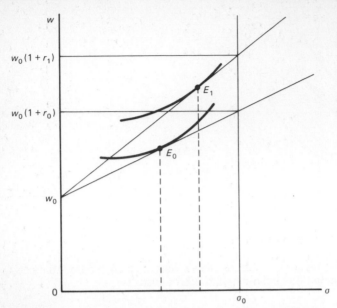

Figure 7.2 The agent's response to a higher rate of interest.

is not, so the conclusion that more risk is being borne implies at once that more bonds are being held at a higher rate of interest. That is, the higher the rate of interest, the smaller the demand for money. From this analysis it is possible to derive for the individual a speculative demand curve for money that is continuous and downward sloping, unlike the Keynesian approach, which yields a smooth relationship only in the aggregate.

However, the relationship does not *have* to be downward sloping because its nature depends on the indifference curves from which it is derived. It is quite possible to draw these curves so that at a higher rate of interest less risk is taken (that is, more money is held) or indeed so that just the same amount of money is held; these possibilities are shown in Figure 7.3. The nature of the demand-for-money function derived from this analysis depends on the nature of the indifference map underlying it and becomes an empirical matter rather than one of theory. This should not perturb the reader unduly, for such conclusions often emerge in economics.[6]

[6]The possibility of a "backward-bending" supply curve of labor is a famous example of this and, indeed, if we substitute income for w on the vertical axis of Figure 7.1, substitute hours worked for σ on the horizontal axis, interpret the intercept of the budget constraint as being nonlabor income and its slope as being equal to the wage rate, we find that we have exactly the model that can yield this implication.

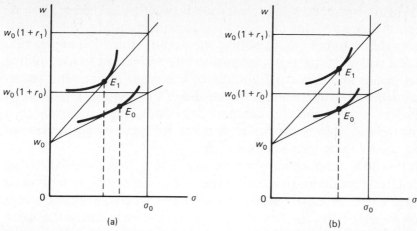

Figure 7.3 (a) An indifference map that yields a higher demand for money at higher rates of interest. (b) An indifference map that yields the same demand for money at different rates of interest.

This is no more than a case of the substitution effect and the income effect (it may be better to call it the *wealth effect* here) potentially working in opposite directions. Consider Figure 7.4, which reproduces Figure 7.2. The movement from E_0 to E_1 can be regarded as partly a movement around an indifference curve and partly a movement to a higher one. The substitution effect $E_0 - E_2$ clearly leads to less money's

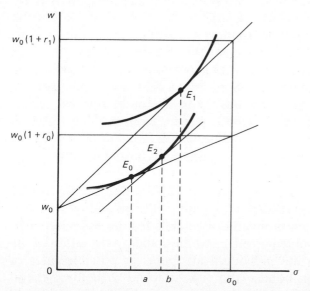

Figure 7.4 The distance a represents a substitution effect, b the wealth effect, and $a + b$ the total effect of the rate of interest being r_1 rather than r_0.

being held at a higher rate of interest, but the wealth effect from $E_2 - E_1$ could go either way. However, so long as an increase in wealth leads people to desire to hold more bonds, the wealth effect of a higher rate of interest will reinforce the substitution effect and lead to the holding of more bonds and hence the holding of less money. Since this seems so reasonable a postulate about the nature of the relationship between the level of wealth and the demand for bonds, the possibility of a perverse relationship between the demand for money and the rate of interest seems to be virtually ruled out.

It should be stressed here that we are dealing with the relationship between the demand for money and the rate of interest of an individual who has a given amount of wealth to allocate between money and bonds at each value of the interest rate. This is not necessarily the same relationship as that between the demand for money and the rate of interest when the rate of interest changes. Changes in the rate of interest leave wealth unaltered only for individuals who are not holding bonds when the rate changes. For those who are holding bonds, a rise in the rate involves a fall in their wealth, and vice versa. So long as the demand for money changes in the same direction as wealth, so long as money has a positive wealth elasticity of demand, these effects will reinforce the already analyzed tendency of the relationship between the demand for money and the rate of interest to be negative.

The effect of changes in the riskiness of bonds on the demand for money should also be discussed. In terms of our diagrams, an increase in the riskiness of bonds involves a shift to the right of σ_0, so that the budget constraint becomes more shallow at a given rate of interest. This is shown in Figure 7.5, where it is clear that greater riskiness of bonds has an effect in every way equivalent to a lower interest rate, increasing the quantity of money demanded. Similarly, a decrease in the riskiness of bonds causes the demand for money to decrease. Interest makes bonds attractive to hold, and riskiness detracts from their desirability. A rise in the interest rate and a decrease in risk are alternative ways of making bonds more attractive to hold, and so it is hardly surprising that they work in equivalent ways.

We have here, then, a theory of the speculative demand for money by an individual that suggests that it depends on the individual's wealth, the rate of interest (which in this theory stands for the expected yield on holding bonds over some period), and the standard deviation of the probability distribution the individual attributes to possible rates of capital gain and loss on bonds—the risk attached to holding them. Though nothing is explicitly said about the price level here, it should be clear that because the utility function underlying this analysis makes

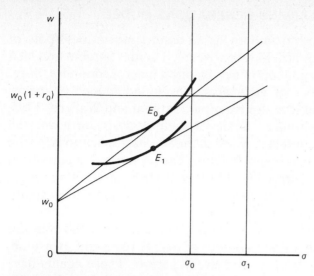

Figure 7.5 The effect of an increase in the riskiness of bonds causes a movement from E_0 to E_1.

utility a function of real wealth, we again have a function in which, other things being equal, the demand for money measured in nominal terms is proportional to the price level.[7]

The key characteristic of this theory, as we have presented it, is that it deals with the allocation of wealth between two assets, the return on one being certain and the return on the other being subject to risk. The reader should also note that there is nothing about the *zero* rate of return on money that is essential to the results generated. It is its *certainty* that matters. If money were to bear a positive, but still certain, rate of return r_m, the only difference this would make to the above analysis would be to shift the intercept of the budget constraint with the vertical axis of our diagrams up from w_0 to some point $w_0(1 + r_m)$. As we shall see in a later chapter, the possibility of money's bearing interest is an important point to consider when deciding how to test hypotheses having to do with the speculative demand for money. For the moment, however, we merely note that this model suggests that some measure of the economy's assessment of the riskiness of assets other than money may be worth including in the demand-for-money function.

[7] But remember that saying the demand for money is proportional to the price level, other things being equal, is not the same as saying that a change in the price level will necessarily lead to a proportional change in the demand for money. The "other things" may not remain equal. (See Chapter 5, footnote 6, page 55.)

MONEY IN THE OVERLAPPING GENERATIONS MODEL

Analysis of the demand for money as an asset is not a monopoly of Keynesian macroeconomics. In recent years, Thomas Sargent and Neil Wallace, two leading exponents of new classical macroeconomics, have, together with a number of associates, developed monetary theory along these lines as well (see, for example, Sargent and Wallace, 1982; Wallace, 1988). Though many details of their analysis are novel and unlike anything to be found in Keynesian theory, its implications for the nature of the demand-for-money function have a surprising amount in common with the older approach. Their analysis is based on the *overlapping-generations* model pioneered by Paul Samuelson (1958), a simple version of which may be described as follows.

Let us divide time into discrete periods, 1, 2, 3, etc., and consider an economy into which a given number of agents (constant over time, for the sake of simplicity) are born every period. These agents have finite lives, lasting two periods, so that at any moment half the economy's population is young and half old; thus the generations overlap. There is no need to confine the length of agents' lives to two periods in such a model, but doing so keeps the analysis of concern to us here transparent. Figure 7.6 will be helpful in visualizing this framework. The horizontal axis represents successive time periods; the overlapping horizontal lines numbered 1, 2, and 3 represent the life spans of the generations born in periods 1 through 3. Though it is possible to analyze production activity in such a framework, for present purposes there is no need to introduce this complication. Instead, let us simply assume that each agent receives at birth a certain endowment of consumption goods, but let these goods be nondurable in the sense that they cannot

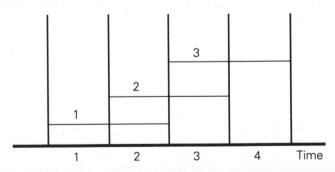

Figure 7.6 The basic structure of the overlapping generations framework. Generation 1 is born in period 1, and lives for 2 periods. Generation 2 is "young" when generation 1 is "old"; and so on.

be stored in the current period for consumption in the next. Each generation enjoys the utility of consuming its endowment of goods during the first period of its life, when young, but during the second period of its life, when old, it consumes nothing and therefore obtains no utility.[8] Crucially, in this initial setup, there is no scope for trade between the generations.

Now suppose that, in some fashion that may be left mysterious, we add a contrivance called "money" to this economy. Let it consist of a stock of pieces of paper that cannot in and of themselves yield any direct flow of utility to the agents who hold them, but that, by a social convention that is expected to persist forever into the future, are exchangeable against consumption goods, and, unlike consumption goods, can be stored between periods. Let this stock of money be placed in the hands of the old generation at the beginning of some time period, say, in the hands of generation 1 at the beginning of period 2. Generation 2, by assumption, knows that money will be acceptable in exchange for goods in period 3. Hence by selling some of its endowment of consumption goods to generation 1 in exchange for money, it can obtain the wherewithal to buy consumption goods in period 3, thereby transferring some consumption from period 2 to period 3. So long as the marginal utility of consumption declines with its volume during any period, generation 2 will gain from doing this. The introduction of money thus gives a windfall gain to generation 1, which, having consumed its entire endowment of goods in period 1, is now enabled to purchase and consume extra goods in period 2. Generation 2 and all subsequent generations also gain from the introduction of money because they are able to smooth out their consumption over time.[9] There is no sleight of hand at work here. What has happened is that the introduction of money has opened up the possibility of intergenerational trade, and the exploitation of this opportunity has brought benefits to all concerned, as trade always does.

At first glance it might appear that money's means-of-exchange

[8] The reader who finds the assumption of zero consumption objectionably unrealistic should note that the results we are about to develop depend only on agents' second period endowment's being smaller than the first. Zero is simply the easiest special case of this to analyze.

[9] The reader might think that, if there will be an end to this economy's existence in some period in the future, call it T, generation 1's windfall comes at the expense of generation T, but this is not valid. In this case, generation T would have no incentive to accept money from generation $T - 1$, since it would have no prospect of spending it in $T + 1$. Generation $T - 1$, knowing this, would have no incentive to accept money from generation $T - 2$, and so on. Money could not be introduced at all into such a finite-lived economy.

role is highlighted by this analysis and that the analysis provides a natural theoretical basis for exploring the implications of this role. However, this first glance is misleading. Suppose that our economy has been endowed with a stock of durable land. By bartering land against consumption goods, agents could have effected exactly the same utility-enhancing smoothing of consumption that we have just analyzed. What really matters in the overlapping generations model is not any capacity to create economies in shopping time, but the durability of money (or land), its capacity to act as a store of value between periods. Or again, suppose that, instead of money, we had introduced a government with powers to tax consumption goods and redistribute the proceeds. That government could have introduced a pay-as-you-go old-age security system and implemented exactly the same rearrangement of consumption patterns as the introduction of money permitted. Here agents' "store of value" would have been their future claim on a portion of the next generation's endowment, guaranteed by the government.

The foregoing arguments do not mean that the overlapping generations model is irrelevant to monetary theory, but only that it provides a vehicle for understanding the demand for money as an asset rather than as a means of exchange. The results it generates in this regard are interesting, though some are problematic. To begin with, if, in this framework, there exists some asset other than pieces of paper, and if that other asset yields a real return to its holder, for example, as productive land would, then agents whose sole motive for holding assets is to smooth consumption over time would not freely hold money unless it, too, yielded an equal return. But in the real world agents do hold money even though the return on other stores of value dominates that on money. That is why advocates of this approach to monetary economics, for example, Wallace (1988), draw attention to the existence of "legal restrictions," such as legal tender laws, that introduce an element of coercion into the decision to hold money. Without wishing to argue that legal restrictions of this sort are completely irrelevant to money-holding decisions, it must be pointed out that they do not seem to be sufficient to explain the holding of rate of return–dominated money. For example, during the period 1797–1821, Bank of England notes were not convertible into gold, were not legal tender, and bore no interest. Indeed, they depreciated as a result of inflation. Nevertheless, they circulated throughout Britain as money and were held by agents.

One can conceive of the monetary authorities generating a positive rate of return on money by creating a steady deflation of the price level. So long as this rate of deflation is just equal to the rate of return on other assets, it can be shown that agents in an overlapping generations model will be indifferent between holding money and other assets; but a small rise in the rate of return on those other assets would have an indefinitely large negative effect on money holding. In the absence of legal restrictions no one in such a model would want to hold money if it was dominated in rate of return. It is worth noting that the infinite elasticity of demand for money as an asset with respect to the rate of return on other assets implied here bears a striking resemblence to the Keynesian prediction that the agent's demand for speculative balances is of an "all or nothing" type. It is also worth pointing out that it is this prediction that underlies the possibility of a liquidity trap in the aggregate demand-for-money function.

This property of the demand-for-money function as it emerges from the overlapping generations model also has implications for the interaction of the supply and demand for money when money, rather than being an intrinsically worthless piece of paper, instead represents a claim to real goods that the issuer of money promises to honor at some definite future date.[10] If each unit of money represents a claim to a well-specified good (if it is a *well-backed* claim, to use the jargon current in this branch of monetary economics), its current purchasing power over goods will be its expected redemption value discounted to the present at the prevailing rate of interest. Variations in the quantity of such well-backed units of money will have no effect on their purchasing power. Any tendency for an increase in that quantity to drive down their value will immediately be met by an indefinitely large increase in the demand for them to take advantage of the higher rate of return implicit in that depreciation; and any tendency for a fall in their quantity to drive up their value will lead to an indefinitely large fall in the demand for them. If money is well backed, then, and the demand for it is purely an asset demand, the standard prediction that, when the economy's level of real income is given, the general price level will move in proportion to the supply of money will not hold. This is a striking implication of treating the demand for money as the demand for a store of value pure and simple, and one that, in principle at least, permits sharp tests of the validity of this approach to be formulated.

CONCLUDING COMMENT

The models of the demand for money that we have expounded in this chapter are certainly "unrealistic" in the sense that they abstract from an aspect of money clearly visible in the real world, namely, its capacity

---

[10] The guaranteed immediate convertibility of paper money into gold, which we associate with the gold standard, is, of course, a limiting case of such a promise.

to function as a means of exchange. The reader, however, should not dismiss the models out of hand for this reason. From the point of view of understanding how the macroeconomy functions and which specific formulation of the general macroeconomic framework set out in Part I of this book is empirically relevant, what matters is not that money is a means of exchange, but whether this fact imparts to the demand-for-money function characteristics that cannot be explained without reference to it. Models of the demand for money as an asset yield predictions about the nature of the demand-for-money function that arise when the means-of-exchange function is ignored. Hence they enable us to formulate empirical questions whose answers might help us to decide whether or not we need take account of money's peculiar characteristics when we construct theories about it. These models tend to predict the sensitivity of the demand for money with respect to the opportunity cost of holding it will be high, and we have seen in Part One that such a characteristic of the demand-for-money function would have important implications for the behavior of the macroeconomy. If for no other reasons than that they draw our attention to this issue and that they yield suggestions about how empirical questions about it might be formulated, these models are well worth our attention.

three

DATA PROBLEMS AND ECONOMETRIC ISSUES

chapter 8

Measuring the Variables of the Demand-for-Money Function

INTRODUCTORY COMMENT

In our theoretical discussions, we have talked about money, the rate of interest, wealth, and the like, as if it were quite clear what these words referred to. The reader has no doubt some rough idea of what is meant by each of these terms, an idea that suffices for understanding the logic of the theories. However, if empirical tests are to be carried out, a precise definition must be given for each term so that data can be gathered, and clearly specified empirical hypotheses, based on various models of the demand for money, can be formulated.

THE MEASUREMENT OF MONEY

Consider first the problem of finding an empirical measure of money. There is no sharp distinction in the real world between money and other assets, but rather there is a spectrum of assets, some more like one's rough idea of money than others. Theories of the demand for money as a means of exchange refer to assets readily acceptable and transferable in everyday transactions. The money concept to which they apply was, until the early 1970s, rather easily defined at least in the context of the U.S. economy. There were but two assets that clearly were readily acceptable and transferable. These were currency and demand deposits at commercial banks. The sum of these assets available to the public at that time was widely agreed to constitute the relevant measure of the money stock as far as theories of the transactions demand for money were concerned.

Matters have become more complicated in the last two decades. In the early 1970s, beginning in New England, there were introduced NOW ("negotiable order of withdrawal") accounts, transferable by check like demand deposits but unlike them bearing explicit interest, albeit at a regulated rate. In 1981, such accounts became available nationwide. More recently, ATS ("automatic transfer service") accounts have become available. These accounts, being transferable by check, clearly belong in any definition of money used to test transactions demand theories against recent United States data.

Each economy raises its own problems in measuring means of exchange. For example, in the British economy, currency and current accounts at commercial banks might be regarded as generally acceptable and readily available means of exchange. But the availability of automatic overdrafts to bank customers has led some to argue that unused overdraft limits also constitute "money" in a meaningful sense. In Canada, certain classes of deposits at trust companies (institutions similar to savings and loan associations) and certain classes of time deposits at chartered banks have long been transferable by check. The charges levied for making these transfers by check are sometimes sufficiently high as to deter people from using such assets as if they were the equivalent of ordinary checking accounts, and so it is far from obvious a priori whether it is appropriate to treat all such assets as equally efficient means of exchange. Moreover, the situation in Canada began to change in the 1970s and 1980s, as the commercial banks introduced new types of interest-bearing low-cost checkable deposits, notably, in 1981, accounts paying interest on a daily basis; these new assets probably belong in a definition of money that is relevant to testing theories about transactions demand.

There is little, if anything, that one can say about these issues that is generally true of all times and places. It is clear which assets are means of exchange and which are not in some economies but not in all. As the above examples show, the dividing lines between means of exchange and other assets do not stay put over time in any particular economy. The boundary shifts as the financial system evolves, and the most that one can say in general is that economists seeking to test transaction demand theories need to be sensitive to the institutional framework of the economy generating their data.

Even if the borderline between means of exchange and other assets was clear-cut, it would be hard to settle on an appropriate and generally acceptable definition of money on a priori grounds. Some theories of the demand for money treat it as a store of value, pure and simple, and ignore its means-of-exchange role. Thus theories of the speculative demand for money emphasize the fact that money's capital value does not vary with the rate of interest. In the United States, currency, demand deposits, and, these days, NOW and ATS accounts have this characteristic to be sure, but they are not the only assets that possess it. Noncheckable time deposits at commercial banks and deposits at mutual savings banks and savings and loan associations are, from the point of view of an asset approach to the demand for money, just as much "money" in the United States as are their equivalents in other economies. Moreover, such assets yield an interest income to their holders at a rate higher than that borne by checkable deposits and currency. Despite this, individuals hold currency and low- or zero-interest checkable deposits in significant amounts, and asset motives for holding money can be of little relevance as far as the demand for such *narrow money* is concerned. Asset motives are more likely to play a role in determining the demand for assets such as noncheckable time deposits at banks and perhaps savings and loan associations, not to mention, in recent years, money market mutual funds. Hence the importance of asset motives can best be tested in the context of the demand for *broad money* defined over a wider spectrum of assets than currency and checkable deposits.

Theories of the demand for money, such as Friedman's, which rest simply on the proposition that money yields a flow of unspecified services to its owners also raise problems. Every asset yields services, and in defining one set of assets as being money and another as not being money, one is really arguing that the services yielded by the various assets in the first category are sufficiently similar to one another as to make it possible to treat those assets as if they were all one asset, and sufficiently different from those yielded by other assets to disqualify those other assets from being put in the same category. It is, however, asset holders rather than the economists studying their behavior who determine which assets are close substitutes for one another and which are not. The only way to find out what asset holders think is to study their behavior; in the context of this more general approach to the problem of the demand for money, the correct definition of money becomes an empirical matter, at least within rather broad boundaries laid down by one's "rough idea" of what money is.[1]

In the light of the foregoing arguments, it is hardly surprising that several definitions of money have been employed in the course of testing theories of the demand for money. For the United States, the bulk of the work carried out down to the mid-1970s confined the definition of narrow money to currency plus demand deposits at commercial banks, "old M_1," as it is now called, or to the definition of broad money for currency plus demand deposits plus time deposits at commercial banks, "old M_2." As we have noted, however, from the 1970s onward, developments in the banking system began to undermine the relevance of these simple notions of what constituted narrow and broad money. In particular, NOW and ATS accounts have come to be included in the narrow money concept ("new M_1"), and the broad concept ("new M_2") has had to be extended to include such assets as, for example, shares in money market mutual funds and money market deposit accounts. The process of financial innovation that has required these adjustments is an ongoing one, and ideas about the "appropriate" definition of money in the U.S. economy will undoubtedly continue to change in the future. Similar developments have taken place in other economies, too. Moreover, even broader concepts of money, including a wider and wider spectrum of assets may, and have been, defined, with labels such as M_3, M_4, and so on. All we can do is warn the reader to take careful note of how the authors of any particular study have measured "money."

One novel approach to measuring money involves the construction of index numbers of its quantity. Instead of simply adding up what are, after all, heterogeneous assets on a dollar for dollar basis, it is argued that those assets that are more readily and cheaply transferred should be given more weight in measuring the aggregate money stock than those that are less liquid. W. Barnett (1980, 1990) has pioneered the use of the Divisia Index to generate aggregate money supply measures for the United States. Here the proportional change in the money supply

---

[1] The notion that the question of the correct way to measure money for purposes of carrying out empirical work on the demand for money and related problems is itself an empirical issue is set out and defended in Laidler (1969) and Friedman and Schwartz (1970, Part I). For a criticism of this approach to the problem, see Mason (1976), who argues with considerable justice that this approach carries with it a grave danger of leading one into circular arguments: The definition of money that enables a theory to work well is chosen as appropriate, and then evidence generated using it is cited as supporting the theory in terms of which the data were selected in the first place. This danger undoubtedly exists in principle, but, as we shall see in Chapters 11 and 12, there seem to be enough results concerning the demand-for-money function that do not depend on the precise variable chosen to measure money that Mason's objection may not be a fatal one.

is computed as a weighted average of proportional changes in its components, the weights being the product of the amount of each component held multiplied by the difference between its own rate of return and some representative rate of interest. The intuition underlying this procedure is that the greater is this difference, the greater must be the "liquidity services" the asset in question yields to its holder, and hence the more is it "money."

There is a difficulty here. The difference between rates of return measures, at best, liquidity on the *margin* rather than the *average* liquidity of particular assets. In a perfectly competitive banking system, where all types of bank liabilities bore interest at the market rate, this differential would be zero, and the Divisia Index would yield the peculiar results that money stock growth was indeterminate.[2] This is a theoretically extreme example, not likely to be encountered in practice. Indeed, the United States banking system is rather heavily regulated and hence is relatively far removed from the competitive ideal; and regulatory changes there can, and do, from time to time lead to significant discrete changes both in the liquidity and rates of return on particular types of deposits. As Barnett (1990) has argued, in such circumstances, the employment of the Divisia Index might be particularly appropriate.

The demand for money has been studied in many countries other than the United States. To discuss the details of definitions of money used in studies of these other countries would require us to deal with their individual financial systems to an extent that would be inappropriate in a book such as this. Suffice it to say that, as far as possible, people working on countries other than the United States have tried to utilize definitions of money roughly corresponding to those used in studying U.S. data. In a number of cases, for example, S. Namba (1983) for Japan and Cockerline and Murray (1981) for Canada, experiments with Divisia Index numbers have also been carried out; but it is a fair generalization that their use leads to much less improvement in the fit of various functions outside of the United States than within that economy.

As we have stressed again and again in the first two parts of this

---

[2] The problems involved here stem from certain fundamental issues in monetary theory that are beyond the scope of this book. The basic point is that in an economy that uses token as opposed to commodity money, the marginal cost of producing real balances is essentially zero. Under competitive conditions real balances become a free good to the economy, and all the difficult questions that arise in general about accounting for the services provided by free goods in measuring income, wealth, and economic welfare are relevant to the case of money. The reader who wants to follow up this issue is referred to Friedman (1969) and Johnson (1969), two of the fundamental papers on the matter. Fried and Howitt (1983) discuss closely related issues.

book, the demand for money is a demand for *real* balances. The concepts of the money stock we have been discussing are measured in nominal terms. To get to a measure of real money from nominal money, it is necessary to divide by an appropriate price index. The selection of the index is relatively uncontroversial. It is generally accepted that a broadly based index such as, in the case of the United States, a gross or net national product deflator is an appropriate choice, but sometimes a consumer price index is used, particularly for those countries where national product deflators are either unreliable or unavailable. By and large, one measure of a broad spectrum of prices moves in harmony with another, and little seems to hinge on such a choice in most cases. Sometimes, though, price indices are distorted by being heavily weighted with officially set prices, particularly in countries where governments seek to control inflation by direct price controls, and this can raise problems in particular instances.

As we shall see, many important empirical results concerning the demand for money are rather insensitive to the precise way in which money is measured and how that measurement evolves over time. However, "many" is not "all," and we shall have to return to some of the issues raised above, particularly those having to do with financial innovation, when we discuss the outcome of empirical work.

INCOME AND WEALTH

The independent variables in the demand-for-money function fall into three groups. First, there are what we shall call the *scale* variables in the relationship, income and wealth; second, there are the *opportunity cost* variables, the yields on assets other than money and the yield on money itself, including the expected rate of inflation; finally, there are the *other* variables that particular approaches to the theory of the demand for money suggest may be relevant, the level of wages, the riskiness of bonds, and so on. We shall now discuss the scale variables.

The level of income is often thought of as standing as a proxy for the volume of transactions in the economy and hence has played an important role in empirical tests of transactions-based theories of the demand for money. It is also important because it is one of the principal arguments in the demand-for-money function utilized in the macroeconomic model presented in Part I. The measurement of this variable presents little problem because, although gross national product series, net national product series and gross domestic product series have been used to measure it, these variables move rather closely together over time and no important difference in results is obtained by using one or the other. Sometimes, instead of national income, consumer expenditure has been used as a transaction proxy.

The empirical measurement of wealth is not so straightforward. For the United Kingdom, it is possible to construct a series on financial wealth, and Khusro (1952) and Grice and Bennett (1984) have used such a series in studies of the demand for money in that country. However, this is a narrow wealth concept, and only for the United States do data exist that permit the construction of long time series for various broad measures of the aggregate level of nonhuman wealth, real as well as financial, owned by the private sector of the economy. An important problem here concerns how much consolidation there should be of disaggregated wealth data in producing an aggregate figure. For example, if households own firms, as they do, should one remove all elements of double counting from the aggregate wealth of the two sectors and treat the value of household wealth alone as constraining the money holding of households and firms combined?

There is no straight theoretical answer to this question, but empirical work by Meltzer (1963) seemed to show that the results achieved are not importantly influenced by the degree of such consolidation in the wealth data used, at least within the private sector. Therefore, he measured wealth as the consolidated net worth of the private sector, including that sector's ownership of government debt.[3]

Even in the context of work in the United States, most economists have been deterred from using this variable by the conceptual problems involved in measuring the "correct" aggregate just discussed and also by Friedman's arguments discussed earlier (Chapter 5, pages 57–58) to the effect that an even more inclusive wealth concept, embodying the value of human as well as nonhuman capital, should be used when measuring the constraint on money holding. To measure this more inclusive concept of wealth presents formidable difficulties of its own, and virtually all attempts to come to grips with them have started from the simple idea that wealth is the discounted present value of expected future income. So long as the rate of discount used can be regarded as constant, wealth varies in exactly the same fashion as expected income. If expected income rises by 10%, so will wealth; if it falls, so will wealth,

---

[3] Meltzer's evidence also suggested, however, that to treat the government as "owned" by the private sector, and hence to add government assets rather than government debt to the assets of the private sector, made a difference in the results achieved. To treat government debt as net wealth to the private sector ignores the possibility that the private sector regards the future tax liabilities inherent in the necessity that the government pay interest on its debt as decreasing its net worth. Meltzer's preferred way of measuring wealth is, therefore, open to criticism inasmuch as it ignores this possibility.

and so on. One is interested in studying the relationship between *variations* in the level of wealth and *variations* in the demand for money and, because this is the case, it is not important whether wealth is measured directly or whether *expected income*, or, as it is often called, *permanent income*, is used as a proxy for this variable. It is to the discussion of this variable that we now turn.

EXPECTED INCOME

No problem in economics has received more attention recently than that of expectation formation on the part of economic agents, but until the mid-1970s it seemed that a remarkably simple approach to modeling the relationship between the actual behavior of a variable and expectations about its future behavior would suffice to produce satisfactory empirical results, and much earlier empirical work on the demand for money employed it. This approach involves applying what is interchangeably known as the *error learning* or *adaptive expectations* hypothesis to data on the actual values of whatever variable agents are thought to be forming expectations about.

Let us call the variable in question X, and let the subscripts $t, t-1$, and so on, refer to the periods during which its value is actually being observed. Let X^e be the value X is expected to take in the future, and let the subscripts $t, t-1$, and so on, refer to the periods during which the expectation in question is held. We can write the change that takes place in the value X is expected to take, the extent to which expectations adapt, between two periods, as $X_t^e - X_{t-1}^e$. The error learning hypothesis postulates that this change is proportional to the difference between the expectation about the value of X_t held in the period $t-1$ and the value X_t actually ends up taking, that is, to the amount by which the initially held expectation turns out to be in error. Thus with λ a positive fraction we can write the error learning hypothesis as

$$X_t^e - X_{t-1}^e = \lambda(X_t - X_{t-1}^e) \tag{8.1}$$

Elementary rearrangement of this expression gives

$$X_t^e = \lambda X_t + (1-\lambda)X_{t-1}^e \tag{8.2}$$

and from this, by continuous back-substitution, it follows that

$$X_t^e = \lambda X_t + \lambda(1-\lambda)X_{t-1} + \lambda(1-\lambda)^2 X_{t-2} \\ + \cdots + \lambda(1-\lambda)^n X_{t-n} \cdots \tag{8.3}$$

In short, the error learning hypothesis implies that the expected future value of a variable can be measured by taking an exponentially weighted average of current and past values of that variable, the very simple assumption underlying this procedure being nothing more than that, in trying to assess the future, people take past experience into account—and take more notice of the recent past than of more distant times.

The error learning hypothesis seems plausible enough in a rough-and-ready sort of way, but to say that this approach is plausible stops a long way short of saying that it is the best that can be done. Work dealing with the so-called *rational expectations* notion, which builds on the seminal contribution of Muth (1961), starts from this simple observation.[4] Suppose that an economic agent did indeed start out using the error learning hypothesis to form expectations of income, but suppose he or she found that this practice was leading to systematic forecasting errors of some sort. For example, suppose the formula usually overpredicted income at times when it was falling and underpredicted it at times when it was rising (as it usually would if income followed a cyclical time path). A rational maximizing agent, as economists always suppose the subjects of their analysis to be, would notice such systematic errors and would modify the way in which information on current and past income was used in forming expectations about its future course until the errors were eliminated. The agent would then no longer be forming expectations by applying Equation (8.3) to the relevant series, but in a way that was *rational* in the sense that any errors would be random over time; anything other than a random pattern of errors would eventually be recognized and allowed for in the expectations formula used.

If we take this line of reasoning seriously, it still might lead us to the proposition that the agent will form expectations about income (or any other variable for that matter) by applying some sort of averaging process to current and past values of the variable in question, but that process will not in general be the simple special case of exponentially declining weights described in Equation (8.3). Just what the averaging process will be in any particular case must depend on the way in which the variable about which expectations are being formed moves over time. There is no general formula to describe what a statistician would call an "optimal time series forecast" of income. Even so, the idea that

[4] The rational expectations idea has, of course, been more widely applied in models of inflation than in the context of the demand for money per se. In particular, it has been used by Lucas (for example, 1973) and Barro (for example, 1977, 1978) to deal with some of the issues concerning the interaction of aggregate supply and demand in the short run that were raised in Chapter 3, pages 34–36.

the demand for money might respond with a more complex lag pattern to the behavior of real income than one which can be captured in exponentially declining weights has been incorporated in a number of studies, as we shall see. Letting the data find the appropriate weights to apply to current and lagged values of income (at least within certain bounds) might be interpreted as coming quite close to the idea of measuring permanent income as an optimal time series forecast of income, and a good deal of empirical work does just that.

One can carry the rational expectations notion further. There is no good reason why maximizing agents should use only information about the past behavior of the variable they are trying to forecast. Rather, they might be expected to make use of all information that seems to be relevant to their forecast. If we set aside the considerable practical problems of the costs of data acquisition and processing, this observation may be translated into the proposition that in forecasting the future value of any variable, economic agents will act as if they were using a complete econometric model of the system generating that variable, a system of which, as often as not, their own behavior will be a part. This version of the rational expectations notion has had a considerable impact in the area of economic theory in the last 15 years or so, and has been applied in the empirical analysis of expected inflation (see, for example, Barro, 1977, 1978).

The implications of the foregoing discussion for the measurement of alternative scale variables for the demand-for-money function are easily summarized, although somewhat disheartening. At least one very influential theory of the demand for money suggests that a rather inclusive notion of wealth is the appropriate scale variable to utilize, and although direct measurement of such a variable has always been recognized as virtually impossible, it looked for a while as though this problem could be circumvented by replacing wealth with the expected or permanent stream of income it yields, a variable that could in turn be measured for the aggregate economy quite easily by applying the error learning idea to data on current and past values of real national income. Although this simple procedure has been widely used, and, as we shall see, with considerable success, the notion of rational expectations casts considerable doubt on its validity. The results generated by this earlier work must therefore be treated with skepticism and interpreted with great care, as must those of studies that postulate a distributed-lag relationship between the demand for money and real income and permit the data to determine the lag pattern. We shall return to this matter later (pages 123–130 and 165–167).

RETURNS ON ALTERNATIVE ASSETS

Now let us turn to the problem of measuring the opportunity cost variables that might be included in the demand-for-money function. Consider first the question of choosing an appropriate variable to measure the nominal yield to be earned on holding assets other than money. In practice, the availability of data limits the choice to one or two series, particularly when long time periods are to be studied. Thus, for the United States, though there are several available candidates when only post–World War II data are to be studied, notably, for example, the yields on 3-month treasury bills or on savings and loan association deposits (or shares as they are usually called), the series used for studies on longer periods have usually been either the yield on 20-year corporate bonds or on 4–6-month commercial paper. They are the yields to be earned on instruments having 20 years (or 4–6 months) to run to redemption, yield being defined as the ratio to its current market price of the average income per annum to be earned from holding to maturity the instrument in question. This yield thus includes any change in the price of the asset that must take place to bring its current price into equality with its redemption price.

As it happens, the two series in question move closely together over time, and, for the purpose of testing for the presence of a rate of interest variable in the demand-for-money function, one is probably as good as the other. Moreover, there are reasonable a priori arguments as to why either one is an appropriate selection. On the one hand, the long rate is representative of the average rate of return on capital in the economy at any time, and hence it is a good indicator of the general opportunity cost of holding money. On the other hand, short maturity instruments are closer substitutes for money than longer bonds, so that the yield on them is particularly relevant among the alternatives that are forgone by holding cash. There is merit in both these arguments, but they should be weighed in the light of work on the term structure of interest rates, the interrelationship of yields on assets of varying maturity. The most satisfactory theory of the term structure appears to be that (with suitable adjustment for risk) expected holding-period yields on assets of various maturities tend to be equalized by the market. The yield expected to be earned over any week, say, by owning 20-year bonds, tends to be brought into equality with that to be earned on instruments of all other maturities. This expected holding-period yield, of course, includes capital gains and losses made over the period. Now, if this is the case, then the yield on 4–6-month commercial paper, say, is more likely to be a good measure of short-holding-period yields on assets other than money, and hence of the opportunity cost of holding money over short periods, than is the yield to maturity on 20-year bonds.[5]

Nevertheless it has been pointed out by Laidler (1971, pp. 129–130), Karni (1972), and Friedman (1977) that the holding period for money is itself chosen by agents, so that, in principle, the whole term structure of interest rates is relevant to measuring the opportunity cost of holding money at any moment. This argument is further strengthened by McCallum's analysis of the shopping time model of the demand for money, which stresses that current holdings of money are one element in an overall strategy that is influenced by expectations about future short-term interest rates as well as their current values. Heller and Khan (1979) have attempted to obtain a summary measure of the term structure by, for each observation, running the regression of yield on term to maturity and term to maturity squared and then using the coefficients thus obtained as measures of the level and maturity structure of interest rates. Though they obtained reasonable results, their methods have not been followed up by others, perhaps because, as we have noted, results on the role of the opportunity cost of money holding on the demand for money are not all that sensitive to the precise measure chosen. As the reader will see below, it seems much more important to include some interest rate variable in the demand-for-money function than whether it is a short rate, a long rate, or some hybrid such as that constructed by Heller and Khan.

One implication of the foregoing arguments is that there exist assets on which the rate of return over that short holding period is subject to little uncertainty. This in turn suggests that theories of the speculative demand for money have little scope for application in practice because of the existence of such assets, and that the liquidity trap hypothesis may better be conceived of as dealing with the behavior of long-term relative to short-term interest rates than with the behavior of the rate of return on assets other than money relative to the rate of return on money itself. Nevertheless, the issue raised here is an empirical one. Even a little uncertainty about the holding-period yields on other assets may be enough to give speculative elements an important role

[5] The reader who wishes to pursue this matter further should start with Michaelson (1973). Note that the yield to maturity on a short instrument will not be a perfect proxy for the relevant holding period yield on a long one. The latter is likely to be higher to compensate agents for holding a riskier, or less "liquid," asset. On this, see Fried and Howitt (1983) who argue that the level of the "liquidity premium" involved here is likely to rise and fall with the general level of interest rates.

in determining the demand for money, particularly broadly defined money.

Rates of return on bills and bonds are not the only opportunity cost variables that have been used in demand for money studies. We have already mentioned the rate of return on financial intermediaries' liabilities. Hamburger (1966, 1977b) has argued that physical assets might also be good substitutes for money, and has used as an opportunity cost variable the rate of return on equities as measured by the ratio of dividend yield to price (and hence exclusive of capital gains and losses). This variable in principle measures the real return on physical capital and in inflationary situations needs to be supplemented by some variable incorporating an inflation rate measure, and in fact Hamburger's work has always involved the use of such an extra variable. (Just what it should be is discussed on pages 107–110.) Finally, it should be noted that Hamburger (1977a) was also one of the first to realize that when modeling the demand for money in open economies, the rate of return to be earned on foreign securities is worth considering as an opportunity cost variable. He applied this idea to the cases of the United Kingdom and Germany, arguing that foreign interest rates might influence the demand for money in those countries; other writers, for example, Poloz (1980, 1982), have more recently investigated the role of U.S. interest rates in influencing the demand for money in Canada.

THE OWN RATE OF RETURN ON MONEY

Though much of the theoretical work dealt with in Part II treated money as an asset bearing a zero nominal rate of return, such an assumption is hardly empirically accurate. NOW accounts, time deposits, and such in the United States, and their equivalents in other countries explicitly bear interest; and variations in the rate of return they yield ought to influence the demand for money defined broadly enough to include them. Though in many economies cartel arrangements among the banks—sometimes sanctioned by government regulation—have resulted in demand deposits' bearing no explicit interest, this is not universally the case. It was only in 1933 that it became illegal for banks in the United States to pay interest on their demand deposits. Moreover, we have already seen (page 96) that interest-bearing checkable accounts have been reintroduced in recent years, while in Canada interest-bearing deposits on which checks can be drawn have long been available. In any event, if explicit interest is not paid to depositors, banks can still evade cartel arrangements by making indirect payments to their customers. Setting service charges at a level below the cost of

operating an account, making loans to depositors at preferential interest rates, giving free advice on business and tax problems, to say nothing
of more obvious promotional schemes offering free gifts, are among the
methods available to banks for making payments to depositors without
explicitly calling those payments interest. Thus, it is an error to suppose
that even narrowly defined money necessarily does not pay a return to
those who hold it, and variations in such a return ought to lead to
variations in the quantity of money demanded.

Despite the foregoing arguments, the great majority of the empirical studies dealt with below have treated money, whether broadly or
narrowly defined, as bearing interest at a zero rate or, at least, at an
unvarying rate, which can therefore be ignored. Some workers, however, have been more careful and have included explicit measures of the
own rate of return on money in their studies. So long as interest is
explicitly paid on bank deposits, there is no problem in measuring their
own rate of return. However, if it is not paid explicitly, as in the case
of demand deposits in the United States after 1933, difficulties arise.
Two broad approaches have been taken to this issue. First, it might be
assumed, as for example by Feige (1964) and Lee (1967), that banks vary
the interest rate they pay to their customers only by varying the charges
they levy for servicing checking accounts. Then variations in the ratio
of the total value of service charges to the volume of demand deposits
can be treated as being inversely correlated with the rate of interest on
demand deposits and can be used as a proxy for that variable. Barro and
Santomero (1972) refined this approach and used data from a survey of
commercial banks for the period 1950–1968 to discover how remitted
service charges actually varied with the size of the deposit held and in
this way derived a measure of the rate of interest on demand deposits.

An alternative approach is that of Klein (1974a, 1974b), who starts
with the idea that banks manage to avoid completely any cartel arrangements and do in fact pay, albeit by covert means, what he terms a
competitive rate of return to their customers. Klein calculates the
competitive rate of return on demand deposits in the following way. The
main cost any institution bears in having a demand deposit outstanding
rather than some nonmoney liability is the interest it forgoes on the
proportion of its newly acquired assets that must be held in non-interest-
bearing reserves against that liability. If demand deposits were truly
non-interest-bearing, and no other marginal costs were involved, the
return to be made by having an extra dollar's worth of deposits outstanding would be the interest earned on the non-reserve fraction of that
dollar which the bank could invest in interest-earning securities. Thus,

if the market rate of interest were 5%, and the reserve ratio to be held against demand deposits 20%, a bank that did not pay any interest on demand deposits could earn a rate of return of 4% on every dollar deposited with it. Klein's basic postulate is that competition forces the bank to pass this marginal profit on to its depositors. Hence, in our simple example, demand deposits would bear interest, covertly paid, at the rate of 4%.

Klein's actual computations are more complex than this simple example because they allow for other implicit costs and subsidies inherent in U.S. banking regulations, but they follow the broad outlines just set out. He applies a similar procedure to computing the competitive rate of return on time deposits also, for although these bear explicit interest, the rate at which it is paid is also subject to cartel arrangements and regulations. He then computes the own rate of return on narrow money as a weighted average of the zero rate borne by currency and his estimate of the competitive rate on demand deposits. When dealing with broad money, the competitive rate on time deposits is included in a similar average.

Klein's measure of the own rate of return on demand deposits assumes that banks pay their customers a competitive rate of return on demand deposits and is open to criticism for making this assumption. Certainly, the Barro-Santomero results suggest that the rates paid by banks were below the competitive level at the time of their study. Later work by Startz (1979) based on a direct study of banks' expenses comes to the same conclusions. Judd and Scadding (1982b) cite two unpublished studies, Axilrod et al., (1977) and Becker and Bental (undated), as also suggesting that Klein's estimates of the own rate of return on demand deposits are too high. Thus Klein's work on this issue, ingenious though it is, needs to be interpreted with care.

THE EXPECTED INFLATION RATE

The final opportunity cost variable we should discuss is the expected rate of inflation. Here, as with expected (or permanent) income, the adaptive expectations hypothesis was widely used in early studies, notably by Cagan (1956), who used it to generate a series for the expected rate of inflation in a pioneering study of the demand for money in hyperinflations. Thus, the expected inflation rate has frequently been measured as an exponentially weighted average of current and past values of the actual inflation rate. The error learning hypothesis is, of course, just as open to criticism based on the rational expectations idea when applied to measuring expected inflation as when applied to measuring expected income. How good an approximation it provides to the expectations that would be formed by a rational maximizing agent depends very much on the nature of the time path followed by the inflation rate at a particular time and place, and although the approximation in question turned out to be a good one in Cagan's study, this cannot be the case in general.[6]

As in the context of measuring permanent income, so the practice of letting the data find the weights to be attached to current and past rates of inflation, instead of imposing exponentially declining weights, as adopted by, for example, Shapiro (1973) and the many more recent studies using error-correction techniques (see pages 130–132), goes some way to meeting these difficulties. Furthermore, particularly in studies of the influence of expectations about inflation on the so-called inflation-unemployment trade-off, some workers (for example, Barro, 1977, 1978) have carried the rational expectations idea further still. It has been argued that because in a fully employed economy the price level moves in proportion to the money supply, the expected rate of growth of the money supply, generated from a model of the underlying processes governing money creation, can be used to measure the expected inflation rate. Perhaps it can, but the proportional relationship between money and prices underlying this practice arises only in long-run equilibrium in an economy in which, among other things, the demand-for-money function is stable over time. A measure of the expected inflation rate that presupposes the stability of the demand-for-money function is not ideally suited for use in tests designed to investigate that stability.

For some times and places there exist data on inflation expectations generated by opinion surveys of one sort or another, and these have occasionally been used, for example, by Goldfeld (1973), in demand-for-money studies.[7] However, the operation of market mechanisms provides us with a simple indirect way of coping with the role of expectations about inflation in the demand-for-money function, at least for advanced economies with well-developed and competitive capital markets. Bonds, bills, and commercial paper, like money, are nominal

[6] See Mussa (1975) for an analysis of the conditions under which adaptive expectations are rational.

[7] Survey data often produce qualitative data on expectations rather than quantitative evidence. They tell us whether people expect inflation to be higher or lower, but not by how much. See Carlson and Parkin (1975) for a pioneering attempt at extracting quantitative information about expectations from such qualitative evidence.

assets whose real value depreciates with inflation. Thus, when inflation is expected, the public is reluctant to hold them unless the rate of return they bear is adjusted upward to compensate for the expected erosion of real capital value brought about by inflation. The higher the expected rate of inflation, the greater such an adjustment must be; but this is to argue that variations in the expected rate of inflation will be reflected in variations in these rates of return. To include the rate of return in a nominal asset in the demand-for-money function is thus to include a measure of the expected inflation rate therein. Moreover, the measure in question is produced by market forces, and its reliability does not depend on any particular hypothesis about how inflation expectations are formed.

The foregoing reasoning takes us a long way toward solving the problems of finding an appropriate measure of the expected inflation rate to use in demand-for-money studies, but it does not take us all the way. To begin with, only if asset markets were free of all distorting influences, not least those stemming from the fact that the nominal returns agents earn from asset holding are subject to taxes, would we expect fluctuations in nominal interest rates to reflect perfectly fluctuations in inflation expectations. As it is, for economies such as the United States, though the relationship is probably close enough to be useful, it is far from perfect. Moreover, in many economies well-developed asset markets that generate reliable data on nominal interest rates do not exist, and in others, though they exist, they are so strictly regulated that the data they generate on interest rates are quite misleading. In such cases, other expedients to measure expected inflation might be available. For example, when Frenkel (1977) came to investigate the Weimar hyperinflation (one of those included in Cagan's pioneering study), he noted that foreign exchange was a relevant alternative asset to domestic money and measured the opportunity cost of holding money by the forward premium in the foreign exchange market, arguing that this premium measured directly the expected rate of inflation. Here again, however, we do not always have data on foreign exchange rates, so Frenkel's solution to the problem of measuring expected inflation cannot be universally applied.

In short, there are many instances, particularly when less-developed countries are studied, in which the problem of measuring expected inflation cannot be circumvented by resorting to the use of indirect measures such as we have just been discussing. In such cases, there is no universally applicable solution to the problem of measuring expected inflation, and an important aspect of judging any study of the influence of expected inflation on the demand for money must be an assessment of the adequacy of the measure of expected inflation used.

OTHER VARIABLES

Relatively little needs to be said about the other variables that may, according to one or another of the theories discussed in Part II, play a role in the demand-for-money function. The real-wage rate, which theories of the demand for money as a means of exchange suggest might be important, has been used in several studies. Khan (1973), Dutton and Gramm (1973), and Karni (1974) used long runs of United States data (1900–1965, 1919–1958, and 1919–1968, respectively), and Dotsey (1988) included a real-wage variable in equations explaining the U.S. demand function for currency (that is, Kevin Dowd (1990) studied quarterly data on personal-sector money holdings in the United Kingdom for the period 1974–1985. Diewert (1974) and Philips (1978) studied the demand-for-money equation as one among several that emerged from a rather general model of household behavior very much in the spirit of McCallum's analysis described in Chapter 6 above. The results obtained do not seem to have been sensitive to the particular choice of wage variable. For example, Dutton and Gramm used an economy-wide, average real-wage variable, Karni used average hourly earnings, and Dowd used hourly after-tax earnings, but all found the variable to be significant.

A study by Slovin and Sushka (1983) has incorporated a measure of the riskiness of bonds, and a series that measures variations in the inflation rate has been developed by Klein (1975). Inasmuch as such variations may reduce the predictability of the value of money, Klein's measure can be regarded as capturing fluctuations in the liquidity of money, and he used it as a variable in an empirical study of the demand for money in the United States (Klein, 1977), as did Laidler (1980). The distribution of income has not been directly incorporated into empirical work on the demand for money as yet. However, several studies, notably those by Bordo and Jonung (1981, 1987, 1990) as well as Siklos (1991) for five countries (the United States, Canada, the United Kingdom, Sweden, and Norway) and one by Klovland (1983) for Norway, have tried to investigate the effects of long-run institutional change on the demand for money along lines suggested by Fisher's analysis (see page 47 above). They have used, for obvious enough reasons, such variables as the proportion of the labor force employed outside of agriculture, the ratio of population to bank offices, the ratio of currency to the total money stock, and the ratio of nonbank financial assets to total financial assets to measure the degrees of monetization and financial development of the economies they studied.[8]

CONCLUDING COMMENT

As we have now seen, giving empirical content to the theoretical notions that form the bases of the theories of the demand for money discussed in Part II of this book is far from straightforward, and by no means all of the problems that arise here have satisfactory and universally applicable solutions. More detailed discussion of the issues this raises is best carried on in the context of specific studies. Before we can turn to these, however, we need to say something about some of the econometric problems that arise in the context of studies of the demand for money. These form the subject matter of the next chapter.

[8] It is worth noting that Bordo and Jonung explicitly refer to Knut Wicksell's (1898) exposition of the classical quantity theory, rather than Fisher's, as the inspiration for their work.

chapter 9

Some Econometric Issues

INTRODUCTORY COMMENT

We are mainly interested in the demand for money because we are concerned about the way in which the quantity of nominal money in circulation in an economy interacts with other factors to influence the behavior of interest rates, real income, employment, and the price level. We are concerned with the aggregate demand-for-money function, and in the previous chapter we discussed some of the issues involved in measuring the variables used in empirical studies of that function. It is not necessary to enter into a discussion of the technical details of various econometric techniques in order to bring out the main lessons that have been learned from their application, but their use does raise certain questions of which readers must be conscious if they are to interpret with an appropriately critical attitude the empirical work we shall soon discuss.

THE IDENTIFICATION PROBLEM

Any theory of the demand for money leads to propositions about the nature of the relationship between the quantity of money agents in the economy want to hold and the variables that underlie that decision, those variables typically being some real income or wealth measure representing the scale variable in the function, some interest rate or rates measuring the opportunity cost of holding money, and, of course, the price level, if we are dealing with the demand for nominal money. The first thing to note here is that we cannot be sure that we ever actually observe the quantity of nominal money demanded. What we see is the quantity of money in circulation, and it is only by assuming that this money is all willingly held that we can treat it as measuring the dependent variable of our function. Moreover, though it may be true that variations in real income, the price level, and some representative interest rate lead to variations in the nominal quantity of money demanded, it is also true that variations in the nominal quantity of money supplied (among other variables) lead to variations in income, the price level, and the rate of interest. When we are confronted by time series data on these variables, it is far from obvious that the relationships among them that can be given quantitative content do indeed reflect the structure of the demand-for-money function rather than the combined influences of all the other behavior relationships that make up the structure of the economy. That is to say, it is far from clear that the demand-for-money function can be *identified*.

To see better what is involved here, it is helpful to set aside the complications of dealing with a complete macroeconomic model and to consider instead the way in which the identification problem arises in the context of the simple supply-and-demand apparatus with which we began Part I of this book. In Figure 9.1, therefore, we show the demand for some good X as a negative function of its own price and the supply function as a positive function of that price. Let the problem be to measure the relationship between the demand for X and its price from observations generated in this market. As can be seen from Figure 9.2(a), this will be possible if the supply function shifts while the demand function remains stable. In this case, all observed values lie on the demand curve. If only the demand function shifts, the supply curve will

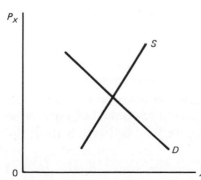

Figure 9.1 The supply and demand for X.

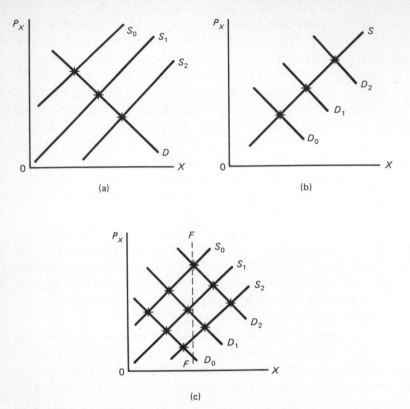

Figure 9.2   (a) Only the supply curve shifts, ensuring that all observations (marked with crosses) lie on the demand curve. (b) Only the demand curve shifts, so that observations outline the supply curve. (c) Both curves shift, yielding a set of observations that, if regression analysis is applied to them, will produce a curve such as *FF*, which is neither a supply function nor a demand function. *X* is the dependent variable.

be observed, as in panel (b). If both functions shift, a situation such as that shown in panel (c) will arise, and we will obtain a scatter of observations that lie between the demand curve and the supply curve, telling us nothing about either, though we can still use regression analysis to fit a function such as the line *FF* to them. In fitting such a curve, however, it is clear that we do not obtain a measure of the relationship between the demand for *X* and its price.[1]

Of course, econometricians have worked on means of overcoming the problems we are illustrating, and the outlines of a satisfactory solution to them are easily enough grasped in the context of the simple supply-and-demand apparatus used in Figure 9.2. To begin with, if the

---

[1] The classic article on identification of supply and demand curves is Working (1927, reprinted 1953) and is still worth reading.

demand curve for X does shift around, that can be allowed for by including those factors causing it to shift as extra exogenous variables in the demand function to be fitted. Then, so long as at least one of the variables causing the supply curve of X to shift does not appear in its demand function, so long as at least some of the shifts in the supply function of X are *independent* of any shifts of the demand function, it has been shown that it is indeed possible to identify the relationship between the demand for X and its price. In these circumstances, the use of regression analysis to estimate a relationship between the quantity of X traded, its own price, and the other variables affecting the demand for X will yield estimates of the parameters of the demand function for X, including that linking quantity demanded to price.[2]

The important point here is that to ensure that workers studying the demand curve for X can identify it, they must know about certain properties of the entire supply-and-demand system generating their observations. In particular, they must know which exogenous factors cause the supply and demand curves to shift and whether or not they vary independently of one another. If we apply these principles to the matter of estimating a demand-for-money function, their implications are reasonably clear. Suppose that we believe the demand for nominal balances to depend on the level of real income, the price level, and a representative interest rate, and the supply of nominal balances to depend on that same interest rate and the stock of base money available in the economy. Then, if fluctuations in the stock of base money are independent of fluctuations in real income and prices or of any other variable, including random factors that might cause the demand for money to vary, the parameters of the demand function will be identified. If the latter condition does not hold, then they will not be.

As the reader will see, some workers have paid attention to the identification problem when studying the demand for money, but, as Cooley and Leroy (1981) have argued, even where the problem has been addressed, efforts to ensure that conditions under which the demand-for-money function is identified do in fact hold have been rather perfunctory. In the example given above, as they point out, any tendency for the monetary authorities to accommodate shifts in the demand for money with base money changes would undermine identifiability. In any event, far too often the whole identification problem has been ignored. The fact that parameter estimates obtained for the

---

[2] The reader well versed in econometrics will realize that, strictly speaking, for the above conclusion to be true, the demand curve must be just identified—it must be possible to derive one, and only one, value for each of its parameters. If it is overidentified, other techniques whose details need not concern us here must be applied.

demand function when the problem has been ignored tend to be much like those generated in studies where it has been explicitly addressed certainly suggest that this issue may often not be a critical one, but Cooley and Leroy are nevertheless right in arguing that this fact stops far short of demonstrating conclusively that this is the case. "Often" is not "always," and we shall have reason to return to this question when we discuss so-called short-run demand-for-money functions below.

Another approach to the identification problem as it arises in the context of the demand-for-money function is worth some comment. Suppose we chose to fit the relationship in real rather than nominal terms, treating the quantity of real money as the dependent variable. In an economy in which the price level fluctuates freely and endogenously, there is no separate supply function for real balances. In this case, we have but a single equation to worry about and hence need not concern ourselves with the identification problem as we have just discussed it. Provided we are willing to take it for granted that the demand for real balances is independent of the price level, rather than asking that this property of the function be tested, and, crucially, provided we are willing to argue that all factors affecting the demand for real balances are determined elsewhere in the system independently of the demand function, we are able to identify the other parameters of the relationship.[3] Again, though, we must note that if the price level tends to be sticky in the short run, this argument will not apply to short-run functions.

SIMULTANEITY

Once it is pointed out that the price level and therefore the quantity of real money are endogenous variables, it is hard to ignore the fact that so, usually, are real income and interest rates. The endogeneity of the variables on the right-hand side of our demand-for-money function, whether it be formulated in nominal or real terms, raises a set of issues for regression analysis, which is often used to estimate demand-for-money functions, that econometricians call *simultaneous equations bias*.

Even if all of our data were measured with perfect accuracy, and if the arguments of our demand-for-money function were capable of

---

[3] This latter condition, theoretically speaking at least, will hold if the economy generating our data is operating at full employment. Such an economy is described in the flexible-price vertical aggregate supply curve analysis presented in Chapter 3 (pages 30–32), and it is argued there that the supply and demand for money determine only the price level, with real income and interest rates being determined elsewhere in the system.

explaining every scrap of variation in the quantity of money demanded, the identification problem would still arise. This problem is not peculiar to the application of regression analysis, which takes it for granted that some residual fluctuations of the dependent variable of the relationship being studied are unexplained and should be attributed to an *error term*. The additional problem of simultaneous equations bias arises in the presence of such error terms. To be specific, when variables endogenous to the economic system turn up as explanatory variables on the right-hand side of the demand-for-money function, the simultaneity problem arises because these variables in their turn are determined elsewhere in the system and because their determination, too, is subject to residual error.

If the economic system as a whole is from time to time subject to random shocks, these might be expected to cause simultaneous random fluctuations in all endogenous variables of the system. The random fluctuations will be correlated with one another, not because there is any question that the relevant fluctuation in one endogenous variable causes a fluctuation in another, but simply because they have a common cause elsewhere in the system. When one performs the "ordinary" least squares regression of real-money balances on, say, real income and the rate of interest, one is, of course, treating all systematic, as opposed to random, variations in one endogenous variable as being the result of those in two other such variables. To the extent that the system to which these variables belong is subject to the kind of common shocks we have just discussed, the quantitative estimates we obtain of the parameters of the function will, if we ignore their presence, be biased by the influence of errors common to the three variables, but having their cause elsewhere in the system.

The most common way in which economists cope with this problem is to remove the offending errors from the right-hand-side variables of the demand-for-money function.[4] This may be accomplished, at least in principle, by performing the regression of each of these variables on variables that are truly exogenous to the economic system and using their predicted values from such a regression to replace their actual values on the right-hand side of the demand-for-money function. This technique, known as "two-stage least squares," and variations on it deal adequately with the problem of simultaneous equations bias of ordinary least squares in principle, but in practice they are effective only to the

---

[4] Though it is the most commonly used method, it is not the only one, by any means. See, for example, Johnston (1972, Chapter 13) for a concise account of this and other approaches.

extent that the choice of "truly exogenous" variables (often referred to as *instruments*) is appropriate. To call a variable exogenous does not make it so.

Two-stage least squares has been used quite frequently when demand-for-money functions have been fitted, but in many cases this does not seem to have made much difference to the results obtained. This might be because simultaneous equations bias is not a major problem in the context of the demand for money, or it could be because, as Cooley and Leroy (1981) have suggested, an inappropriate choice of instruments has left the two-stage least squares estimates of the function just as biased as those obtained by simpler methods. For reasons that will become apparent, I am inclined to think that Cooley and Leroy are unduly pessimistic about this matter, just as they are about the extent to which the identification problem may be solved in practice, but this is nevertheless an issue readers must bear in mind as they make up their own minds about the quality of existing evidence on the demand-for-money function.

PERIOD AND FREQUENCY OF OBSERVATIONS

At first sight, it might seem that the length of time for which we have observations on variables to be used in tests of the demand-for-money function and the frequency with which those observations occur have little to do with econometric issues per se. However, this is not the case. To begin with, long runs of data are often time trended, and this raises estimation problems; and the extent to which a particular set of data might suffer from the kind of errors that lead to simultaneous equations bias can be related to the length of the time period it covers and to the time interval over which individual observations are averaged. Also, as we shall see in a moment, a whole set of econometric issues having to do with the appropriate treatment of time lags in the demand-for-money function arise in this context, too.

The availability and quality of data with which demand-for-money functions may be tested vary greatly from country to country. For some countries, for example, the United States, the United Kingdom, Canada, Italy, Norway, and Sweden, there are data series going back well into the nineteenth century. As might be expected, the further back one goes, the patchier are the sources from which such series can be constructed, and long consistent runs of data only exist for annual observations of the relevant variables. For more recent times, especially since World War II, relevant data are available on a quarterly basis for many countries, and some series are available for monthly, weekly, or even daily observations. However, it is the least frequently observed variable that determines the frequency of observations used in any particular study, and the lack of real-income data for any period shorter than a quarter means that most studies of the demand-for-money function have used quarterly or annual data. Some investigators, notably Friedman and Schwartz (1982), taking advantage of the extremely long period for which United States and United Kingdom data are available, have opted for an even higher degree of time aggregation in their work, using observations averaged over business cycle phases (upswings and downswings) lasting on average 2 years or more, Friedman (1959) even used data averaged over whole cycles.

Long runs of data reaching back into the beginning of this century or even earlier tend to be dominated by time trends; but regression analysis is, strictly speaking, valid only if the values of the variables it deals with are the outcome of processes that ensure that the variable's underlying average value is constant over time, if the process in question is *stationary*. Clearly, a variable subject to time trend is not stationary, but its first time difference might be.[5] Some studies of the demand for money have used first-differenced data to eliminate the effects of time trend; others have used velocity (money divided by income) as a dependent variable, rather than money alone, for a similar reason. More recently, a powerful new technique called *co-integration analysis*, which will be discussed below, has been introduced to overcome such problems.

A great advantage of long periods of data is that they permit a relatively high degree of time aggregation to be used, and this, too, helps with the simultaneity problem. The more one averages a variable over time, the more random fluctuations in it tend to cancel out. If a series observed monthly is averaged to produce quarterly observations, the consequences of short-term random shocks, whose effects persist for only a few weeks, are purged from the data and the resulting series is smoother than the monthly one. Averaging up to annual observations has a further smoothing effect, and so on. In short, there is a presumption that studies using annual data are less subject to simultaneous equations bias than those using quarterly data and that those using cycle phase average data are even less suspect in this regard.

Using data with a rather high degree of time aggregation also helps us with the problem of measuring expectational variables. The difference between the average actual value of a variable and the average

---

[5] But, if the series rises at a rising rate, its first difference will still be subject to a time trend. Then, second differences might do the trick, and so on.

value agents expected it to take over the relevant period obviously shrinks as we move from quarterly to annual to cycle phase data, and Friedman and Schwartz (1982), for example, use the actual rate of inflation to measure the expected rate over cycle phases. Also, using a theorem from growth theory, they use the rate of growth of real income to measure the real rate of return on capital, so that for them the opportunity cost of holding money is given by the rate of growth of nominal income, which is, of course, the sum of the real growth and inflation rates.

However, using data with a high degree of time aggregation has its costs. The number of observations in any time series is obviously reduced by aggregation. Moreover, though unwanted random error is averaged out of the data, so are other variations, which, though short-term, might well be systematic and could potentially throw extra light on the nature of the demand-for-money function. Some econometricians, for example, Hendry and Ericsson (1983, 1991a), have been particularly critical of Friedman and Schwartz for aggregating data over time because of the potential destructive effect this has on the data's information content. One will never discover how serious a matter this is without actual experiments. Thus, there are excellent reasons why, despite the extra problems it generates, students of the demand for money have carried out much of their work using quarterly and, where available, monthly data.

ADJUSTMENT COSTS AND THE SHORT-RUN DEMAND-FOR-MONEY FUNCTION

Theories of the demand for money as a means of exchange do not make predictions about how much cash the individual agent or even the economy as a whole will be holding at each and every moment. Agents engaged in market activity will plan to have their cash balances fluctuate over time as a result of the unsynchronized nature of receipts and payments. Theories of the transactions and precautionary demands for money are explicitly based on just this consideration, and more general approaches, such as Friedman's, in treating money as a "temporary abode of purchasing power," also acknowledge it.[6]

The "demand for money" that such theories seek to explain is a demand for a *target level* of money holding that agents seek to achieve *on average over time* and not at each and every moment. For cycle phase

---

[6] Economists taking this approach to monetary economics often refer to money as a "shock absorber" or a "buffer stock." See Laidler (1984) for a discussion of the issues raised by this approach. See also pages 175–178 below.

average data for a whole economy such as Friedman and Schwartz (1982) use, this might not matter much. By the time money holdings have been added up over agents to obtain a figure for the whole economy and then added up again over time, departures of individual cash holdings from their desired levels at any particular moment will, like as not, have been averaged out of the data. But suppose we stopped at annual data or quarterly data? Could we then make the same claim? Most researchers using annual data and virtually all of them using quarterly data have concluded that such a claim should not be made, and though the methods they have used to deal with the resulting problems have often been far from satisfactory, an understanding of these methods is vital to an appreciation of what we have and have not learned from their empirical work on the demand for money.

The most common of these methods involves the notion of "adjustment costs." In order to understand that notion in the context of empirical work on the demand-for-money function, the reader should note first that many studies of the demand-for-money function postulate that the demand for real balances takes a constant elasticity form

$$\frac{M_t}{P_t} = kX^{\beta_1} r_t^{\beta_2} E_t \tag{9.1}$$

where X is some scale variable, r is the interest rate, and E is an error term. The reader should also note that if we rewrite this relationship in logarithms, using lowercase, boldface, italic letters for logs, it reduces to a convenient linear form particularly suitable for estimation by way of regression analysis.[7] Where $\beta_0 = \log k$, we have

$$(\boldsymbol{m} - \boldsymbol{p})_t^* = \beta_0 + \beta_1 \boldsymbol{x}_t + \beta_2 \boldsymbol{r}_t + \boldsymbol{e}_t \tag{9.2}$$

I have attached an asterisk (*) to the dependent variable of this relationship to indicate that it denotes the target, or long-run, value of real balances determined by the right-hand side of the equation. Suppose that Equation (9.2) referred to the demand for money of an individual agent, and suppose that we allowed for the possibility that the agent's money holding might from time to time depart from its target value. We

---

[7] The β's are clearly elasticities in Equation (9.1). Consider β_2. It follows from (9.1) that

$$\frac{\delta(M_t/P_t)}{\delta r_t} = kX_t^{\beta_1} \beta_2 r_t^{\beta_2 - 1}$$

so that

$$\frac{\delta(M_t/P_t)}{M_t/P_t} = \beta_2 \frac{\delta r}{r_t}$$

might argue then that the agent would encounter costs of two kinds. First, because the agent is away from target money holdings, he or she is enjoying less benefits from money holding than otherwise; and second, an agent who adjusts money holdings over time to move back toward the target will also encounter costs involved in making the necessary trades.[8] For reasons that will become apparent in an instant, suppose that both of these costs may be described in quadratic functions so that their total K is

$$K = \alpha[(m - p)_t^* - (m - p)_t]^2 + \alpha_2[(m - p)_t - (m - p)_{t-1}]^2 \quad (9.3)$$

A maximizing agent will attempt to control money holding over time so that these costs are at a minimum, and what this implies may be discovered by taking the derivative of K with respect to $m_t - p_t$, the variable under the agent's control, and setting it equal to zero. Because of the quadratic form of Equation (9.3), to do this yields the convenient linear expression

$$(m - p)_t - (m - p)_{t-1} = \frac{\alpha_1}{\alpha_1 + \alpha_2}[(m - p)_t^* - (m - p)_{t-1}] \quad (9.4)$$

If we define $\beta_3 \equiv \alpha_1/\alpha_1 + \alpha_2$ and then substitute the right-hand side of Equation (9.2) for $(m_t - p_t)^*$ in (9.4), we end up with

$$\begin{aligned} (m - p)_t = {} & \beta_3\beta_0 + \beta_3\beta_1 x_t + \beta_3\beta_2 r_t \\ & + (1 - \beta_3)(m - p)_{t-1} + \beta_3 e_t \end{aligned} \quad (9.5)$$

Moreover, if we estimate the parameters of this so-called short-run relationship, we may recover those of the original long-run function by dividing the former by 1 minus the coefficient of the lagged dependent variable. This adjustment cost formulation of the short-run demand-for-money function has been widely used in empirical work on the demand-for-money function, and the results it has generated have often seemed to be satisfactory. However, this does not alter the fact that the interpretation of results based on it is fraught with difficulty. The analysis from which we derived it seems plausible enough if we swallow the rather arbitrary quadratic form of Equation (9.3), but closer inspection reveals that this plausibility is superficial indeed. The problems here are both econometric and economic, as we shall now see.

[8] The reader who is familiar with the empirical literature on the demand for investment goods and consumer durables will recognize these arguments. They were explicitly borrowed from this source by economists working on the demand for money in the 1960s. See, for example, Chow (1966).

ECONOMETRIC PROBLEMS WITH
THE LAGGED DEPENDENT VARIABLE

Consider the error term e in Equations (9.2) and (9.5), which is there to capture the effects of all factors, systematic and random, that affect the demand for money, but are not explicitly included as independent variables in our function. If this error term moves completely randomly over time, then (provided that none of the other problems we shall discuss in due course are relevant) an ordinary regression equation like (9.5) fitted by least squares to time series data would yield unbiased estimates of the parameters of the long-run demand-for-money function and of the adjustment parameter underlying the short-run relationship. However, if there is any systematic component to the error term, caused perhaps by the influence of some omitted variable on the demand for money which itself moves systematically over time, then we have a problem.

A simple example will illustrate the difficulty. Suppose that e depends on its own once-lagged value and that its behavior displays *first-order autoregression*. Write, with u_t a serially uncorrelated random variable having a zero mean,

$$e_t = \rho e_{t-1} + u_t \qquad (9.6)$$

Then write the long-run demand function ... $\beta_0 + \beta_1 x_t + \beta_2 r_t$ as $f(Z)$ to save space. Substitute the right-hand side of this expression into Equation (9.5) in order to get

$$(m - p)_t = \beta_3 f(Z) + (1 - \beta_3)(m - p)_{t-1} + \beta_3 \rho e_{t-1} + \beta_3 u_t \qquad (9.5')$$

Basic regression analysis is premised on the assumption that the error term displays no autoregression. If such analysis was applied to estimating Equation (9.5) when (9.5') was the true expression, then the influence of e_{t-1} on the demand for money would be attributed to the variable $(m - p)_{t-1}$. Of course, e_{t-1} is already a component of this variable, so that, if ρ is positive, the resulting estimate of $1 - \beta_3$ will be biased upward, adjustment will appear to be slower than it really is, and our estimates of the long-run parameters of the demand-for-money function will also be biased upward; and vice versa. Furthermore, if the short-run dynamics implicit in our data are unstable, then our estimates of $1 - \beta_3$ and of the long-run parameters will also be unstable over time, even perhaps when the true long-run process generating the data is not.

These problems are not insoluble. Techniques for allowing for autocorrelation in the residuals of regression equations of both the first and higher orders do nowadays exist. Nevertheless, in the context of time series work on the demand for money, particularly with quarterly data, autocorrelated residuals are both a common and an important phenomenon. Thus, empirical estimates of short-run demand-for-money functions based on expressions like Equation (9.5) cannot always be taken at face value. Apart from anything else, the relevant estimation techniques have only been developed relatively recently and were not widely available to people working in the 1960s and 1970s when much pioneering work on the demand for money was done.

The adjustment cost hypothesis is not the only means of introducing a lagged dependent variable into the demand-for-money function. If the appropriate scale variable in the relationship was permanent income, and if it was decided to proxy this variable by applying the error learning hypothesis (see Chapter 8, page 100) to the logarithms of current income, which would amount to postulating that agents revised their expectations of income according to the ratio of the actual value of income to the previous expectation of its value, we would have for the long-run demand-for-money function

$$(m - p)_t = \beta_0 + \beta_1 y_t^p + \beta_2 r_t + e_t \tag{9.7}$$

with the log of expected income y_t^p being given by

$$y_t^p = \lambda y_t + (1 - \lambda)y_{t-1}^p \tag{9.8}$$

If the reader carries out the so-called Koyck transformation on the above expression, by substituting Equation (9.8) into (9.7), then subtracting from the resulting expression Equation (9.7) multiplied through by $1 - \lambda$ and lagged one period, this will yield[9]

$$\begin{aligned} (m - p)_t = &\lambda\beta_0 + \lambda\beta_1 y_t + \beta_2 r_t - (1 - \lambda)\beta_2 r_{t-1} \\ &+ (1 - \lambda)(m - p)_{t-1} + e_t - (1 - \lambda)e_{t-1} \end{aligned} \tag{9.9}$$

To be sure, this is not the same expression as Equation (9.5) would yield if we used current real income as the scale variable in the long-run demand function, but it is sufficiently like it that, if (9.9) was in fact the true model of the demand-for-money function, then those who fitted (9.5) would obtain rather good results, and vice versa.[10] They might also

---

[9] This widely used manipulation is named after L. M. Koyck, the Dutch econometrician who discovered it. See Koyck (1954).

[10] The truth of this assertion is not logically necessary. Rather it follows from the empirical fact that the rate of interest is a highly serially correlated variable, so that to omit its lagged value from an equation containing its current value results in the explanatory power, if any, of the lagged variable's being attributed by the regression to the current value. Note that the argument above amounts to saying that lags in the empirical relationship might derive from problems of measuring the arguments in the long-run function. Goodfriend (1985) analyzes a much more general version of this argument.

be misled into believing that adjustment lags were an important factor in the demand-for-money function, when in fact they were not. It is possible to attempt to distinguish between these expectations and adjustment cost approaches to introducing a lagged dependent variable into the demand-for-money function. It is also possible to treat adjustment lags and expectation lags as complementary phenomena and to allow them both to appear in the function by substituting y^p for X in Equation (9.5) and then applying the Koyck transformation to the resulting expression. As we shall see in Chapter 12 (page 165), some people working on the demand for money have indeed pursued this line of enquiry, so the lesson of the foregoing argument is not that the adjustment lag hypothesis is untestable in principle. Rather it is that empirical demand-for-money functions utilizing lagged dependent variables must be interpreted with great care since they do not necessarily reflect the workings of adjustment mechanisms.

ECONOMIC PROBLEMS WITH
THE LAGGED DEPENDENT VARIABLE

As was remarked earlier, the adjustment cost model of the short-run demand for money raises problems having to do with economic theory as well as econometric estimation. The reader will recall that models of the transactions and precautionary demand for money, such as were discussed in Chapter 5, postulate that agents face transactions costs in adjusting their money holdings in order to derive what in the context of the present discussion is properly called the long-run demand function. The costs discussed there were lump sum in nature, but it was pointed out that it was possible to extend the relevant models to incorporate variable costs, albeit at the expense of a considerable increase in their analytic complexity. There is no need to go into such analysis explicitly to make the following important point: It is awkward to postulate, as do, for example, Santomero and Seater (1981), at least implicitly, one kind of adjustment cost to derive the long-run demand-for-money function and then, having done that, to postulate another kind to justify the introduction of a lagged dependent variable into the relationship for purposes of empirical work. If it is thought that both kinds of costs are important, then, as Milbourne, Buckholtz, and Wasan (1983) argue, both need to be introduced simultaneously at the beginning of the analysis in order to derive valid results. Studies of the demand for money that claim to be testing transactions demand for money models, but rely on lagged dependent variables introduced on adjustment cost grounds in order to obtain satisfactory empirical results, are thus highly suspect.

The dependent variable of Equation (9.2) is the log of real balances. That is appropriate enough, since all of our theories of the demand for money tell us that the demand for money is indeed a demand for real balances. However, when we apply the adjustment cost argument to that equation, we end up with Equation (9.5), which tells us that economic agents will adjust their real balances slowly over time in response to changes in the scale variable of the demand-for-money function (expected real income, say) and the rate of interest. As far as the individual agent is concerned, the price level is at least as much an exogenous variable as are expected real income and the interest rate, and to attain a given level of *real balances*, the agent must take the price level as given and vary his or her holdings of *nominal balances*.

This is important because Equation (9.5) implies that, when the price level changes, nominal balances adjust instantaneously to keep real balances constant. It is not obvious that agents' adjustment to price level changes should be instantaneous when their adjustment to changes in other variables is slow, and some economists have concluded that Equations (9.3) and (9.4) are inappropriate as applications of the adjustment cost idea to the demand for money, arguing that they should be cast in terms of nominal rather than real balances. If that is done, instead of Equation (9.4) we have

$$m_t - m_{t-1} = \frac{\alpha_1}{\alpha_1 + \alpha_2}(m_t^* - m_{t-1}) \equiv \beta_3(m_t^* - m_{t-1}) \quad (9.4')$$

and Equation (9.5) becomes, again writing the long-run function as $f(Z)$ to save space,

$$(m - p)_t = \beta_3 f(Z) + (1 - \beta_3)(m_{t-1} - p_t) + \beta_3 e_t \quad (9.5'')$$

This expression differs from (9.5) only in having the current rather than the lagged value of the log of the price level on the right-hand side. Given that the price level is a highly autocorrelated variable, particularly in quarterly data, it is a fair generalization to say that if the "real adjustment" version of the short-run demand-for-money function we discussed earlier performs well, then so will this "nominal adjustment" version. However, the two forms are not the same. It is possible in principle to distinguish between them; the underlying economics of the two versions of the function do differ. Once more, we have a reason for taking great care about interpreting the results of demand-for-money studies that use lagged values of the dependent variable as right-hand-side variables.

INDIVIDUAL AND MARKET ADJUSTMENTS: MONEY HOLDINGS AS BUFFER STOCKS, AND IDENTIFICATION AGAIN

The arguments about adjustment costs presented earlier were cast in terms of the behavior of the individual agent, but the empirical applications concerned the aggregate demand-for-money function. It is a common enough practice in economics to construct a model of the behavior of a representative agent in an individual experiment and then to argue that in the market experiment the economy as a whole acts "as if" it was simply a scaled-up version of that individual agent. However, that does not make it safe to do so, because what is true of the individual is not always true of the aggregate of individuals acting together. It is always possible to commit fallacies of composition when going from propositions about individuals to propositions about the whole economy, and the following important fallacy of composition permeates the foregoing discussion, as we shall now see.[11]

The variable under the control of the individual agent is nominal balances, and he or she varies these in order to attain a desired level of real balances. This consideration underlay our derivation of the nominal adjustment short-run function (9.5″). However, throughout the analysis of the economy as a whole set out in Part I of this book, we treated the nominal quantity of money as an exogenous variable determined on the supply side of the market. If we take that analysis seriously as a framework for discussing the interaction of the quantity of money and other variables in the economy, then however plausible arguments about nominal adjustment may be at the level of the individual agent, they are, quite unequivocally, logical nonsense when applied at the level of the economy as a whole. Nominal money cannot simultaneously be a variable that is exogenous to the arguments of the aggregate demand-for-money function and a variable that responds endogenously to variations in them.

As we saw in Part I, equilibrium between the supply and demand for money in the flexible price version of our macroeconomic model is maintained by having the price level vary. When a flexible price economy is pushed off its long-run demand-for-money function, it moves back to equilibrium by way of the influence of price level changes on the

[11] Care in distinguishing between individual and market experiments is, of course, a distinguishing feature of Patinkin's (1965) analysis. The following arguments are developed at greater length in Laidler (1982, Chapter 2), and Gordon (1984). Lane (1990) presents a more general formulation of them, developed in the context of a complete macroeconomic model. See also Laidler (1984).

stock of real balances. Laidler (1982, Chapter 2) and Lane (1990) have shown that, if the price level is perfectly flexible, such adjustment is instantaneous, and only a long-run aggregate demand-for-money function is observable. However, if prices move less than instantaneously, we would observe the economy moving slowly to equilibrium over time by way of the influence of price level changes on the quantity of real balances. The effects of being out of equilibrium on agents' plans would, according to this view, be absorbed by fluctuations in their holdings of money, which act as so-called *buffer stocks*. On this basis, some economists have argued that, for the economy as a whole, the real adjustment version, Equation (9.5), of the short-run demand-for-money function is in effect a price level adjustment equation. Their argument will not quite do, however.

To begin with, the distinction between the short-run and long-run demand-for-money functions arises from costs encountered by the individual agent when attempts are made to alter money holdings, not from the existence of some degree of price level stickiness at the level of the economy as a whole. Such stickiness is a consequence of the way in which the economy responds to exogenous shocks, not least in the supply of nominal money, and to interpret Equation (9.5) as an appropriately specified price level adjustment equation, we would have to argue that it is possible to capture in one simple parameter, β_3, the entire transmission mechanism whereby the price level responds to discrepancies between the supply and demand for nominal money. This might be possible, though it seems implausible to say the least. If we are suspicious of this one parameter, however, we must of course be suspicious of all other parameters estimated using a real adjustment equation like (9.5).

Also, it may reasonably be pointed out that the assumption of an exogenous nominal money supply is an extreme one. In real-world economies, the nominal money supply does respond endogenously to changes in the variables underlying the demand for money. Such endogeneity can, for example, arise when monetary authorities are attempting to maintain some control over the level of interest rates by increasing nominal money when market forces are tending to drive them up, and vice versa. It can also arise through the balance of payments when the authorities are trying to control the level of the foreign exchange rate. In such cases, it might make sense to postulate that the nominal money supply adjusts slowly to changes in the demand for it, but this does not make the nominal adjustment version (9.5″) of the short-run demand-for-money function an appropriate form to use. One cannot use the

existence of time lags in the *supply-of-money* function to justify including a lagged dependent variable in what purports to be a *demand-for-
money* function. As we have seen, whenever supply and demand functions interact to produce data for us, we must be concerned about the
identification problem, and the above argument amounts to saying that
it is not clear that the structure of the short-run demand function is
properly identified in an equation like (9.5) or (9.5″). In this respect,
it provides an economic complement to the econometric arguments of
Cooley and Leroy (1981) referred to earlier.

It is only relatively recently that economists have become fully
aware of the problems discussed in the preceding few paragraphs, and
much of the literature dealing with empirical work on the demand-for-
money function, particularly that using quarterly data, either ignores
them altogether or treats them in a rather perfunctory manner.[12] However, some workers, notably those associated with Dr. Clifford Wymer,
have addressed these issues head on. They have taken the view that the
appropriate way to deal with the adjustment of cash holdings to a target
value (among other problems) is to construct an explicit model of that
adjustment process and to estimate it as a complete system, all of whose
parameters are properly identified. Wymer's procedure involves, first,
specifying a complete macroeconomic model in which the transmission
mechanism for monetary policy is highlighted and, second, estimating
the parameters of the long-run demand-for-money functions simultaneously with all the other parameters of the model, including those that
purport to capture the process whereby not just the demand for money,
but all other endogenous variables, move over time toward their equilibrium values. This procedure is complex and requires a great deal of
effort on the part of its users. It is not surprising, therefore, that it has
more often been used by those whose main interest is, in any case, in
building complete macroeconomic models of particular economies,
rather than by those more concerned with studying just one of the
components of such a model, namely, the demand-for-money function.
Also, this technique is vulnerable to the criticism that any error made
in specifying one component of the system can, in principle at least,

---

[12] As is often the case, however, full awareness of a set of issues has come with
a rather long time lag after they were raised. Important elements of the foregoing
arguments are to be found in Walters (1967), Starleaf (1970), Tucker (1971), Akerlof
(1973), Artis and Lewis (1976), Jonson (1976a, 1976b), and Lewis (1978). More recently
they have been developed by Knoester (1979), Laidler (1980, 1982), Carr and Darby
(1981), Goodhart (1982), Coats (1982), Judd and Scadding (1982a), and Kanniainen and
Tarkka (1983).

undermine the reliability not just of estimates of that component, but of the rest of the model as well.[13]

CO-INTEGRATION AND ERROR-CORRECTION ANALYSIS

The foregoing arguments tell us that the short-run demand-for-money function, as it is often specified, may not be properly identified and that procedures that might help with this problem may render any study of the demand for money extremely vulnerable to problems arising from specification errors. These problems arise with respect to the short-run function, but, as we have already argued, they may well contaminate our ability to estimate the parameters of the long-run function as part of the structure underlying the short-run relationship. A relatively recently developed body of econometric techniques involving *co-integration* and *error-correction analysis* help us to surmount this impasse. They enable us, in principle at least, to estimate long-run relationships without simultaneously having to take a strong position on how to model short-run dynamic processes and to generate statistical descriptions of the latter while remaining agnostic about the economic processes underlying them.[14]

We noted earlier that the absence of stationarity in economic variables makes the application of regression analysis to them problematic. However, the fact that a particular variable does not always tend to move back toward the same average value over time does not mean that its behavior is not susceptible to further investigation. Thus, the income velocity of money V_y and the nominal interest rate r might be nonstationary. Then we could write

$$V_{yt} - \mu r_t = e_t \tag{9.10}$$

where e is the component of velocity's behavior not related to r. If e itself fluctuates around a mean value of zero and always tends to return to that value, then it is a stationary variable, and the variables V_y and r are said to be co-integrated. Moreover, if we began our investigation with the economic hypothesis that V_y was in fact causally dependent on r, the parameter μ might be interpreted as a structural parameter of the economy, relating V_y to r, that is, a parameter of the economy's long-run aggregate demand-for-money function.

[13] Jonson (1976a), Jonson, Moses, and Wymer (1976), Gandolfo and Padoan (1984), and Laidler and Bentley (1983) all use Wymer's techniques to investigate the existence and nature of a monetary policy transmission mechanism in complete (though sometimes small, Laidler and Bentley use but 5 equations) macroeconomic models.

[14] The reader in search of a more technical, but still highly accessible, account of these techniques is referred to Dickey, Jansen, and Thornton (1991).

The above argument holds only if e is stationary and regardless of the dynamic behavior it displays over time. So long as that dynamic behavior tends to make e converge on zero, so long as the *error* in Equation (9.10) is ultimately *corrected*, the argument is valid. Techniques of statistical time series analysis, whose details would take us far beyond the scope of this book, are available, however, to model the dynamic behavior in question and to test for the tendency of e to return to a stationary mean value. Indeed, such tests are critical in deciding whether or not variables such as V_t and r are co-integrated. To say that an error-correction process that forces e to tend to converge on a time invariant mean value does not exist is to say that V_t and r are not co-integrated, and vice versa.

Though the concepts of co-integration and error correction help us to analyze data on the demand for money, they do not solve all our problems. To begin with, if we deal with more than a pair of variables, there is no guarantee that the array of parameters linking them (corresponding to μ in Equation (9.10)) will be unique. There might be more than one *co-integrating vector* linking them, and there is no way in which the data alone can tell us which vector (if any) corresponds to the parameters of the long-run demand-for-money function. Second, there are several techniques of testing for co-integration, and they do not always give the same results, particularly when applied to the rather small runs of time series data available to students of the demand for money.

Third, and finally, though statistical techniques can help us describe the dynamic behavior of money holdings, or velocity, as they fluctuate around their long-run equilibrium time path, they can tell us nothing about the economic forces driving that behavior. We may formulate specific economic hypotheses about the forces producing that dynamic behavior, compare their predictions to the statistical description of the data that error-correction techniques provide, and reject or tentatively accept those hypotheses depending upon the outcome of the comparison. But we cannot carry out such an exercise without first formulating the hypotheses to be tested. In short, like any other statistical technique, error-correction analysis is a complement to, not a substitute for, economic theory.

Nevertheless, none of the above qualifications detracts from the main message we are trying to convey here, namely, that, because they enable us to investigate the nature of long-run equilibrium relations without having to take a prior position about the short-run dynamic processes generating our data, the techniques that may be grouped under the general headings of co-integration and error-correction analysis represent an important advance in our capacity to investigate empirically various hypotheses about the demand for money.

CONCLUDING COMMENT

By now the reader will be wondering whether any satisfactory empirical study of the demand for money—or of any other relationship for that matter—is possible. There is indeed an important sense in which such skepticism is justified. It is impossible to think of a single study of the demand-for-money function in which all of the difficulties discussed above are simultaneously dealt with. However, we do not have to rely on any one piece of work when trying to answer questions about the demand for money. There have, by now, been hundreds of empirical studies of the relationship. Each one of them, taken in isolation, is open to criticism for neglecting some econometric problem or another, but, taken together, the body of work now available to us has faced up to all the problems we have discussed in this chapter (and to others that space has not permitted us to discuss). When a particular result on the nature of the demand-for-money function comes through in a number of studies, conducted by different techniques, on different bodies of data, it seems reasonable to believe that the result in question tells us something about the empirical characteristics of that function and that the result ought not to be explained away as a statistical quirk caused by neglect of the identification problem, simultaneity, autocorrelated residuals, or anything else.

    Moreover, the problems we have discussed in this chapter, though always important in principle, may not always be important in practice. If one maintains, rather than tests, the hypothesis that the demand for nominal money is proportional to the price level, the demand-for-real-money function is more likely to be identified. The chances of simultaneity's being a problem are reduced if data are highly aggregated over time. The addition of a lagged dependent variable to the demand function when shorter time periods and lower degrees of time aggregation are being used, together with some attention to autocorrelation in the error term of the equation to be fitted, does not guarantee success in filtering out the effects of short-run adjustments in the economy on demand-for-money relationships, but it may be good enough in some circumstances. Such procedures cannot always be counted on to provide satisfactory estimates of the parameters of the long-run demand function, but one must not conclude, on this basis, that they never have done nor ever will do so.

In short, the issues discussed in this chapter do not give grounds for a nihilistic attitude about the possibility of satisfactory empirical work in monetary economics. Rather, they raise a series of warnings about taking empirical results at face value, about naively believing that the facts can be trusted to speak for themselves. The facts cannot be so trusted, but they can still tell us a great deal if their message is interpreted in the light of the considerations we have discussed in this chapter. One cannot be more specific than this without dealing with the outcome of particular studies, and it is to this task that the next, final, part of this book is devoted.

four

THE EMPIRICAL EVIDENCE ON THE DEMAND FOR MONEY

chapter *10*

An Overview
of the Evidence

THE ISSUES TO BE ADDRESSED

Earlier chapters of this book have generated various questions worth asking about the demand-for-money function. The most important are:

1. Is the rate of interest an important variable in the function?
2. In assessing the responsiveness of the demand for money to market rates of interest, is it important to pay attention to variations in the own rate of return on money?
3. Is it ever the case that the interest elasticity of demand for money becomes infinite or unstable over time, as certain theories of the demand for money as an asset predict?
4. Does any particular interest rate appear to be more relevant for the demand for money than others?
5. What influence does the expected rate of inflation exert on the demand for money?
6. Is the demand for money measured in nominal terms proportional to the price level?
7. Should income or wealth or perhaps both be included in the demand-for-money function?
8. Does the level of wage rates play a role in determining the demand for money as theories of the demand for money as a means of exchange suggest?
9. Are there significant economies of scale in money holding as many of these same theories of the demand for money as a means of exchange imply?

10. Is institutional change an important factor influencing the demand for money over time?
11. Are there any important instabilities in the behavior of the demand for money which the above-mentioned factors leave unexplained?

Chapters 11 and 12 present a detailed survey of the literature that attempts to answer these questions, along with specific references to particular contributions. This chapter provides a preliminary overview of the contents of that literature, without attempting to attribute particular results to particular authors.

A SUMMARY OF THE EVIDENCE

The answers that can be given to the above questions vary from quite confident to extremely tentative. An endemic difficulty in testing propositions about economic behavior is that it is impossible to hold "other things equal" and investigate only one issue at a time. The world does not provide data in such a convenient form. In testing a particular relationship, it is necessary to assume something about the nature of other relevant relationships. One cannot deal with the influence on the demand for money of the rate of interest using data generated by an actual economy without also including a variable such as income or wealth in the function fitted to the data, and the outcome of such a test may critically depend on which of these other variables is chosen and on the particular form of functional relationship chosen for fitting. Moreover, different tests address econometric issues—for example, identification and simultaneity—with different degrees of seriousness, and there is always a chance that the outcome of a particular test will depend on the econometric technique employed. However, it turns out that the answers one obtains for many of these questions are insensitive to this kind of problem. Regardless of the other variables used, the form of the functional relationship fitted, and the econometric techniques used, the results are essentially the same, and this is true for an encouraging number of issues.

The importance of the rate of interest for the demand for money is now established beyond any reasonable doubt, and the evidence is only a little less clear that the interest elasticity of demand for money never becomes infinite. At the same time, studies that have directly confronted the issue find that the own rate of return on money has a measurable effect on the demand for money. The evidence is not clear-cut on the choice between a long and a short interest rate for inclusion in the demand-for-money function. Some studies point one way and others another. However, there is evidence that the rates of return on such close substitutes for money as (for example, in the United States) savings and loan association shares are of particular importance. Furthermore, for open economies such as the United Kingdom and Canada, foreign interest rates appear to be relevant measures of the opportunity cost of holding money.

There seems to be little doubt that the expected inflation rate influences the demand for money under conditions of hyperinflation and also during rapid inflations such as those widely experienced in Latin America. Though most earlier studies could not find a role for the expected inflation rate during the extremely mild inflations that characterized most advanced economies until the mid-1960s, more recent work in the United States has taken account of the effects of the higher inflation rates experienced since then and has found the expected inflation rate to be important in the demand-for-money function. In any event, inflation had a marked effect on nominal interest rates in the 1970s and 1980s, and evidence about the importance of these variables in the function provides strong indirect support for the hypothesis that expected inflation affects the demand for money. As to the role of the price level, a considerable body of evidence supports the proposition that the demand for nominal balances is proportional to the price level.

If we must choose between the two, then wealth, or, more precisely, permanent income, rather than measured income appears to be the superior scale variable for the demand-for-money function. At first sight, this result would seem to favor interpreting the demand for money as if money was an asset or a consumer durable good. However, it is well known that consumption expenditure is related to permanent income, and, as we have seen, at least one model of the demand for money based on money's means-of-exchange role, namely, McCallum's shopping time model, predicts that money holding and consumption are simultaneously chosen outcomes of an agent's broader market strategy. Such evidence as we have on choosing between these two views tends to support interpreting the data as pointing to the importance of money's means-of-exchange role in the economy.

The Keynesian approach to the theory of the demand for money suggests that both wealth and income might be relevant to the demand for money, the latter being particularly important as far as the transactions and precautionary demand is concerned. It is inherently difficult to get results that find a role for both variables at the same time because wealth and income move closely together and it is hard to distinguish between their separate influences. And, in any event, a loose interpretation of the shopping time model suggests that an agent's money holding, consumption, and labor income might all be the chosen outcomes of a maximization process into which wealth enters as the critical constraint. Studies that treat income and wealth as alternative or separate influences of the demand for money are open to the criticism that they may not have investigated carefully enough the processes generating the function.

Analysis of the demand for money as a means of exchange suggests, as we have seen, that real wages belong in the relationship. A number of studies have looked at the role of real wages in the demand-for-money function, and all have found them to be important. Also, there is a considerable body of evidence that the demand-for-money function is characterized by economies of scale, and this result, too, points to the importance of transaction and precautionary motives. The fact that economies of scale turn up most frequently when the demand for narrowly defined money is studied strengthens this conclusion.

It does appear that institutional change is an important factor influencing the demand for money. Although much of the impetus toward investigating this matter has come from the apparent instability in the demand-for-money function that has recently been observed in the United States and elsewhere, such change turns out, with the benefit of hindsight, to have been important for a long time and in a rather wide variety of countries. Moreover, failure to account for institutional change in many early studies of the demand for money obscured the existence of the economies of scale in the function to which we have alluded above.

In recent years, even when such change is taken into account, there still remain apparent problems of stability with estimates of the demand-for-money function. These probably have as much to do with the problems of estimating adjustment processes discussed in the preceding chapter (pages 123 ff) as with difficulties having to do with the underlying long-run demand-for-money function.

With this brief summary of the evidence in mind, let us now turn to the tests that provided it, beginning with the question of the importance of opportunity cost variables in the function.

chapter 11

The Influence of the Opportunity Cost of Holding Money

EARLY WORK ON THE ROLE OF INTEREST RATES

Much empirical work, particularly early work, on the demand-for-money function took it for granted that the crucial issue to be investigated was the relationship between the demand for money and the rate of interest. This view led economists to design tests that concentrated on this variable and were based on quite simple notions about the role of the other variable or variables. In early studies of the United Kingdom by Brown (1939) and of the United States by Tobin (1947) and Bronfenbrenner and Mayer (1960), the distinction between active and idle balances was maintained, and only the demand for the latter was treated as responsive to the rate of interest. To obtain a measure of idle balances, the following broad procedure was followed (with details differing among studies). It was assumed that the demand for active balances is proportional to the level of income and that, at some time when the ratio of total money holdings to income is at its lowest observed value, idle balances held are equal to zero. This lowest ratio was then postulated as measuring the parameter k in the equation

$$\frac{M_d}{P} = kY + l(r) \qquad (11.1)$$

so that, if at other times the supply and demand for money are in equilibrium, idle balances can be measured as being equal to

$$\frac{M_s}{P} - kY$$

and the demand for them related to the rate of interest.

Differences among these studies in the precise definitions of the variables used need not concern us here. They all concluded that a distinct negative relationship between the demand for idle balances and the rate of interest could be observed. Khusro (1952), in updating Brown's work on the United Kingdom, treated the ratio of idle balances to liquid assets as varying with the rate of interest and hence provided the first example of evidence to the effect that some, albeit very narrowly defined, wealth variable plays a role in the demand-for-money function.[1] He also used multiple regression techniques to estimate the value of k, the ratio of active balances to income, rather than using the much cruder method described above. He found that this, too, improved the explanatory power of his equations, which always displayed a significant inverse relationship between idle balances and the interest rate. Bronfenbrenner and Mayer, as an alternative to the very strict assumptions about the nature of the demand-for-money function implicit in their initial work, postulated that the demand-for-money function was of the form

$$\frac{M_d}{P} = kY \cdot r^{\beta_2} \tag{11.2}$$

so that, with equilibrium assumed between the supply and demand for money, they were able to measure the interest elasticity of the demand for money β_2 by way of the equation

$$\frac{M_s}{PY} = kr^{\beta_2} \tag{11.3}$$

They fitted this to successive pairs of years, relating the change in the logarithm of the ratio of money holdings to income to the change in the logarithm of the interest rate, and found again the β_2 was generally negative and that this parameter was a better predictor of the direction of change in the demand for money than the hypothesis that this direction of change is a random variable.[2]

---

[1] Grice and Bennett (1984) provide evidence that such a variable remained important to the demand of the broad money in the United Kingdom over the period 1963–1978.

[2] That β_2 is the interest elasticity of demand for money follows from the argument presented in footnote 7, page 121.

. A somewhat similar study by Latané (1954) began with the follow-ing demand-for-money function:

$$\frac{M_d}{P} = aY + bYr^{-1} \qquad (11.4)$$

from which can be derived

$$\frac{M_d}{PY} = a + br^{-1} \qquad (11.5)$$

Latané used regression analysis to show that the parameter b was significantly positive, indicating that the demand for money is nega-tively related to the rate of interest. He also found that the equation he fitted seemed to have some predictive power over data generated out-side the time period to which it was initially fitted.

LATER RESULTS

The drawback to all the tests just described is that they assume that the demand for money is proportional to the level of income, a postulate that would be challenged by those who regard wealth as a more ap-propriate variable to include in the function, as well as by those who suspect that there may be economies of scale in money holding. Even so, the tests consistently point to the importance of the rate of interest as a determinant of the demand for money, and other work, which does not rest on such strict assumptions, confirms this result. Much of this work is based on regression analysis and its main results have more recently been widely confirmed by exponents of co-integration and error-correction techniques.

One can, and much work on the matter has done so, postulate that the demand-for-money function can be approximated by the log-linear form

$$\frac{M_d}{P} = kX^{\beta_1} r^{\beta_2} E \qquad (11.6)$$

where X stands either for the level of income Y, the level of nonhuman wealth W, or the level of permanent income Y^P, the β's are elasticities, and E is a multiplicative error term, and let a regression equation simultaneously find the values of both elasticities. Some investigators, however, have preferred a semi-log relationship between the demand for money and the rate of interest, that is, they have made the log of money holdings depend on the natural value of the interest rate.

Work carried out by Allan Meltzer (1963) for the United States fitted log-linear functions for the period 1900–1958, using all three possible substitutes for X and definitions of money that excluded time deposits at commercial banks (old M_1), included them (old M_2), and added deposits at mutual savings banks (M_3). Using the rate of interest on 20-year bonds for r, Meltzer found a significant negative relationship between the demand for money, however defined, and the rate of interest, regardless of the other variable included in the function. Moreover, when Meltzer divided his time period into decades, fitting a separate velocity function to each decade, he found a remarkable similarity in the relationship between the velocity of circulation and the rate of interest for various decades. Recently, Robert E. Lucas, Jr. (1988) took Meltzer's (1963) quantitative estimates of the parameters of the demand-for-money function and showed that data for the 1960s, 1970s, and 1980s all lay roughly along the velocity function that those parameters implied. Lucas's work thus provides striking evidence of the robustness and stability over time of the influence of the rate of interest on the demand for money in the United States.

Also in 1963, Meltzer in collaboration with Karl Brunner (Brunner and Meltzer, 1963) used U.S. data for 1900–1958 to investigate the properties of a number of velocity functions. These functions used various permutations and combinations of variables, including income, permanent income, and nonhuman wealth. For each one, a regression equation was fitted to the first 10 years of data and its parameters were used to predict the velocity of circulation in the eleventh year; then the second through eleventh years were used to predict velocity in the twelfth year. This process was carried on through the time series. The average errors in prediction made by the various functions were computed, and it was found that the rate of interest played an important role in allowing accurate predictions to be made, while the interest elasticity of demand for money appeared to remain relatively stable regardless of which other variables were included in the function.

Demand functions like Equation (11.6), using successively a short and a long rate of interest and using permanent income as the other variable, were fitted by Laidler (1966b) to United States data for the period 1892–1960, and again, regardless of whether the definition of money used included time deposits or excluded them, statistically significant negative interest elasticities of demand for money were found. It was also found that the relationship between either interest rate and the demand for money was much the same during the independent subperiods 1892–1916, 1919–1940, and 1946–1965. In similar work on United Kingdom data for the period 1900–1965, Laidler (1971) found interest rate variables to have a significant effect on the demand for money. Kavanagh and Walters (1966) found the same in an earlier study in which a measured-income formulation of the demand-for-money function was tested against data drawn from the years 1877–1961. Bordo and Jonung (1981, 1987) fitted permanent-income formulations of velocity functions, in which they paid careful attention to institutional change, to data for Canada, the United States, the United Kingdom, Norway, and Sweden, for the period 1870–1975 and found interest rate variables to be important. In a more recent study, Bordo and Jonung (1990) extended their data to 1986 and confirmed its importance. Klovland (1983) in his detailed study of Norway for the period 1867–1980 and Spinelli (1980) in his work on Italy over the period 1867–1965 obtained similar results. In addition, and with no attempt to be comprehensive, we may cite the following studies as finding significant interest rate effects: Macesich (1970), Clark (1973), Clinton (1973), Poloz (1982) for Canada, Teigen (1971) for Norway, Leponiemi (1966) for Finland, Niehans and Schelbert-Syfrig (1966) for Switzerland, Lewis (1978) for Australia, Adekunle (1968) for a number of less-developed countries, Namba (1983) for Japan, and Gandolfi and Lothian (1983) for eight advanced countries.

NEGATIVE RESULTS ON INTEREST RATE EFFECTS

Few studies of the demand for money have failed to find a significant negative relationship between the rate of interest and the demand for money, and there are usually good reasons to discount such results when they have occurred. Thus, Laidler and Parkin (1970), studying the demand for money in the United Kingdom with quarterly data for the period 1955–1967, found that it did not respond systematically to the treasury bill rate. However, the Bank of England (1970), for almost the same period, found evidence of the importance of other interest rate variables in the function; consideration of the rather special role treasury bills played in the British financial system at that time (a description of which need not detain us here) suggests that Laidler and Parkin's choice of variable was inappropriate. Or again, Gray, Ward, and Zis (1976) treated the group of ten major industrial countries as if they were a single economy and found a coefficient for the interest rate not significantly different from zero; its value was negative, nevertheless, so that their results were indecisive rather than definitely suggesting that the interest rate was not important; and similarly indecisive results have turned up elsewhere from time to time.

Friedman's (1959) work on U.S. data for the period 1869–1957 presents more subtle problems. He reasoned that since by far the greater part of variations in the rate of interest take place within the business cycle, a demand-for-money function fitted to data that abstracts from the cycle, if it is used to predict cyclical fluctuations in the demand for money, should yield errors in prediction related to the rate of interest. He therefore took data on the average values of the variables concerned over each business cycle. The variables used were money defined to include time deposits and permanent income, and to them was fitted a log-linear regression whose parameters were then used to predict annual variations in the velocity of circulation. Friedman found no close relationship between the errors of prediction and the rate of interest. This procedure is reliable only if abstracting from the business cycle totally frees the data from the influence of any relationship between the demand for money and the rate of interest, but there was a slight downward trend in interest rates in the data Friedman used. By omitting the interest rate from his cycle average regression, Friedman thus measured the relationship between the demand for money and permanent income erroneously, so that his annual predictions based on it were not reliable. When a test similar to Friedman's was carried out by Laidler (1966b), the rate of interest was included in the initial cycle average regression, and this inclusion was found to increase the predictive power of the function for annual data, thus confirming the importance of the rate of interest as a determinant of the demand for money.[3] In a subsequent paper, Friedman (1966) himself acknowledged the interest rate to be an important variable in the function, while his work with Anna J. Schwartz (Friedman and Schwartz, 1982) on the role of money in United States and United Kingdom economies over the years 1867–1975 accords a significant role to the interest rate (measured by the rate of change of nominal income) in the demand function.

ECONOMETRIC ISSUES

Now most of the studies cited above used either real-money balances or the velocity of circulation of money as their dependent variable and dealt with long periods of data. Hence, the arguments advanced in a previous chapter (page 116) suggest that they probably have coped adequately, if implicitly, with the identification problem. However, a number of relatively early studies, for example, Brunner and Meltzer (1964) for the period 1930–1959 and Teigen (1964) for the period 1929–1959, addressed this and the related simultaneity issue explicitly, while esti-

---

[3] It was not possible to obtain interest data for Friedman's entire period, so that the data used began in 1892.

mating both demand and supply functions for money for the United States. The Brunner and Meltzer demand function used nonhuman wealth and the long rate of interest and, even with explicit attention being paid to the identification problem, the interest elasticity of the demand for money appeared to be close to −0.7. This is essentially the same estimate as Meltzer (1963) obtained in his single-equation study. Teigen, using the level of income, a short rate of interest, and the lagged money stock, as well as a slightly different specification of the supply function, found an interest elasticity of demand for money of about −0.15. This estimate is very like that obtained by Laidler (1966b) with a single equation. Frowen and Arestis (1976) studied supply and demand functions for money in West Germany and reported that their estimates of the parameters of the demand-for-money function were relatively insensitive to the extent to which they took explicit account of the presence of the supply function in obtaining them. Moreover, Jonson (1976b) estimated a demand-for-money function as one component of a complete econometric model of the United Kingdom for the period 1880–1970. He used Wymer's method of simultaneous estimation (see page 129), and, with the real income elasticity of demand for money constrained to be equal to one, obtained an estimate of the interest elasticity of demand for money that was little different from those yielded by the work of Kavanagh and Walters (1966) and Laidler (1971).

Evidence such as this suggests that as far as investigating the role of the interest rate in the demand-for-money function is concerned, the identification problem is not usually a serious one, nor it would seem is the problem of simultaneity. Thus, Feige's (1967) study of the United States for the period 1915–1963 was one of the first to use two-stage least squares estimation (see page 117); he obtained an estimate of the interest elasticity of demand for money (as well as of other parameters) that was both significantly negative and of about the same order of magnitude as that obtained by other workers (for example, Laidler, 1966b, using ordinary least squares). Klovland (1983), in his study of Norway for 1867–1980, explicitly tested for simultaneous equations bias and found it negligible. Similar results have been obtained by people working with shorter time spans of data where simultaneity might be expected to be more of a problem. For example, Poloz (1980) and Gregory and McAleer (1981) conclude that simultaneity raises at best minor problems for interpreting recent Canadian data.

Mention was made in Chapter 9 of serially correlated residuals. These are mainly of concern when lagged dependent variables are in the function, but even so, with the notable exception of Courchene and

Shapiro (1964), many early demand-for-money studies took no account of the problems they raise. However, as the reader will recall, the techniques associated with co-integration and error-correction analysis are specifically designed to cope with, indeed to exploit, the time series properties of data, so much so that Hendry and Mizon (1978) entitled one of the pioneering applications of error-correction modeling to the demand for money "Serial Correlation as a Convenient Simplification, Not a Nuisance. . . . " None of the work that exploits these new techniques casts doubt on the existence of an important inverse relationship between the demand for money defined in a variety of ways, and/or the velocity of circulation, and some representative interest rate.

The following list of references supports this contention. For the United States, we have MacDonald and Taylor (1991) using annual data for the years 1874–1970, Rasche (1987) using quarterly data on M_1 for 1933–1985, Rose (1985) also using quarterly data for the period 1953–1983. For the United Kingdom we have Hendry and Ericsson (1991a) using annual data (1874–1970) and a series of studies by Cuthbertson and Taylor using more recent data for a variety of broad and narrow definitions of money; see Cuthbertson and Taylor (1990) for an example and Cuthbertson (1991) for further citations. For Canada, we have Caramazza, Hostland, and Poloz (1990) using quarterly data on both broad and narrow money for the period 1968–1988; for Japan, Yoshida (1990) using quarterly data on broad money for 1968–1989, and Rasche (1990) using narrow money, again quarterly, for 1955–1988. For five industrial countries (the United States, the United Kingdom, France, Germany, and Japan) using narrow and broad money for various periods bounded by (1973–1985), we have Boughton (1991) and so on. The studies of Hendry and Ericsson (1991a) and MacDonald and Taylor (1991) use data down to 1970 because they have arisen in the context of a debate about Friedman and Schwartz's (1982) study of *Monetary Trends in the United States and the United Kingdom*. What is striking here is the fact that modern techniques, deployed in the case of Hendry and Ericsson by economists highly critical of Friedman and Schwartz's application of regression equations to highly time-aggregated data, nevertheless lead to the same conclusions as those reached by Friedman and Schwartz.

The foregoing list is by no means comprehensive, though it is reasonably representative. The point to be stressed in the current context is that whatever problems exponents of these new techniques of time series analysis may or may not have uncovered, their work has done nothing to change, and a good deal to confirm, earlier views about the existence of a systematic effect running from the interest rate to the demand for money.

THE OWN RATE OF RETURN ON MONEY

The introduction into the picture of the own rate of return on money in no way undermines the robustness of results concerning the importance of the rate of interest in the demand-for-money function. Lee (1967) used such a variable in a study of the effects of the rate of return on such near monies as savings and loan association shares on the U.S. demand for money, and Klein (1974a, 1974b) used his estimates of the competitive rate of return on money described earlier (pages 106–107) in somewhat similar exercises, although for a much longer time period (1880–1970) than Lee. Instead of using the interest differential between money and other assets, as did Lee, Klein entered the two rates of return separately and in finding that they took coefficients of opposite signs but similar orders of magnitude was able to confirm, rather than take for granted, the appropriateness of using the interest differential as a single variable.

Klein's results are also notable in that they suggest that studies that ignore the own rate of return on money underestimate the sensitivity of the demand for money to the opportunity cost of holding it. When market interest rates rise, so does the own rate of return on money, so that the interest differential between money and other assets changes less than the value of market interest rates. The observed change in the demand for money under such circumstances should, according to Klein's results, be attributed to this relatively smaller change in interest differentials rather than the relatively larger change in the overall levels of interest rates. In this respect, Klein's results supplement those of Barro and Santomero (1972), who reached a similar conclusion by including their measure of the own rate of return on demand deposits in an equation fitted to 19 annual observations on the demand for money of the U.S. household sector. Moreover, though Startz (1979) has criticized Klein's estimates of the own rate of return on money, Startz's work did not refute the basic qualitative result Klein sought to establish, namely, that the variable in question does affect the demand for money in the direction economic theory would predict and that its presence in the demand-for-money function does not undermine evidence on the importance of the rate of return on alternative assets.

In recent years, it has become a not unusual practice to include a measure of the own rate of return of money in the analysis of the demand for broadly defined aggregates that include bank deposits of a type that bear explicit interest at market-determined rates. In such studies, the own rate is represented by, for example, the rate of interest paid by banks on those time deposits included in the definition of money employed rather than any more subtle variable constructed along the lines that Klein's work might suggest is appropriate. (See Cuthbertson and Taylor, 1990, for a typical example.) As far as narrow money is concerned, where explicit interest is paid at low and stable over time rates or not at all, the variable is often omitted, despite the warning implicit in Klein's work that it may be important.

THE LIQUIDITY TRAP

The liquidity trap hypothesis states that at low levels of the rate of interest the demand for money becomes perfectly elastic with respect to that variable. It is not possible to fit directly by regression analysis a function that has a negative slope over part of its range and no slope at all over another part, but less direct tests are not hard to devise. If the liquidity trap hypothesis is true, it must be the case that the interest elasticity of demand for money becomes greater as the rate of interest falls, since this is the only way it can pass from a finite to an infinite value. There appears to be little evidence that this is in fact the case.

As mentioned above, Bronfenbrenner and Mayer (1960) investigated the interest elasticity of M/PY with respect to the interest rate for successive pairs of annual observations. Over the period they dealt with, 1914–1957, they noted no tendency for the interest elasticities they measured to be higher at low rates of interest. Laidler (1966b) divided the time period 1892–1960 between the years when the rate of interest was above its average value for the period and those when it was below. Such a division was made for both the long and short rates of interest, and regressions of the money stock on the level of permanent income and the interest rate were performed for the two sets of data separately. Definitions of money including and excluding time deposits were employed, and hardly any tendency was discovered for the interest elasticity of demand for money to be higher for low-interest observations than for high-interest ones; nor was there any evidence that the function was any less stable at low rates of interest.

A more direct approach to the question was taken by Pifer (1969). He argued that to fit a log-linear function to the relationship between the demand for money and the interest rate was to take for granted that the minimum conceivable value for the interest rate is zero, because such a constant elasticity demand curve is asymptotic to the horizontal axis. He then noted that an equation that has the form of Equation (11.6) is simply a special case of

$$\frac{M_d}{P} = kX^{\beta_1}(r - r^{\min})^{\beta_2}E \quad \cdot \cdot \tag{11.7}$$

where $r^{\min}$ is set equal to zero. The relationship between the demand for money and the rate of interest implicit in such a relationship is asymptotic to $r^{\min}$. Pifer then substituted a series of values for this variable into an equation like Equation (11.7), starting at zero and stopping just short of the lowest value actually observed for r. He argued that if an equation with a positive value for $r^{\min}$ fitted his data significantly better than the equation that set the variable at zero, it would be evidence in favor of the liquidity trap hypothesis. Pifer applied this test, and a variation on it in which the interest rate rather than the quantity of money was treated as a dependent variable, to U.S. data for the period 1900–1958 and found no evidence to suggest that there is any well-defined floor above zero for the value of the interest rate.

Kostas and Khouja (1969), using a method somewhat similar to that of Pifer also on U.S. data, found some evidence that a long interest rate can take a minimum value above zero, but not a short rate, this phenomenon being important in the late 1940s, however, rather than the 1930s. Their estimation techniques were criticized by Kliman and Oksanen (1973), and since the late 1940s was precisely the period in which U.S. policy was geared to maintaining the rate of interest on government bonds constant by varying the money supply, there must be some suspicion that Kostas and Khouja discovered a perfectly elastic supply-of-money function rather than a perfectly elastic demand function for those years; for once the identification problem may have been important. Eisner (1971) and Spitzer (1976), both of whom reworked Pifer's tests with more sophisticated econometric techniques and found evidence of a minimum value for the long interest rate, explicitly expressed concern at the absence of any attempt to confront this issue of identification in their own work.

The liquidity trap hypothesis arises when it is postulated that a "normal" value for the interest rate plays a role in the demand-for-money function. Starleaf and Reimer (1967) computed such a variable as a geometrically weighted average of present and past values of the actual rate, took the difference between this variable and the current rate, and related the demand for money to this very Keynesian variable. They found virtually no evidence of its importance as far as the United States was concerned. Robert Crouch (1971) examined the behavior of the interest rate over time in the United States. He found no evidence that it tended systematically to return to some normal value and no evidence that any kind of average of its past values was a better predictor of its future value than was its current value. Such evidence as this goes against the very basis of the theory of the speculative demand for money on which the liquidity trap hypothesis is based, but it is worth noting that, in their elaborate study of the Canadian monetary sector, Courchene and Kelly (1971) found evidence consistent with the playing of a role by a "normal" interest rate variable in asset demand functions, though not to the extent of generating a liquidity trap.

Thus, most evidence goes against the liquidity trap hypothesis, but the results of Kostas and Khouja, Eisner, and Spitzer are, on the face of things, in its favor. These results, however, all depend on the use of a long interest rate. There is no sign of a trap when short rates are used, and this suggests that these workers may be dealing with a phenomenon associated with the term structure of interest rates rather than the demand for money. More likely, the fact that long rates were at a minimum in the late 1940s, when monetary policy was geared to keeping such rates low and stable, rather than in the 1930s, when the economy was deeply depressed, points to the possibility that the behavior of the money supply function rather than the money demand function may underlie them. Until these conjectures are investigated explicitly, however, the conclusion to which I subscribe, that the liquidity trap hypothesis is of no empirical significance, rests on some degree of personal judgment.

THE ASSET DEMAND FOR MONEY AND MONEY'S BACKING

The liquidity trap hypothesis is, as we saw in Chapter 7, an implication of an asset demand approach to modeling the demand for money. We also saw there that certain other variations on the asset approach, particularly those associated with the work of Sargent and Wallace (for example, 1982) suggest that, if the monetary asset is "well backed" in terms of its future convertibility into goods, then the demand for it will be highly sensitive to the expected yield on holding it. Also, as a corollary, even large variations in its supply will be absorbed in money holdings and hence exert no important influence on the price level.

Two studies by Smith (1985a, 1985b) claim to find evidence in favor of this prediction in the monetary history of various North American colonies during the eighteenth century. Large variations in the quantity of paper money seem to have occurred in some of these colonies without accompanying variations in the price level, and Smith attributes this to the quality of the backing of these issues. However, this conclusion has been strongly criticized by Michener (1987) and Bordo and Marcotte (1987). Both point out that substantial quantities of metallic (gold and silver) money also circulated in North America at that time, and they suggest that fluctuations in the quantity of paper money were perhaps offset by the export and import of metallic money through a balance of payments mechanism. Those who are not expert on colonial history must approach this debate with caution, because the evidence required to settle it definitively does not exist. For example, there are not enough data on income, interest rates, and the quantity of money to estimate even the simplest demand-for-money functions. Thus, again, there is an element of personal judgment in my own tendency to accept the arguments of Smith's critics, pending the outcome of further research.

This conclusion, however, does not mean that expectations about the future reliability of money's purchasing power cannot affect the demand for it. Sargent (1986, Chapter 3) has argued that, at the end of hyperinflations, expectations about the future viability of a country's fiscal regime (and hence about the likelihood of the government's resorting to inflationary finance in the future) have a marked effect on the demand for money. Siklos (1989) confirms this conclusion with a detailed study of the demand for money during the Hungarian hyperinflation of 1945–1946. Such results are quite compatible with the idea that the demand for money is the outcome of an intertemporal maximizing strategy, such as emerges in McCallum's shopping time model, for example, because, as we argued in Chapter 6 above, a model of this type leads to the conclusion that variations in the future opportunity cost of holding money will affect its current demand. And, in any event, neither Sargent's results nor those of Siklos point to anything approaching an infinite elasticity of demand for money with respect to the cost of holding it.

THE STABILITY OF THE DEMAND FOR MONEY–INTEREST RATE RELATIONSHIP

Asset demand models of the demand-for-money function and the liquidity trap hypothesis in particular are closely related to the proposition that the relationship between the demand for money and the rate of interest may be unstable over time. In fact, this relationship seems to be remarkably stable. If we consider the United States over the period 1892–1960, the work of Laidler (1966b) shows that the elasticity of demand for money M_2, with respect to the short rate of interest, appears to have varied between roughly -0.12 and -0.15 and, with respect to the long rate of interest, between -0.2 and -0.6. (If M_1 is used instead, the relevant elasticities are -0.17 to -0.20 and -0.5 to -0.8, respectively.) These variations seem small, and when Khan (1974) applied formal econometric tests designed to discover the presence of a structural change in the demand-for-money function over a similar period, he found no sign of any such change. The order of magnitude of the interest elasticity estimates found by Laidler (1971) for the United Kingdom over the period 1900–1964 seems to be similar to that implied by United States data and again shows little variation between subperiods. Similarly, Friedman and Schwartz (1982) fitted the same demand-for-money function both to the United States and the United Kingdom over the period 1867–1975 and to various subperiods and found little variation in their interest elasticity estimates. Recent application of co-integration and error-correction techniques to the same long runs of data by Hendry and Ericsson (1991a) for the United Kingdom and MacDonald and Taylor (1991) for the United States produced essentially similar results.

Teigen (1964) estimated supply and demand functions separately for both pre– and post–World War II data for the United States, but found no important difference between the two periods in the interest elasticity of the demand for money. Meltzer's (1963) procedure of fitting velocity functions decade by decade revealed a slightly lower interest elasticity of the demand for money in the 1930s than at other times, while Brunner and Meltzer's prediction test, which excluded the years 1941–1950 because of the interest rate pegging money supply policy pursued in those years, found that regressions weighted heavily with observations taken from the 1930s produced a function that was able to predict the velocity of circulation in the 1950s with no marked falling off in accuracy relative to other times. Similarly, Laidler's variation on Friedman's test, which employed cycle average data to generate a demand-for-money function then used to predict annual variations in money holding, showed no tendency to be less accurate in its predictions for the 1930s than for other times.

Lieberman (1980) found evidence of a break in the stability of the relationship between U.S. demand for narrow money and the rate of interest in 1933, but that is precisely the year in which U.S. authorities began to prohibit the payment of interest on demand deposits. Lieberman argued that although the underlying demand-for-money function was stable at this time, the resulting change in the behavior of the own rate of return on money gave the appearance of instability in tests that ignored the influence of the own rate of return. This result is of considerable interest because, as we shall see below, the 1970s and 1980s generated a good deal of data that have cast doubt on the stability of the demand-for-money function. Subsequent work has shown that institutional changes can account for some, though not all, of these problems. See Judd and Scadding (1982a) and page 170 below. Lieberman's work suggests that there is nothing new in such a phenomenon.

The evidence cited in the last few paragraphs seems to show that instability in the relationship between the demand for money and the rate of interest has never been a factor of particular importance as far as the economic history of the United States and the United Kingdom in the present century is concerned. Moreover, work on other countries, such as that of Bordo and Jonung (1981, 1987, 1990), Klovland (1983), and Spinelli (1980), though it did not explicitly address this issue, gives no reason to believe that such instability has been a problem in economies as diverse as the United States, the United Kingdom, Sweden, Canada, Norway, and Italy. This evidence, like that on the closely related liquidity trap hypothesis, comes from studies using a variety of data and techniques. Some of the tests cited above used a short rate of interest and a narrow definition of money; others used both broad and narrow money concepts and both short and long interest rates. The tests used functions using wealth, income, and expected income as their scale variable, and the conclusions seem invariant with respect to the many possible permutations and combinations of data involved. Like the conclusion that the rate of interest is an important determinant of the demand for money, the conclusion that the instability hypothesis and related doctrines are of little empirical relevance does not seem to depend in any way on a particular formulation of the demand-for-money function.

THE CHOICE OF INTEREST RATE

The results on the role of interest rate variables in the demand-for-money function are clear enough then. Such variables ought to be included in the relationship; there is little reason to suppose that a liquidity trap exists or that there is an inherent instability in the relationship between the demand for money and the interest rate. Which interest rates, however: a short rate or a long rate; the rate of return on some financial asset, such as a savings and loan association share, which may be regarded as a close substitute for money; an interest rate on foreign securities; the rate of return on equity capital; the whole term structure of interest rates; or some combination of the above? As we have seen, some studies have used one and others another of these alternatives, and for many purposes nothing seems to hinge on the choice. For example, for long runs of United States and United Kingdom data, Laidler (1971) showed that there is no systematic difference between a long and a short rate as far as explanatory power is concerned. Perhaps this result is not too surprising since, as we have suggested, a single interest rate in the function is best interpreted as standing as a representative measure of the rates of return to be earned on holding the many assets that agents could substitute for money in their portfolios, rather than as the "correct" indicator of the opportunity cost of holding money.

A good deal of recent work, much of it using post–World War II data and the bulk of it for the United States, supports this conjecture. Heller and Khan (1979) showed that over the period 1960–1976 their measure of the whole term structure of interest rates performed better than any single interest rate in explaining variations in the demand for money. Hamburger (1966, 1977b) has shown that the addition to a function explaining the U.S. demand for narrow money of the real yield on corporate equity improves its explanatory power significantly, even if that function already contains a long-term bond rate and the savings deposit rate, while his (1977a) work in the United Kingdom and West Germany shows that the yield on foreign securities supplements, rather than replaces, that on domestic assets.

One striking feature of much work is the consistency with which the returns on "near monies" (assets that might themselves be included in some broader measures of money) turn out to be significant in explaining variations in the demand for relatively narrowly defined money. For example, when using old M_2 as his dependent variable, Lee (1967) found the interest differential between time deposits and savings and loan association shares important, while in 1969 he found that the yield on corporate equities supplemented rather than supplanted the influence of the rate of return on savings and loan association shares on the demand for narrow money. Goldfeld (1973) found the time deposit rate important when using a narrow definition of money, even when he also included a short-term market interest rate—that on 4–6-month commercial paper—in his equation. Cagan and Schwartz (1975), in comparing quarterly data for 1921–1931 and 1954–1971, found a rate of return on savings deposits (computed as an average of the rates of return offered on a variety of such assets) to be important, particularly in the latter period.

These results are typical of the time series evidence surveyed by Feige and Pearce (1976) and confirm the evidence generated by several studies of portfolio behavior surveyed by Feige (1974). They show rates of return on near-money assets to exert a systematic influence on the demand for demand deposits and time deposits at commercial banks.

The role of rates of return on money substitutes has not been so closely studied for other countries, but it is worth noting that the Bank of England (1970) found the rate of return on deposits with local authorities an important argument in the demand-for-money function for almost the same time period over which Laidler and Parkin (1970) obtained indecisive results with the treasury bill rate.

It is not too difficult to sum up the implications of the foregoing evidence. Because rates of interest on a wide variety of assets tend to move together, it is possible to obtain reasonable enough results when studying the demand for money by including just one representative rate in the function. This is important because the kinds of models of the macroeconomy in general and of the demand for money in particular that we discussed in the first two parts of this book often rely on a simplification like this. It is good to know that the simplification is not so drastic as to remove those models from all contact with the real world. Nevertheless, it is clear that the real world is more complicated than the models and that, in fact, money-holding agents treat a rather wide variety of assets as alternatives to money in their portfolios. There is nothing surprising about this; indeed, it would be startling had things turned out otherwise. However, it does mean that as the menu of assets available to money holders changes over time, we might expect their behavior vis-à-vis money holding also to change as a result. This is a potentially important point when recent stability problems with the demand-for-money function are considered.

THE ROLE OF EXPECTED INFLATION

The significance of the expected rate of inflation as a factor influencing the demand for money is well established. Although Cagan's (1956) study of European hyperinflations was criticized by Jacobs (1975) for using statistical methods that exaggerated the closeness of the relationship between these variables, there is no reason to believe that Cagan's results are entirely a statistical artifact. Furthermore, despite the fact that Cagan measured the expected inflation rate by applying the error learning hypothesis, it turns out that error learning was very close to rational behavior as a means of forming expectations as far as the inflations he studied were concerned. This is particularly the case with respect to the Weimar Republic's hyperinflation, and in this case Frenkel's (1977) use of the forward premium in the foreign exchange market to measure expected inflation may be considered a pioneering attempt to apply the rational expectations hypothesis to the study of the demand for money. It is noteworthy, therefore, that he found expected inflation so measured to be just as important a determinant of the demand for money as did Cagan. The results of Sargent (1986) and Siklos (1989), cited above in connection with the potential influence of the quality of money's backing on the demand for it, also imply that the expected inflation rate is important in influencing money holdings during hyperinflation. Rational agents would be expected to take account of the future viability of the fiscal regime in assessing the likely future course of inflation.

Numerous other studies of rapid inflations—some using error learning to proxy expected inflation, some using lagged actual inflation, and some not using formal econometrics at all—have all come to the conclusion that variations in the expected inflation rate systematically influence the demand for money. Studies have been made on the Confederate States of America (Lerner, 1956), a group of 16 Latin American countries (Vogel, 1974), Chile (Harberger, 1963; Deaver, 1970), Argentina (Diz, 1970), Brazil and South Korea (Campbell, 1970), and Nationalist China (Hu, 1971). Moreover, Perlman (1970) showed that cross-country variations in the proportion of a country's assets held in liquid form are related in a systematic fashion to cross-country variations in the average inflation rate. Although early work on the United States by Selden (1956) and Friedman (1959) could not find any systematic influence of the rate of inflation on the demand for money, studies by Shapiro (1973) and Goldfeld (1973) did find one in post–World War II data, regardless of whether the expected inflation rate is measured as some weighted average of past actual rates of inflation or, as in the case of some of Goldfeld's work, generated from opinion survey data. Moreover, it is worth noting that Brown (1939), in his pioneering study of the demand for money in the interwar United Kingdom, found that variations in the inflation rate influenced the demand for "idle" balances and that Melitz (1976), in a study of France, found the expected inflation rate a more important opportunity cost variable than any market interest rate.

Quite apart from all this, there is an overwhelming amount of indirect evidence on the issue. As we have seen, there can be no reasonable doubt that variations in rates of interest influence the demand for money, and in every study cited in this chapter at least one of the rate of interest variables used has been the rate of return on a nominal asset.[4]

---

[4] Indeed, of the commonly used interest rate arguments in studies of the demand for money, only the dividend price ratio favored by Hamburger (1966, 1977b) is a real interest rate that does not encompass the expected inflation rate. See Laidler (1980, Appendix B) for a brief discussion of this. However, Hamburger did not use this rate by itself in his work. He always included a nominal interest rate variable, such as a bond rate, in his functions as well.

Economic theory suggests that such rates of return should vary systematically with the expected inflation rate, and a large body of empirical evidence, some of which is surveyed in Laidler and Parkin (1975), confirms that they in fact do. These two factors taken together thus imply the existence of an indirect, but nevertheless well-determined channel whereby variations in the expected inflation rate influence the demand for money. Because, for reasons not well understood, variations in nominal interest rates do not fully reflect variations in the expected inflation rate, this particular channel of causation still leaves room for the expected inflation rate to play a direct role in the demand-for-money function over and above that played by nominal interest rates as, for example, the results of Brown, Melitz, Shapiro, and Goldfeld show. All four found a role for the expected inflation rate in a function that also contains a nominal interest rate variable.

CONCLUDING COMMENT

Whether one thinks of the demand-for-money function as being sensitive to income, wealth, or permanent income; whether one defines money broadly or narrowly; whether one ignores problems of identification, simultaneity, and autocorrelated residuals or deals with them; whether one uses a short rate of interest, a long one, a measure of expected inflation, the return on financial intermediaries' liabilities, a foreign interest rate, the return on equity, or even an index of the level and structure of interest rates in general; whether one ignores the own rate of return on money or takes explicit account of it, there is an overwhelming body of evidence in favor of the proposition that the demand for money is stably and negatively related to the opportunity cost of holding it. Of all the empirical issues in monetary economics, this is the one that appears to have been settled most decisively.

chapter *12*

Other Variables and the Question of Stability

THE INFLUENCE OF THE PRICE LEVEL

The hypothesis that the demand for money is a demand for real balances, that other things being equal the demand for nominal money is proportional to the general price level, is crucial for the economy's behavior. Furthermore, all of the theories of the demand for money discussed in Part II of this book imply the truth of this proposition. The hypothesis is an important one, then, and has been widely tested.

Many of the studies we dealt with in Chapter 11 took this prediction for granted, and the demand-for-money functions fitted in the course of carrying them out were cast in real terms. That is, the original data on nominal wealth, income, and the money stock were divided through by the price level before they were used for regression analysis.[1] The reason for this is as follows. If the demand-for-money function under test is, say,

$$\frac{M_d}{P} = kX^{\beta_1} r^{\beta_2} E \tag{12.1}$$

where X stands for the scale variable in the function and E is a multi-

---

[1] It is also worth noting that because most of our theories of the demand for money are concerned with the behavior of the individual agent, one might expect the demand for money in the economy as a whole to grow in proportion to the population. This does indeed appear to be the case, and it is usual in studies of the demand for money to measure relevant variables such as money, wealth, and income in per capita terms.

plicative error term, one of the pieces of information one requires is the value of the β's. If it is taken for granted that the demand for nominal balances is proportional to the price level, this function can be rewritten in nominal terms by multiplying both sides through by P; thus

$$M_d = kPX^{\beta_1} r^{\beta_2} E$$

This is not the same function as

$$M_d = k(PX)^{\beta_1} r^{\beta_2} E \qquad (12.3)$$

which is what would be fitted if the data were left in nominal terms, for here β_1 would measure an average of the wealth or income elasticity of demand for money and the price level elasticity of the demand for money. The former can, in principle, take any value, while in Equation (12.2) the latter is assumed to be equal to 1.

   If the price level elasticity of the demand for money is equal to 1, the estimate of the wealth or income elasticity of the demand for money coming from an expression like Equation (12.3) will be biased toward 1. In order to avoid such a bias, formulations like Equation (12.1) have generally been preferred for empirical work. This procedure is all right so long as one is convinced that the price level elasticity of demand for money is indeed equal to 1. If it is not, to divide an expression like

$$M_d = kP^{\beta_4} X^{\beta_1} r^{\beta_2} E \qquad (12.4)$$

through by P yields not Equation 12.1, but rather

$$\frac{M_d}{P} = kP^{(\beta_4-1)} X^{\beta_1} r^{\beta_2} E \qquad (12.5)$$

That is, if Equation (12.4) rather than Equation (12.2) is correct, the demand for real balances will also depend on the level of prices, and the omission of this variable may show itself in instability and poorness of fit in any test that uses data measured in real terms. The fact that such instability has not appeared in a wide variety of studies suggests strongly that the price level elasticity of demand for money is indeed 1 and that the price level does not influence the level of real-money holdings.

   The evidence just cited is indirect, as is an even larger body of evidence bearing on the matter which is worth mentioning. The macroeconomic proposition that the demand for money is a demand for real balances is closely related in logic to the microeconomic proposition that equilibrium demands and supplies of goods and services depend only on their *relative* prices and not on the level of money prices. If the latter hypothesis were falsified, then so would be the former, but an extremely large literature in empirical microeconomics bears witness to the fact that successful work in that area is consistent with the proposition that relative prices alone are important.

The evidence alluded to here is worth taking seriously, but one always feels more comfortable with a result when indirect support of it is supplemented by direct evidence. Meltzer's (1963) study is an early source of such direct support. First, he fitted functions (using wealth and income in different formulations) to both data cast in nominal terms and data cast in real terms. That is, he measured β_1 in the context of both an expression like Equation (12.1) and an expression like Equation (12.3). His results show a distinct tendency for the estimate of β_1 to be closer to 1 in the latter case, as one would predict if the demand for nominal balances were proportional to the price level. Meltzer went on to fit directly to the data a regression based on Equation (12.4), obtaining a direct estimate of β_4. The resulting estimate was, to all intents and purposes, equal to 1. Laidler (1971) carried out a similar test to Meltzer's on United Kingdom and United States data over the period 1900–1965 (a little shorter than Meltzer's) and, with a different specification for the rest of the function, nevertheless obtained similar results on the role of the price level. A variation of such a test is to take an equation like (12.5), already cast in real terms, and estimate $\beta_4 - 1$. The parameter should, of course, not be different from zero. Friedman and Schwartz (1982) did just that to the demand functions fitted to U.K. and U.S. data for the years 1867–1975 and did indeed get a zero coefficient. Klovland (1983) reports similar results for Norway for the period 1867–1980.

Long runs of annual data are particularly suitable to testing the hypothesis that the demand for money is a demand for real balances, because, as we have argued above, problems of identification and simultaneous equations bias are likely to be at a minimum in such cases. However, tests have also been performed using shorter periods of quarterly data as well. For example, Goldfeld (1973), using postwar U.S. quarterly data, included the price level in a demand-for-real-balances function and found that the elasticity of demand for real balances with respect to the price level was zero, thus confirming that the coefficient β_4 in Equation (12-4) indeed takes a value of unity. In their study of postwar quarterly data for the U.K., Laidler and Parkin (1970) followed essentially the same procedure as Meltzer (1963) and obtained similar results, and the Bank of England (1970) produced evidence suggesting that the demand for nominal balances varies in proportion to the price level but perhaps with a lagged response. However, not all studies of the short-run dynamics of the demand for money yield this result. Boughton and Tavlas (1990) applied error-correction techniques to estimating demand-for-money functions for the United States (broad money), Germany (broad money), France (narrow money), Japan (broad and narrow money), and the United Kingdom (broad and narrow money) and allowed the data to determine the implied long-run price level elasticity of the demand for money. In four cases, Germany, Japan (narrow money only), and the United Kingdom (broad and narrow money), values noticeably different from 1 were found. A later study by Boughton (1991) confirmed these problematic results.

The fact that the hypothesis that the demand for money is a demand for real balances is so fundamental to economic theory, combined with the large amount of evidence, both direct and indirect in its favor, makes one suspect that these results of Boughton and Tavlas arise as a by-product of some misspecification in the functions that they fitted to the data which generated them; but the results should be noted as an uncomfortable anomaly requiring further investigation. Given the tendency of economists to publish only a subset of the empirical results they obtain, noted, for example, by Cooley and Leroy (1981), and perhaps to be unduly prone to select for publication only those subsets that confirm their initial hypotheses, one cannot, much as one might like to, rule out the possibility that Boughton and Tavlas's results are more representative of those which modern techniques of dynamic modeling generate than mere inspected of published work might indicate.

THE CHOICE OF A SCALE VARIABLE

Theoretical arguments like those set out in Part II of this book have prompted economists to treat as an important empirical issue whether income or some wealth variable or perhaps some combination of the two should play the role of the scale variable in the demand-for-money function. As we shall see, if one casts the issue in either-or terms, then the evidence is on balance in favor of a wealth variable, but the interpretation of this result is not straightforward.

It was explained (pages 99–100) that two wealth concepts have been thought to be relevant to the demand for money. First, directly measured data on the value of assets, at least for the U.S. economy, have been aggregated to produce a series for nonhuman wealth for that economy. Second, permanent income, measured as an exponentially weighted average of current and past levels of net national product, has been employed as a proxy for a more inclusive concept that treats the present value of future labor income as part of the current stock of wealth. For long runs of U.S. data, either concept appears to be able to explain more of the variation in the demand for money than current income. Such a conclusion clearly emerges from the early work of Meltzer (1963), Brunner and Meltzer (1963), Chow (1966), and Laidler (1966a, 1971).

Meltzer performed regressions that contained both income and wealth variables and regressions that contained each separately. He found that wealth (nonhuman wealth, in this case) provided a more stable demand-for-money function than income and, also, that if both variables were included in the function, wealth showed itself sufficiently closely related to the demand for money to leave nothing for income to explain. He also fitted one or two functions using permanent income and found that this variable, too, explained more than measured income did. These results appear to hold regardless of whether money is defined to include or exclude time deposits, although Courchene and Shapiro (1964) argued that the results were not robust when allowance was made for autocorrelated residuals. Chow, for the period 1897–1959, fitted regressions using permanent income and measured income as alternatives and found that as far as the long-run demand-for-money function was concerned, the former variable performed better, although Lieberman (1980) questioned the reliability of Chow's results, particularly for data generated since 1933.[2]

Further evidence that wealth (or permanent income) performs better than measured income as a scale variable in the U.S. demand-for-money function comes from Brunner and Meltzer's (1963) prediction tests mentioned earlier (page 144). They used both broad and narrow definitions of money and found that, regardless of the definition of money used, functions containing a wealth variable gave more accurate predictions of the velocity of circulation than those containing income. They also found that the superior predictive power of wealth was not the product of one short time span, but rather that it characterized the entire period from the beginning of this century. Brunner and Meltzer's conclusion is strengthened by evidence produced by Laidler (1966a). He used a rather different technique, whose details need not concern us here, to analyze essentially the same body of data. He, too, found that, for either definition of money, wealth or permanent income performed better than measured income. Laidler (1971) also carried out tests on United Kingdom data using measured- and permanent-income vari-

---

[2] Lieberman replicated Chow's work making explicit allowance for autocorrelation in the residuals of the equation in a way that Chow had not. As we have seen (page 123), the presence of serially correlated residuals presents special econometric problems when lagged dependent variables are also included in the function, and we have also seen that to measure permanent income using the error learning hypothesis does just that.

ables as alternatives in straightforward log-linear functions and found that permanent income provided systematically better results. Clark's (1973) work on Canada and Klovland's (1983) on Norway both led to a similar conclusion. Diz's (1970) study of Argentina generated evidence in favor of a permanent-income variable, though Deaver's (1970) work on Chile produced results that were indecisive in this respect.

The permanent-income series used in all the tests described here was generated by applying the error learning hypothesis to data on measured income. Though the logarithm of permanent income measured in this way does not have quite the same value that would be obtained by taking a weighted average of past values of the logarithm of measured income—the former being the logarithm of a weighted average of incomes and the latter the weighted average of the logarithms of income—one would certainly be a good approximation of the other, and if one does insist on using error learning, there is no a priori reason for preferring to express the errors from which we postulate agents to learn as differences rather than ratios.

We saw in Chapter 9 that if we supplement a log-linear demand-for-money function of the form

$$(m - p)_t = \beta_0 + \beta_1 y_t^p + \beta_2 r_t + e_t \qquad (9.7)$$

with the following, also logarithmic, error-learning formulation for permanent income,

$$y_t^p = \lambda y_t + (1 - \lambda) y_{t-1}^p \qquad (9.8)$$

we end up with

$$(m - p)_t = \lambda \beta_0 + \lambda \beta_1 y_t + \beta_2 r_t - (1 - \lambda) \beta_2 r_{t-1} \\ + (1 - \lambda)(m - p)_{t-1} + e_t - (1 - \lambda) e_{t-1} \qquad (9.9)$$

We also saw that Equation (9.9) is very similar, though not identical, to that obtained by applying the real adjustment cost hypothesis to modeling a short-run demand-for-money function in which current income is the scale variable. This procedure would yield, if we substitute y_t for x_t in Equation (9.2),

$$(m - p)_t = \beta_3 \beta_0 + \beta_3 \beta_1 y_t + \beta_3 \beta_2 r_t \\ + (1 - \beta_3)(m - p)_{t-1} + \beta_3 e_t \qquad (9.5''')$$

The only difference between the two is that Equation (9.9) contains a lagged-interest-rate term, and (9.5''') does not. The similarity between Equations (9.9) and (9.5''') opens up the possibility that the apparent superiority of permanent income as a scale variable in the demand-for-money function implied by early studies reflects nothing more than the existence of important adjustment lags in a function whose scale variable is, in fact, measured income. A number of other early studies—Teigen (1964), DeLeeuw (1965), Bronfenbrenner and Mayer (1960), and Goldfeld (1973) for the United States, and Fisher (1968) for the United Kingdom, to cite a few examples—included a lagged dependent variable in what they regarded as a measured-income formulation of the function and found it to play an important role.

From the late 1960s until the early 1980s, a considerable amount of work was carried out that attempted to distinguish between these two conceptually different, but observationally almost equivalent hypotheses. We may cite here, in addition of Feige's (1967) original study of the United States, work by Laidler and Parkin (1970) for the United Kingdom, Spinelli (1980) and Calliari, Spinelli, and Verga (1984) for Italy, Kohli (1981) for Canada, and Khoury and Myhrman (1975) for Sweden. The technical details of this work need not concern us here. After a promising start with Feige's study, which seemed to show that the permanent-income formulation of the function was clearly superior, this line of inquiry ended up producing indecisive results. As the reader will see, everything hinged on the role of the lagged-interest-rate variable in the function, and empirical relationships here proved too fragile to bear the weight of the questions being investigated.

The basic problem here arises from the fact that the adjustment lag and error learning hypotheses are both highly restrictive in the way in which they model the dynamics of the short-run demand-for-money function. Even in the 1970s, certain workers—for example, Goldfeld (1973), Shapiro (1973), and Meyer and Neri (1975)—were experimenting with formulations that permitted more complexity and flexibility in this regard, and successfully so, too. As we noted earlier, co-integration analysis, which came on the scene in the 1980s, permits the nature of the long-run demand-for-money function to be investigated independently of postulates about short-run dynamics, and the error-correction techniques, which are complementary to it, permit an almost indefinite degree of flexibility to modeling those dynamics. The application of these techniques enables us to see clearly why earlier work had such limited success in producing consistent answers to questions about the source of lags in the short-run demand-for-money function, as will now be explained.

The first point to note here is that in the long-run equilibrium situations which co-integration techniques permit us to investigate, current and permanent real income are indistinguishable from one another. The latter is the long-run steady state value of the former. That is why we attach the adjective *permanent* to it in the first place. The second point to note is that error-correction techniques provide a means of statistically describing short-run dynamics, not of discovering the nature of the economic processes generating them. One can, however, formulate specific hypotheses about the processes that make predictions about dynamics and then compare those predictions to the description of the data yielded by error-correction analysis. It is a fair generalization that the specific predictions of error learning, simple adjustment cost models, and even combinations of the two are too simple to be compatible with the complex patterns of behavior revealed by error-correction studies. In short, we now know that we were unable systematically to distinguish between the alternative hypotheses because both are wrong.

But the results of recent work are not all negative. Cuthbertson and Taylor have carried out a series of studies (see Cuthbertson and Taylor, 1990, and Cuthbertson, 1991, for references to these), mainly for the United Kingdom, but also making some use of data for the United States. These studies suggest that a combination of expectational effects, portfolio adjustment costs, and lags in the response of the price level, output, and interest rates to discrepancies between the money supply and the desire of agents to hold money are responsible for the complex dynamics of money holdings. To cite another example, Boughton and Tavlas (1990), in their study of five industrial countries' demand-for-money functions, found that the short-run dynamics of the relationship are more prone to shift around over time than is the underlying long-run function.

In any event, it is important to recall that our interest in the dynamics of the demand for money initially grew out of concern with the choice of scale variable for the function, and that recent work has shown not that current income is after all an adequate scale variable, but that its relationship to a more appropriate variable is complex. In this context, it is noteworthy that Mankiw and Summers (1986), Faig (1989), and Sumner (1990a, 1990b) all find that consumption is a useful scale variable in the function. Consumption is well known to be more closely related to permanent income than to current income and hence is a good proxy variable for the latter. The existence of this relationship, however, also means that we should be careful about interpreting permanent income as a wealth constraint on money holding and hence as being associated with an asset demand approach to the demand for money. Would not consumption, after all, be a good proxy variable for transactions, perhaps better than current income? That is what McCallum's shopping time model suggests, and we shall return to this question in the next chapter.

THE REAL WAGE, ECONOMIES OF SCALE, AND INSTITUTIONAL CHANGE

The evidence about the appropriate scale variable to include in the demand-for-money function leaves open the possibility that models of the demand for money as a means of exchange are empirically relevant. The shopping time model of the demand for money suggests that the wage rate belongs in the function as a measure of the value of the time that is saved by holding and using money for trading. The wage rate may also be interpreted as a proxy variable for the brokerage fee, which plays a key role in transactions and precautionary theories of the demand for money. A number of studies have investigated its empirical importance.

One of the earliest, by Dutton and Gramm (1973), used U.S. annual data for the period 1919–1958 and included an interest rate and nonhuman wealth in the function. A variety of alternative measures of wealth were employed, all of which differed from that used by Meltzer in excluding government debt (see page 99), and a variety of interest rate variables were also used. The wage rate proved to have a systematic positive effect on the demand for money, regardless of precisely which other variables were included in the function. In Karni's (1974) study, data for a slightly longer time period (1919–1968) were used, and the model of the demand for money that underlay the empirical function was more closely related to an explicit inventory-theoretic approach to the demand for money. Here, too, however, Karni found a wage variable (real hourly earnings) to have a systematic influence on the demand for money. Khan (1973) also formulated a model based explicitly on an inventory-theoretic approach and found the wage rate to be important for U.S. data over the period 1900–1965. Diewert (1974), fitting a complete model of households' demand for consumption, households' demand for money, and households' labor supply, found the level of wages to affect the demand for money, as also did Phlips (1978). Of course, one would like to see the importance of the wage variable investigated across a far wider variety of specifications of the demand-for-money function than these before concluding definitely that this work has unearthed another important factor influencing money holding, but the results cited here are nevertheless highly suggestive. More recently, Dotsey (1988) found wages important for the demand for currency in the United States, and Dowd (1990) has confirmed the importance of such a variable (real after-tax hourly earnings) in the United Kingdom demand-for-money function over the period 1976–1985.

The evidence on the existence of economies of scale in money holding, another prediction of transactions and precautionary theories, also favors these approaches. It is true that if one looks at earlier studies of long runs of U.S. annual data, such as Friedman (1959), Laidler (1966b, 1971), and Meltzer (1963), or of long runs of British data, such as Kavanagh and Walters (1966) and Laidler (1971), or of data for such countries as Chile (Hynes, 1967) and Argentina (Diz, 1970), one has the impression that economies of scale in money holding are nonexistent. And the results of applying co-integration techniques to long runs of U.K. and U.S. data, for example, Hendry and Ericsson (1991b) and MacDonald and Taylor (1991), are similar. Broader definitions of money on the whole produce higher estimates of the income or wealth elasticity of the demand for money than narrower ones, but it is a fair generalization to say that unity puts a lower bound on the range of the estimates yielded by the above-cited studies.

However, as already noted, several of these studies also present estimates of the demand-for-money function for subperiods, and these results seem to show that the elasticity in question has fallen over time. Thus Laidler (1971), using annual data for the United States, estimated that the permanent-income elasticity of demand for money defined to include time deposits was 1.39 for the period 1900–1916, 1.28 for 1919–1940, and 0.65 for 1946–1965. For the United Kingdom, also using broad money, the relevant estimates were 1.24, 0.79, and 0.68 for the same time periods. These results are representative of a considerable body of evidence. Furthermore, studies using a narrow definition of money are more prone to yield income or wealth elasticities of demand below unity. In particular, the existence of economies of scale in the post–World War II demand-for-money function for both the United Kingdom and the United States is confirmed by several studies of quarterly data; see, for example, Shapiro (1973) and Goldfeld (1973) for the United States and Laidler and Parkin (1970) and the Bank of England (1970) for the United Kingdom. The results for 13 countries surveyed by Fase and Kure (1975) were all generated by postwar quarterly data and show a heavy preponderance of evidence that economies of scale exist. Moreover, a multicountry study by Boughton (1979) shows evidence of economies of scale in the demand for narrow money over the years 1960–1977, though not for broad money. Such results are not affected by the precise specification of the demand function fitted.

At first, it may seem appropriate to conclude on the basis of such evidence that the nature of the demand-for-money function has changed over time, so that economies of scale that did not exist, say, before World War I are now important, particularly for narrow-money concepts. Bordo and Jonung (1981, 1987), in their studies of five advanced countries, show that this conclusion may be misleading. They argue that in this earlier period institutional change, which involved a widening of the proportion of national income going through the market sector, was taking place. The effects of this change were, of course, correlated with the growth of real permanent income, and if they are ignored, the permanent-income elasticity of demand for money in this earlier period appears to be greater than unity. When these effects are allowed for, by introducing the institutional variables mentioned (page 110) into the function, they reduce estimates of the permanent-income elasticity of demand for money to below unity. More recently, Bordo and Jonung (1990) have updated their work, adding more than a decade of new data to their original sample, without changing its conclusions, and Siklos (1991) confirms their results using co-integration analysis. Klovland's (1983) work on Norway confirms this result, and that of Friedman and Schwartz (1982) in the United States and the United Kingdom is at least not inconsistent with it. Although Friedman and Schwartz do not introduce explicit measures of institutional change into their equations, they nevertheless acknowledge its importance.[3]

In short, the earlier studies cited at the outset of this section were perhaps misleading on the matter of economies of scale. Holding institutional factors constant, these economies have probably always been present in the demand-for-money function. However, they are a more important characteristic of demand functions for narrowly defined money than for broader concepts. This is, of course, consistent with the particular significance of transactions and precautionary motives in determining the demand for narrow, as opposed to broad, money.

INSTABILITY IN THE DEMAND-FOR-MONEY FUNCTION

The discussion so far will have given the reader the impression that empirical work has taught us a great deal about the nature of the demand-for-money function, and indeed it has. However, it would be wrong to conclude that, in the process of learning about the demand for money, we have not encountered setbacks from time to time or that the puzzles those setbacks have generated have all been definitively solved. The fact

[3] Rather, Friedman and Schwartz adjust their data prior to estimation for the effects of such change in pre–World War I United States and employ dummy variables to allow for once-and-for-all shifts of the relationship at other times. It should be noted that Bordo and Jonung investigated the potential influence of overall uncertainty about economic matters as measured by the variability of real income per head, but found this to have a measurable influence only in the case of the United Kingdom.

is that two decades ago it was possible to be much more confident about the robustness of our knowledge of the demand-for-money function than it is now. The reason for this is evidence generated over the last 20 years, notably in the United States, but in other countries as well, evidence that shows that certain widely accepted formulations of the demand-for-money function have performed badly in recent years.

The problem first revealed itself, as far as the United States was concerned, in the years 1972–1974, when the demand for money began to grow much more slowly than would have been expected on the basis of past relationships; and this was followed, more recently, by an equally surprising upward shift of the demand for money in 1981–1982. "The Case of the Missing Money," as Goldfeld (1976) aptly termed it, may be described as follows. By the early 1970s, it was widely accepted, particularly among economists working in the Federal Reserve system, that a certain formulation of demand-for-narrow-money function was to be preferred for policy-related analysis. This formulation used current real income as its scale variable, a nominal interest rate as an opportunity cost variable, and because it was typically employed to deal with quarterly data, it was cast in short-run terms; that is, a lagged value of the dependent variable of the relationship, real balances, was added to the right-hand side of the relationship to account for adjustment phenomena. Such a function, essentially identical to Equation (9.5‴), had been shown (for example, Goldfeld, 1973) to fit data from the 1950s and 1960s at least as well as any other, but in the mid-1970s it began to fail a certain kind of prediction test by an increasing amount.

The test in question involved fitting the function to an initial time period and then using the parameters thus obtained to forecast the demand for money beyond the end of the sample. In making forecasts, new observations of real income and the interest rate were, of course, introduced, but the value of the lagged dependent variable utilized, rather than being an actual observation, was instead the value of the demand for money the equation itself had predicted in the previous period. Such "dynamic simulations," as they are called, of the relationship produced a systematic and increasing overprediction of the demand for money after 1974. In a dynamic simulation, once a relationship overpredicts the value of its dependent variable, the error is compounded over time as it is fed back period after period into the value of the lagged dependent variable. However, there is more to the missing money puzzle than the simple arithmetic of dynamic simulation. Laidler (1980) showed that if a "static simulation," which uses the actual instead of the previously predicted value of the lagged dependent variable, is carried out for a function very like the one Goldfeld used, the breakdown of the relationship, though less dramatic, is still readily observable. However, it takes the form of a once-and-for-all shift rather than a cumulative collapse. All in all, the puzzle here is probably a real one, rather than a statistical artifact. This conclusion gains credibility from the fact that, though the United States suffered from the problem first of all, instability in previously satisfactory formulations of the demand-for-money functions appeared there again in the early 1980s and in other economies, too, as the 1970s and 1980s progressed.

Attempts to explain these difficulties may be grouped into three categories. First, some workers suggest that the basic demand-for-money functions that generated the puzzle were misspecified to begin with. Second, some suggest that, although the relationships in question might have been properly specified for the 1950s and 1960s, they need to be modified to take account of the institutional change that took place in the 1970s and 1980s. Third, some suggest that, regardless of whether the long-run demand-for-money functions were correctly specified or not, the techniques available for modeling short-run dynamics in the 1970s were inadequate to cope with the data generated in those and subsequent years and that much apparent instability stems from this inadequacy, rather than from problems with the underlying long-run demand functions.

The stability of the demand-for-narrow-money function in the United States has recently been investigated using co-integration techniques. Some studies, for example, Rasche (1987), Miller (1991), and Hafer and Jansen (1991), find no evidence of a shift in the underlying relationship in the early 1970s, but Dickey, Jansen, and Thornton (1991) show that whether or not such a break is apparent seems to depend on the precise nature of the statistical techniques employed. This evidence certainly suggests that short-run dynamics are responsible for some part of the stability problems we are discussing here, but it does not rule out the existence of specification problems in the long-run function. We shall now discuss some of the work that has attempted to assess the importance of these specification problems.

POSSIBLE SOURCES OF INSTABILITY IN THE LONG-RUN DEMAND-FOR-MONEY FUNCTION

Perhaps the most obvious potential misspecification in Goldfeld's demand function involves Goldfeld's use of current income rather than wealth or permanent income as a scale variable. The evidence discussed earlier in this chapter suggests that current income is almost certainly the wrong variable to use. However, we have seen that measuring permanent income with the error learning hypothesis gives us a form for the short-run demand-for-money function very like that actually used by Goldfeld (see page 165), and Laidler (1980) was able to confirm that instability of the function after 1974 could not be attributed to the use of current rather than permanent income. If the scale variable of the function is not seriously misspecified, the opportunity cost variable might well be. In Chapter 11 we saw that although a single bond or bill rate serves well enough in many formulations of the function, it does seem possible to do better with a little effort. Thus, Heller and Khan's (1979) function, which attempted to relate the demand for money to the whole-term structure of interest rates, was fitted to the period 1960–1976 and did not appear to create any special problems of goodness of fit for these later years. However, simulation tests similar to Goldfeld's carried out by Porter and Mauskopf (1978) and cited by Judd and Scadding (1982a) suggest that this particular line of enquiry does not solve the problem at hand,

As early as 1966, Hamburger argued that the dividend-price ratio ruling in the stock market should be included in the demand-for-money function. Stock market prices fell dramatically in the 1972–1974 period, while dividends did not, and Hamburger (1977b) was able to show that his version of the demand-for-money function generated little or no sign of a missing money puzzle. This result could be a coincidence, and as Judd and Scadding note, citing Hafer and Hein (1979), it does seem to depend rather specifically on Hamburger's assuming an income elasticity of demand for money of unity in his tests. However, the equally puzzling increase in the demand for money in the early 1980s was also associated with a marked fall in the dividend-price ratio, as Hamburger (1983) was quick to point out.[4]

Work by Slovin and Sushka (1983) shows that changes in the variability of interest rates in the 1970s might also have a role in explaining these phenomena. Since such variability is a plausible proxy variable for the riskiness of holding bonds, a factor that Tobin's approach to modeling the demand for money suggests belongs in the function, this postulate, like Hamburger's, is a suggestion worth further

[4] Although it has already been argued that the scale variable in the demand function is probably not to blame for the missing money puzzle, it is worth noting that B. Friedman (1978) has shown that much of the variation in Hamburger's dividend-price ratio over the relevant period was in the price term. He argues that this variable may well be picking up the effects on wealth of variations in the stock market rather than in the opportunity cost of holding money. He then shows that there is evidence to suggest that the addition of wealth to Goldfeld's equation improves its performance after 1974. It would be of interest to see if this argument is supported by data drawn from the 1981–1982 episode.

attention. Certainly, this line of enquiry is more plausible than that which attributes shifts in the demand for money to changes in the variability of the price level. Klein (1975) developed a measure of such variability and showed that over the period 1880–1973 it seemed to have a systematic positive influence on the demand for money (Klein, 1977). Unfortunately, as Laidler (1980) showed, this relationship completely broke down after 1974 and cannot solve the missing money puzzle.[5]

We have already noted that the missing money puzzle involved a narrow (old M_1) definition of money. If the problem was to be completely resolved by attributing it to the absence of the dividend-price ratio or the variability of interest rates, we might expect to find the demand for a broader monetary aggregate, such as old M_2, also giving trouble in the 1970s. After all, bonds and equity are just as much alternative assets to broad money as they are to narrow money. However, evidence of instability in the demand for broad money over the 1970s is much less pronounced than in the case of narrow money, as Laidler (1980) showed and as recent studies using co-integration techniques (for example, Dickey, Jansen and Thornton, 1991) have confirmed.

In a substantial body of work, surveyed in Barnett (1990), he and his associates have shown that in the United States the demand function for various Divisia indices of money remained stable at times when those far more conventionally defined aggregates appeared to shift; and Barnett himself points out (1990, p. 248) that the use of Divisia aggregates is particularly appealing in the context of a moderately regulated financial system, such as that of the United States. This suggests that the source of shifts in the demand for narrow money might be sought, at least in part, in institutional changes within the banking system particularly, though not exclusively, in those associated with the regulatory environment. In this context, it has been noted that the rapid inflation and high market interest rates of the 1970s gave the United States banking system, which was prohibited from paying any explicit interest on demand deposits and was also subject to a ceiling on the interest it could pay on time deposits, particularly strong incentives to find ways of providing assets to its customers that furnished them with services similar to those yielded by more traditional forms of bank accounts, while evading the regulations on interest payments. Such institutional innovations, once induced, would remain in place so that one might expect to find a *permanent* downward shift of the demand-

---

[5] For a discussion of theoretical and statistical problems involved in distinguishing between the effects on the demand for money of the expected inflation rate and its variability, see Eden (1976).

for-money function to be associated with the *temporary* appearance of high nominal interest rates. Entzler, Johnson, and Paulus (1976) were among the first to investigate the presence of such a ratchet effect in the relationship between the demand for money and nominal interest rates, and they found evidence in favor of this hypothesis. Moreover, Garcia and Pak (1979) claim to have isolated an important factor contributing to the ratchet effect in the emergence of large-scale use by firms of repurchase agreements as a means of holding liquid assets.

Such results as these certainly provide a plausible approach to the missing money puzzle, and they are consistent with evidence discussed earlier on the role of institutional change in influencing the demand for money, not least that developed by Lieberman (1980) in the context of the effects of the introduction of a prohibition on interest payments on demand deposits in 1933. Such effects are nothing new, as we have seen. It is also worth noting that regulatory changes in the Japanese banking system in the 1980s seem to have caused the demand for broad money to have shifted there as well, though the application of co-integration analysis suggests that the long-run demand for narrow money remained stable over the same period (see Yoshida and Rasche, 1990, and Rasche, 1990).

If institutional change in response to regulations was all there was to recent problems of stability with the demand-for-money function in the United States and elsewhere, then one would not have expected other countries, where regulatory changes did not take place, to have encountered stability problems with their demand-for-money functions. However, they have, not least Canada where, it should be noted, there are essentially no regulations governing the payment of interest on various classes of deposits. There, as Freedman (1983) showed, the introduction of daily interest-bearing checking accounts, which are, technically speaking, notice deposits and therefore excluded from M_1 statistics, undermined the stability of the demand for M_1 in the late 1970s and early 1980s. In this case, it seems to have been changes in technology, largely associated with a rapid increase in the availability of low-cost computers and associated devices, that brought changes to the nature of the banking system, rather than any disturbance of the regulatory environment.

POSSIBLE SOURCES OF INSTABILITY IN THE SHORT-RUN DYNAMICS OF THE DEMAND FOR MONEY

The foregoing explanations focus on sources of instability in the underlying long-run demand-for-money function. A complementary line of enquiry has investigated the possibility that some of the problems of instability in recent years have stemmed not from problems with the long-run function, but from inadequate modeling of the short-run dynamics characterizing departures from the long-run relationship, from the econometric characterization of various adjustment processes. The work of Gandolfi and Lothian (1983) showed that, in the cases of quarterly data for no fewer than eight advanced economies (the United States, the United Kingdom, the Netherlands, Japan, Italy, Germany, France, and Canada) over the period 1975–1976, estimates of the adjustment coefficients attached to a lagged dependent variable are very sensitive to the way in which the autocorrelation structure of the residuals from the relevant regression equations is specified. Since that autocorrelation structure itself might plausibly be thought of as reflecting adjustment processes of some unspecified kind, the implication of this evidence is that such processes are complicated, volatile, and ill understood. Moreover, Laidler (1980) not only found evidence of a shift in the demand-for-narrow-money function in the United States around 1974, but also found that after that date the autocorrelation pattern in the residuals from the relevant equation changed. The latter finding suggests that something in the dynamic mechanisms at work in the economy changed at around the same time.

In light of the above arguments, in the 1970s, when money supply behavior was, in comparison to earlier years, extremely volatile in a large number of countries, it would not be surprising if those rather simple econometric devices for dealing with the dynamics of the interaction of money and the variables affecting the demand for it, which worked in those earlier years, began to break down. A number of workers (Carr and Darby, 1981; Laidler, 1980; Judd and Scadding, 1982b; Gordon, 1983) have investigated or discussed this potential source of instability in demand-for-money functions, mainly for the United States, though Carr and Darby's work extends to the same eight countries dealt with by Gandolfi and Lothian. The details of the functions postulated and statistical techniques used vary quite widely among individual studies, but all of them place particular emphasis on explicitly modeling short-run adjustment as involving the responses of endogenous variables, in particular the price level (but also sometimes interest rates and output; see Laidler, 1980), to changes in the money supply, rather than as simply reflecting the movement of real balances over time in response to changes in the arguments of the demand-for-money function.

The studies in question that highlight money's potential role as a buffer stock (see page 128) met with mixed success, and it would be wrong to claim that they made a systematic contribution toward clearing up puzzles concerning the stability of the demand-for-money function in the 1970s and 1980s. Thus, when Lothian, Darby, and Tindall (1990) updated, with new data, the functions originally estimated by Carr and Darby, the functions were found to be unstable; though the Gandolfi-Lothian equations first estimated in 1983 survived this test. Moreover, MacKinnon and Milbourne (1988) have argued convincingly that a simple reinterpretation of the short-run demand-for-money function as an equation that reflects the dynamics of the price level's response to changes in the money supply, such as Carr and Darby (1981) suggested, is not compatible with empirical evidence. If it was, one should be able to take nominal money from the left- to the right-hand side of an equation like (9.5''') (page 165), leaving the price level as a dependent variable and obtain satisfactory results; but this procedure simply does not work. Recent work by Hendry and Ericcson (1991b) on the demand for narrow money in the United States and the United Kingdom since the early 1960s gives further support to MacKinnon and Milbourne's argument.

Even so, the fact that there is no simple solution along the above lines does not mean that the basic insight underlying this line of investigation is invalid. The hypothesis at stake is that economists working on the short-run demand for money have failed properly to model the interaction of money supply changes and the endogenous variables of the macroeconomic system. Such mechanisms form the subject matter of Part I of this book, and one important point made there is that it is unlikely that causation runs directly from money to prices without also affecting interest rates and real income. Moreover, the structure within which these variables interact is likely to be volatile and to react to the conduct of monetary policy. Such a conclusion emerges because, as Robert E. Lucas (1976) has argued, the behavior of economic agents that underlies the mechanisms in question depends on those agents' expectations about the conduct of the very policy to which they are responding.

In this regard, it is highly suggestive that, though the application of co-integration techniques tends to make the long-run demand-for-money function appear more robust than did the use of more traditional regression analysis, the error-correction mechanisms that are associated with this approach tell us that short-run dynamics are certainly more complicated than those same traditional methods indicated. It could be that this complexity is always going to be inherent in the transmission mechanism of monetary policy. Without wishing to downplay the significance of omitted variables or institutional change as explanations for puzzles in the behavior of the demand for money in recent years, it is the above line of argument, bringing us as it does face to face with certain fundamental and general issues in empirical macroeconomics, that raises the most significant questions for monetary economists. If it is valid, it suggests that the search for simple and stable adjustment mechanisms in the context of the short-run demand-for-money function is inherently futile.

It must, nevertheless, be noted that recent work by Hendry and Ericsson (1991b) for both the United States and the United Kingdom finds that stable error-correction mechanisms can account for the data generated in both economies over the years 1959–1988 and 1963–1989, respectively. At first sight, these results contradict the foregoing conjecture. However, this work used data which, ex post, accounted for institutional changes that took place during the sample period, and, like Rose (1985), Hendry and Ericsson found that a previously stable U.S. demand-for-narrow-money function did seem to shift as a result of regulatory changes in the early 1980s. It may well be that the stability that Hendry and Ericsson have found is of a kind that can only be discovered with the help of hindsight. Only more work on their relationships, using data generated subsequent to the formulation of their models, will enable this question to be settled.

CONCLUDING COMMENT

We have completed our survey of the evidence on the various questions concerning the demand-for-money function set out at the beginning of Chapter 10. It remains now briefly to assess the significance of this evidence both for the theories of the demand for money discussed in Part II of this book and for the macroeconomic framework described in Part I. These matters are the subject of the next, concluding, chapter of this book.

chapter 13

Tentative Conclusions

INTRODUCTORY COMMENT

As we have seen in the last two chapters, by no means all of the issues raised by macroeconomic theory in general and theories of the demand for money in particular have been settled by empirical work. Nevertheless, on some matters a sufficient amount of evidence does seem to point in a particular direction that it is permissible to come to tentative conclusions. The adjective *tentative* must be stressed, however, because no matter how well established particular results might now appear, there always exists a possibility that evidence generated in the future will cast doubt on them. Not the least important lesson that monetary economists have learned over the last two decades from the missing-money puzzle and related problems discusses at the end of Chapter 12 is that our knowledge of how the real world works, though by no means nonexistent, is fragile. That being said, we have learned other critical lessons from empirical work, and this chapter sets out what seem to be the most important of them. It is convenient to begin with questions about the nature of the demand-for-money function itself.

IMPLICATIONS OF THE EVIDENCE FOR
THEORIES OF THE DEMAND FOR MONEY

The basic question to be asked here is whether or not it pays to base a model of the demand for money on careful and explicit analysis of the motives that lead people to hold money. Let us consider asset demand theories first of all. This analysis does not seem to have produced any predictions that are both unique and empirically important. It tells us that the rate of interest belongs in the demand-for-money function, but so does nearly every other piece of analysis we have considered. Its use of wealth as a scale variable for the demand-for-money function does not set it apart from simpler approaches to the theory of the demand for money, such as that of Friedman, or indeed from modern models of the demand for money as a means of exchange, such as that of McCallum. Its specific predictions about the likelihood of instability in the demand for money–rate of interest relationship and about the possibility of a liquidity trap, particularly when the economy is deeply depressed, receive little support from empirical evidence. Moreover, the very existence of assets whose capital value does not vary with the rate of interest, but which pay a return to their holders at a rate higher than that borne by commercial bank liabilities—assets such as savings and loan association shares in the United States, building society deposits in the United Kingdom, and those deposits with trust companies in Canada on which checks cannot be drawn, to give but three examples—suggests that asset motives cannot dominate the demand for money. If they did, commercial bank liabilities, particularly demand deposits (let alone currency), would not be held in any large amount by the public when, from the point of view of satisfying an asset motive, apparently perfect substitutes exist that pay more interest.

Matters are different when it comes to theories of the demand for money as a means of exchange. Several predictions specific to this approach have been confirmed by much of the evidence discussed above. It does seem that wage levels, standing as a proxy for the value of time, play a role in determining the demand for the narrowly defined money, which is particularly relevant in the context of this approach. The existence of a distinct demand for money as a means of exchange gets further support from studies such as Laidler (1966a) and Goldfeld (1973) that were able to identify separate and stable demand functions for narrow money and for time deposits and from the portfolio studies surveyed by Feige and Pearce (1976) that found the degree of substitutability between narrow money and other assets to be rather limited in scope. Moreover, we noted in Chapter 12 that, though measured income seems to be an inferior scale variable in the demand-for-money function when compared to a measure of permanent income, the latter variable is closely related to consumption, which might plausibly be regarded as a transactions proxy. Faig (1989) and Sumner (1990a, 1990b) have both shown that the pronounced degree of short-run seasonal variation in consumption is also present in money holdings. Faig established this result using narrow money for both Canada and the United States and Sumner used United Kingdom data for narrow and broad money. These findings are hard to square with the idea that money is simply held as an asset, but obviously fit easily with the idea that the primary factor causing people to hold it is its means-of-exchange role.

A key prediction of transactions and precautionary theories is that there should exist economies of scale in money holding, particularly where narrow money is concerned. We have seen that empirical evidence from a number of countries is in favor of this prediction where data for the post–World War II period are concerned. There is less support for data generated in earlier times, but there are a number of reasons to believe that the earlier evidence understates the importance of such economies of scale and that we should hesitate to regard it as casting doubt on their existence. As Fried (1973) has argued, when an economy's income grows over time, two factors affecting the transactions and precautionary demand for money will vary. First, the planned volume of transactions will go up and, other things being equal, if money is held for transaction purposes, one would expect the ratio of money holdings to income to fall as a result of this. Second, at the same time, the level of wages will increase, and, as the opportunity cost of time thus rises, one would expect the volume of money holding associated with any planned volume of transactions to rise. These two forces will operate in opposite directions on the money-income ratio as an economy's income rises, and the effect of rising wages, might well swamp the economies of scale associated with a growing transactions volume. The appropriate way to investigate this suggestion is to include a wage rate variable as well as some other scale variable in the demand-for-money function in order to sort out their relative contributions to variations in money holding. We have seen that Dutton and Gramm, Khan, Karni, Diewert, Phlips, and Dowd did just this, and Karni, who fitted his function with and without a wage rate variable, found that, with a wage rate variable, the wealth elasticity of demand for money fell significantly below unity.

The above argument is highly suggestive, but it does not account for the discrepancy between prewar and postwar results on economies of scale, nor does it account for the steady downward drift over time of the permanent-income elasticity of demand for money that has characterized the demand functions of a number of countries. The most plausible explanation of these phenomena rests on the observation that with the passage of time monetary systems have become more sophisticated. As we have seen, Bordo and Jonung have concluded, after studying this phenomenon in five countries, that estimates of the permanent-income elasticity of demand for money obtained from late-nineteenth and early-twentieth century data are biased upward, if proper account is not taken of institutional change when they are derived. Moreover, the institutional factors that Bordo and Jonung found to be important were all associated with money's means-of-exchange role.

Cagan and Schwartz (1975), building on a suggestion of Alvin Marty (1961), have considered a property of institutional change in the United States that would account for both the fact that economies of scale are more apparent there in post–World War II demand functions than for earlier periods and the fact that the change in question is more clear-cut in the context of narrow money. They argue that one consequence of post–World War II growth of financial intermediaries was a shift in emphasis within the pattern of motivation underlying money holding in the United States. When mutual savings banks, savings banks, and savings and loan associations were relatively unimportant, people held bank liabilities not just for transactions and precautionary motives, but also as a convenient way of storing wealth in a liquid form. Asset motives for holding money can now just as easily be satisfied by holding the liabilities of financial intermediaries and, as these institutions have become important, there has been a transfer of funds to their liabilities, leaving money holding satisfying only transactions and precautionary motives. According to the above argument, in the postwar period, money holding came to be dominated by the transactions and precautionary considerations that lead to economies of scale in money holding in a way that it was not in the prewar period. The reader will note that, to the extent that the missing-money puzzle of the 1970s is explicable in terms of institutional developments, the arguments advanced in that context are similar to those of Marty and Cagan and Schwartz and suggest that such institutional change is an ongoing phenomenon that continues to influence the demand-for-money function.

To sum up then: One can get a long way toward specifying an empirically satisfactory demand-for-money function without being concerned with the role money plays in the economy and the effect that role might have on agents' attitudes toward holding it, as a recent study by Barr and Cuthbertson (1991) was explicitly and successfully designed to show. Nevertheless, it does seem that one can get further by taking specific account of motives stemming from money's role as a means of exchange. Thus, of all the theoretical approaches set out in Part II of this book, these will most likely repay efforts at further theoretical refinement. This conclusion lends strong support to the view of McCallum (1983) that the efforts of Sargent and Wallace and their associates to ground monetary theory in an overlapping generations framework, where the asset they call "money" is a pure store of value, is fundamentally misconceived.

IMPLICATIONS OF THE EVIDENCE
FOR MACROECONOMICS

Let us now turn to what we have learned about the macroeconomic model set out in Part I of this book and its relevance to the actual economy. The evidence on the relationship between the demand for money and the rate of interest described earlier allows a major issue to be settled, because neither of the extreme possibilities whose implications were discussed in Part I turns out to have much empirical content. It is not true that the demand for money is unrelated to the rate of interest, nor does it seem that the function becomes perfectly elastic with respect to the rate of interest at any relevant level of the short rate. It follows from this that although changes in the money supply will shift aggregate demand and cause changes in output and prices, so will real shocks such as those stemming from fluctuations in private-sector investment. Moreover, when it comes to the design of macroeconomic policy, the evidence implies that, in order to assess the effect that some given change in government expenditure, tax rates, or the money supply will have on the economy, one must make use of a complete model of the economy and not concentrate solely on one sector of it.

The fact that the demand for money is systematically related to the opportunity cost of holding it has important implications for the interaction of the quantity of money and the price level in inflationary situations. The model discussed in Part I of this book predicts that if output is fixed at an exogenous full-employment level, the price level changes in proportion to the quantity of money. This "neutral money" conclusion was derived in the context of a once-and-for-all change in the level of the nominal money supply. It would be a short step from this result to the conclusion that the inflation rate—the percentage rate of change of the price level—always equals the percentage rate of growth of the money supply. However, in light of the evidence just cited, such a conclusion would be a misleading oversimplification.

It is certainly true that if real balances are to remain constant while the nominal quantity of money grows, the price level must rise at the same rate as the quantity of money. Thus, holding real balances constant, an increase in the rate of monetary expansion will lead to an equal increase in the inflation rate. However, if the demand for real balances is inversely related to the expected rate of inflation, and if the expected rate of inflation varies with the current rate, it is not valid to assume that real balances remain constant when the rate of monetary expansion, and hence the inflation rate, increases. They will fall, so that, for a while after the increase in the rate of monetary expansion, prices will rise more rapidly than nominal balances. The inflation rate will "overshoot" its long-run equilibrium value. It is only when real balances have fallen to a level compatible with an inflation rate equal to the new rate of monetary expansion that such an equilibrium inflation rate can in fact be generated.

This effect is illustrated in Figure 13.1. On the horizontal axis we measure time, and on the vertical axis nominal money balances and the price level (M and p, respectively). We use a logarithmic scale on the vertical axis, so that a straight line relating a variable to time indicates a constant percentage rate of growth. If we begin with a given rate of money growth at time zero, then prices will rise at the same rate, and the logarithm of real balances will be given by the constant distance $M - p$. If, at time T, the rate of money growth increases, as shown by the kink in the line M-M, we know both that the rate of inflation (the slope of p-p) must increase and that $M - p$ must decrease. It follows that, at T, the line p-p is not merely kinked, but rather is displaced upward. Clearly, if inflation is eventually to settle down on p-p again, it must, for some finite period, run at a rate faster than that given by the slope of that line.

There is no a priori reason to suppose that the time that must elapse for a new equilibrium inflation rate to be reached will be short or that the path by which the inflation rate approaches its long-run

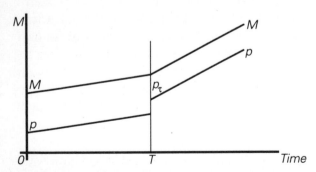

Figure 13.1 The relationship between money and the price level. The broken line p-p depicts the equilibrium time path for the price level, given that money grows along the line M-M. When at time T, money growth increases, so does the equilibrium inflation rate. However, the logarithm of equilibrium money holdings (M-p) must fall at this point too, and so prices must rise at a rate faster than the slope of $p_t p$, in order to restore equilibrium between the supply and demand for money.

equilibrium value after initially overshooting it will be smooth and monotonic. Indeed, it cannot be taken for granted that its equilibrium value will ever be reached. If the demand for money is very sensitive to the expected inflation rate, and if the expected inflation rate is very sensitive either to actual inflation or to the rate of monetary expansion itself, then a self-generating inflation resulting from a so-called flight from money is at least a logical possibility. Empirical work on the relationship between demand for money and expected inflation rate suggests that it is not usually sensitive enough for inflation to become self-generating (see, for example, Cagan, 1956), but if the time path the inflation rate takes toward a new equilibrium value after the rate of monetary expansion changes depends on the behavior over time of the money-holding public's expectations about the inflation rate, then the other less extreme possibilities noted above cannot be ruled out as being empirically important. Thus, Dutton (1971), following up Cagan's (1956) analysis, was able to show that if inflation expectations were formed by an error-learning process, and if all other variables affecting the demand for money remained constant, a cyclical time path for the inflation rate after a once-and-for-all change in the rate of monetary expansion was a distinct empirical possibility.

This same characteristic of the demand-for-money function has implications for the conduct of anti-inflation policy, too. It creates what is often called a *re-entry* problem. It might seem that the monetary policy required to rid the economy of inflation is simple, namely, a reduction in the rate of growth of the nominal money supply. Now it is true that if lower inflation is to be sustained once it is achieved, monetary expansion must be held at a lower level. But during the transition from high to low inflation, agents' demand for real balances will grow. It can be satisfied either by forcing inflation temporarily below its long-run level and allowing real balances to expand by that route or by having nominal money temporarily grow faster than prices are rising. The first of these alternatives might be difficult to engineer, particularly if the target rate of inflation is close to zero, so that falling prices would be needed to get real balances to grow. The second looks more attractive, but requires careful manipulation of the rate of growth of money to achieve a smooth re-entry to lower inflation. Recognizing that other variables, such as output, vary with the inflation rate, and allowing for the fact that the formation of expectations about inflation is likely to be a good deal more complex than a simple error-learning process only make it more likely that the interaction of money and inflation in the real world will be complex. Hence the re-entry to lower inflation problem becomes difficult indeed to cope with.

One further important conclusion follows from all this. The fact that it is difficult to observe a close relationship between fluctuations in the monetary expansion rate and the inflation rate on a quarter-by-quarter or even year-by-year basis does not mean that monetary expansion can be ruled out as a major cause of inflation. Such a relationship should be observable only when the expected rate of inflation is more or less constant and when other variables affecting the demand for money are not changing much, and the real world seldom if ever generates such simple experiments for us.

INTERPRETING INSTABILITY IN THE DEMAND-FOR MONEY FUNCTION

The discussion so far in this chapter has been carried on without reference to the instability problems that were discussed at the end of Chapter 12. It is important to keep a sense of proportion about these difficulties because they have not cast doubt on all we thought we had learned from earlier work. In particular, recent evidence gives us no reason to doubt that the demand for money is systematically related to the opportunity cost of holding it, that current income alone is probably an inadequate scale variable in the relationship, and so on. Rather, recent evidence has shown that when we allow for the effects of the variables which theory tells us are important on the demand for money, there still remain certain systematic shifts that need to be explained. We have seen that two lines of enquiry are promising in this context, and both have rather general implications for the manner in which we think about the role of money in the macroeconomic system.

First, we have seen that institutional change is a plausible explanation of at least some of the changes that have taken place in the demand-for-money function in a number of countries over the last two decades. Furthermore, recent work on earlier periods suggests that such change has been influencing the demand-for-money function for virtually as long as recorded data permit the problem to be investigated. That this should be the case is not really surprising. It has already been noted that money's means-of-exchange role seems to be particularly relevant to explaining the demand for it, and we have also seen that Irving Fisher, whose work summed up a considerable tradition in monetary economics, long ago pointed to the importance of institutional and technical factors as determinants of the aggregate transactions demand for money. However, if this result is unsurprising, it nevertheless has important implications for the way in which we think about monetary policy, because institutional change, which has been a recurring phenomenon in the past, is also likely to be such in the future.

Any monetary authority seeking to ensure that the behavior of the money supply over time is consistent with low and stable inflation and steady growth in real income must constantly be on the lookout for institutional change. To achieve its goals, the authority must adapt the behavior of the supply of whatever monetary aggregate it is controlling to the shifts in demand such change might bring. This in turn means that suggestions, such as that of Friedman (1960), for removing discretion from monetary authorities by seeking to legislate a preannounced manner of behavior for a chosen monetary aggregate, forevermore into the future, simply do not provide a viable way of ensuring monetary stability. This is not just because institutional change is unpredictable, although it often is, particularly when it results from technological innovations. It is also because any attempt to impose some sort of monetary rule on the system will itself be likely to provoke reactions on the part of those particularly affected by it. As was noted above, some of the innovations in the U.S. financial system that took place in the 1970s were probably partly a side effect of regulation. This is not to say that monetary authorities should not announce their policy plans or that they should give up any attempt to control the growth of the money supply, defined one way or another, but it is to say that "Goodhart's Law"—that any monetary aggregate chosen as a policy instrument will quickly see its significance in the financial system change—requires that the authorities constantly monitor the private sector's response to their actions and allow for that response in their own behavior.[1]

The 1970s and 1980s, which generated so many of our concerns about the stability of the demand-for-money function, were also decades of considerable turbulence in the conduct of monetary policy. The second promising line of enquiry into the causes of shifts in the demand for money referred to above starts from the simple proposition that it is unlikely that this was simply a matter of coincidence. As was argued in Part I of this book, we want to know about the demand function for money in the first place so that we may make predictions about the effects of changes in the money supply on variables such as interest rates, real income, and prices. At times when the supply of money is fluctuating rapidly, so, too, will these variables fluctuate. The interaction of the supply of money with the variables determining the demand for it is inherently dynamic; it takes place over time. We have seen, both as an analytic and an empirical matter, that the behavior of expectations

---

[1] Goodhart's law is named after Professor Charles Goodhart, formerly of the Bank of England, and reflects his frustration with the difficulties encountered by that institution in coping with institutional change in the United Kingdom.

about the time path of prices and output plays a key role in the mechanisms linking the supply of money to the variables it influences. Moreover, the rational expectations idea suggests that the behavior of those expectations will be influenced by the behavior of the money supply. Thus, when the money supply fluctuates a great deal and in an unpredictable manner, not only ought we to expect the arguments of the demand-for-money function to fluctuate a great deal, but we ought also to expect the dynamic processes through which the money supply influences those variables to be complex and hence difficult to model empirically. It is precisely these processes that error-correction analysis enables us to describe, and, as we have noted, their application has produced abundant evidence of the complexity in question.

Though the foregoing argument is about the stability over time of the transmission mechanism that links the behavior of the money supply to the variables monetary policy influences, it is of direct relevance to the question of the stability of the demand-for-money function. The demand-for-money relationships that gave the most trouble in the early 1970s were so-called short-run ones, relationships that included a lagged dependent variable among their arguments; it has been argued that the lagged dependent variable is needed in such a relationship to allow for the fact that the adjustment over time of the price level in the face of monetary disturbances is slow. This buffer stock interpretation was advanced or discussed in one form or another by Carr (1983), Carr and Darby (1981), Coats (1982), Gordon (1983), Judd and Scadding (1982a), Laidler (1980, 1982, 1984), and Motley (1983); but, as we have noted, work such as that of MacKinnon and Milbourne (1988) and Hendry and Ericsson (1991b) shows that a simple version of this interpretation, in which money affects only the price level without impinging upon other variables in the demand function, cannot be sustained in the face of empirical evidence. However, as we have also noted, in the present state of knowledge, we cannot rule out the more general conjecture that the error-correction mechanisms, which earlier work tried to summarize in a single coefficient attached to a lagged dependent variable, involve a whole complex of dynamic interactions linking money to prices through a transmission mechanism that involves fluctuations in interest rates and output, not to mention feedbacks to the behavior of the money supply itself. If this conjecture has merit, it is hardly surprising that the traditional short-run demand-for-money function gave trouble in the turbulent 1970s and 1980s, that the error-correction mechanisms which data for those years generate are complicated, and that we are a long way from understanding the underlying processes that generate the dynamic behavior in question.

CONCLUDING COMMENT

A chapter that is itself a summing up needs no long concluding section. Nevertheless, one implication of the preceding argument, obvious though it may be, needs to be addressed explicitly. Our discussion of the dynamics of the short-run demand-for-money function and their relationship to the transmission mechanism of monetary policy and the implications of the rational expectations notion for their stability and predictability has been cast in terms of empirical problems that have been encountered with data generated by the 1970s and 1980s. However, the discussion is quite general in nature. It is relevant to any time and place, although it is likely to be of particular importance in periods of instability in monetary policy. The last twenty years or so has certainly been such a period, but it is by no means the only one for which we have data.

If the arguments we have considered are valid, they ought to have readily observable implications for other times and places as well, for example, the United States in the 1930s or the United Kingdom in the 1920s. Moreover, even data generated by more tranquil times might turn out to be open to reinterpretation in matters of detail in their light. Though it would be surprising if work on these matters radically altered some of the more robust conclusions we have developed in this book— for example, about the superior performance of models of the demand for money based on its means-of-exchange role and about the importance of the rate of interest as an influence on the demand for money— one cannot be sure of such things until the issues have been explicitly addressed. Thus, the reader is reminded of the significance of the word *tentative* in the title of this chapter.

Bibliography

Adekunle, J. O. 1968. "The Demand for Money: Evidence from Developed and Less Developed Countries." *IMF Staff Papers,* 15 (July), 220–266.

Akerlof, G. 1973. "The Demand for Money: A General Equilibrium Theoretic Approach." *Review of Economics Studies,* 40 (January), 115–130.

Artis, M. J., and Lewis, M. K. 1976. "The Demand for Money in the United Kingdom, 1963–1973." *Manchester School,* 44 (June), 147–181.

Axilrod, S., et al. 1977. "The Impact of the Payment of Interest on Demand Deposits." Board of Governors of the Federal Reserve System.

Bank of England. 1970. "The Importance of Money." *Bank of England Quarterly Bulletin,* 10 (June), 159–198.

Barnett, W. 1980. "Economic Monetary Aggregates: An Application of Index Numbers and Aggregation Theory." *Journal of Econometrics,* 14 (September), 11–48.

———. W. 1990. "Developments in Monetary Aggregation Theory." *Journal of Policy Modeling,* 12 (Summer), 205–258.

Barr, D. G., and Cuthbertson, K. 1991. "Neoclassical Consumer Demand Theory and the Demand for Money." *Economic Journal,* 101 (July), 855–876.

Barro, R. J. 1977. "Unanticipated Money Growth and Unemployment in the United States." *American Economic Review,* 67 (March), 101–115.

———. 1978. "Unanticipated Money, Output, and the Price Level in the United States." *Journal of Political Economy,* 86 (August), S49–80.

———. 1984. *Macroeconomics.* New York: Wiley.

Barro, R. J., and Santomero, A. J. 1972. "Household Money Holdings and the Demand Deposit Rate." *Journal of Money, Credit and Banking,* 4 (May), 397–413.

Baumol, W. J. 1952. "The Transactions Demand for Cash: An Inventory Theoretic Approach." *Quarterly Journal of Economics,* 66 (November), 545–556.

Becker, W., and Bental, B. Undated. "Regulation Q and the Effective Rate of Return on Demand, Savings, and Time Deposits." University of Minnesota.

Bordo, M., and Jonung, L. 1981. "The Long-Run Behavior of the Income Velocity of Money in Five Advanced Countries, 1879–1975—An Institutional Approach." *Economic Inquiry,* 19 (January), 96–116.

———. 1987. *The Long-Run Behavior of the Velocity of Circulation: The International Evidence.* New York: Cambridge University Press.

———. 1990. "The Long-Run Behavior of Velocity: The Institutional Approach Revisited." *Journal of Policy Modeling,* 12 (Summer), 165–197.

Bordo, M. D., and Marcotte, I. A. 1987. "Purchasing Power Parity in Colonial America: Some Evidence for South Carolina, 1732–1774: A Comment On The Michener Paper," in K. Brunner and A. H. Meltzer (eds.), *Empirical Studies of Velocity, Real Exchange Rates, Unemployment and Productivity* (Carnegie-Rochester Conference Series, vol. 27). Amsterdam: North-Holland.

Boughton, J. 1979. "Demand for Money in Major OECD Countries." *OECD Economic Outlook* (January), 35–37.

———. 1991. "Long-Run Money Demand in Large Industrial Countries." *IMF Staff Papers,* 38 (March), 1–32.

Boughton, J., and Tavlas, G. 1990. "Modeling Money Demand in Large Industrial Countries: Buffer Stock and Error Correction Approaches." *Journal of Policy Modeling,* 12 (Summer), 433-462.

Bronfenbrenner, M., and Mayer, T. 1960. "Liquidity Functions in the American Economy." *Econometrica,* 28 (October), 810–834.

Brown, A. J. 1939. "Interest, Prices and the Demand for Idle Money." *Oxford Economic Papers,* 2 (May), 46–49.

Brunner, K., and Meltzer, A. H. 1963. "Predicting Velocity: Implications for Theory and Policy." *Journal of Finance,* 18 (May), 319–354.

———. 1964. "Some Further Evidence on Supply and Demand Functions for Money." *Journal of Finance,* 19 (May), 240–283.

———. 1967. "Economies of Scale in Cash Balances Reconsidered." *Quarterly Journal of Economics,* 81 (August), 422–436.

Cagan, P. 1956. "The Monetary Dynamics of Hyperinflation." in M. Friedman (ed.), *Studies in the Quantity Theory of Money.* Chicago: University of Chicago Press.

Cagan, P., and Schwartz, A. J. 1975. "Has the Growth of Money Substitutes Hindered Monetary Policy?" *Journal of Money, Credit and Banking,* 7 (May), 137–160.

Calliari, S.; Spinelli, F.; and Verga, G. 1984. "Money Demand in Italy: A Few More Results." *Manchester School,* 52 (June), 141–159.

Campbell, C. D. 1970. "The Velocity of Money and the Rate of Inflation: Recent Experience in South Korea and Brazil," in D. Meiselman (ed.), *Varieties of Monetary Experience.* Chicago: University of Chicago Press.

Caramazza, F.; Hostland, D.; and Poloz, S. 1990. "The Demand for Money and Monetary Policy in Canada." *Journal of Policy Modeling,* 12 (Summer), 387–426.

Carlson, J. A., and Parkin, J. M. 1975. "Inflation Expectations." *Economica,* NS42 (May), 123–138.

Carr, J. 1983. "Demand for Money: A Reinterpretation." University of Toronto (mimeo).

Carr, J., and Darby, M. 1981. "The Role of Money Supply Shocks in the Short-Run Demand for Money." *Journal of Monetary Economics,* 8 (September), 183–199.

Chow, G. 1966. "On the Long-Run and Short-Run Demand for Money." *Journal of Political Economy,* 74 (April), 111–131.

Clark, C. 1973, "The Demand for Money and the Choice of a Permanent Income Estimate: Some Canadian Evidence, 1926–1965." *Journal of Money, Credit and Banking,* 5 (August), 773–793.

Clinton, K. 1973. "The Demand for Money in Canada, 1955–1970: Some Single-Equation Estimates and Stability Tests." *Canadian Journal of Economics,* 6 (February), 53–61.

Clower, R. W. 1967. "A Reconsideration of the Microfoundations of Monetary Theory." *Western Economic Journal,* 6 (December), 1–8.

Clower, R. W., and Howitt, P. W. 1978. "The Transactions Theory of the Demand for Money: A Reconsideration." *Journal of Political Economy,* 86 (June), 449–466.

Coats, W. L., Jr. 1982. "Modelling the Short-Run Demand for Money with Exogenous Supply." *Economic Inquiry,* 20 (April), 222–239.

Cockerline, J. P., and Murray, J. D. 1981. "A Comparison of Alternative Methods of Monetary Aggregation: Some Preliminary Evidence." Bank of Canada Technical Report 28.

Cooley, T. F., and Leroy, S. F. 1981. "Identification and Estimation of Money Demand." *American Economic Review,* 71 (December), 825–844.

Courchene, T. J., and Kelly, A. K. 1971. "Money Supply and Money Demand: An Econometric Analysis for Canada." *Journal of Money, Credit and Banking,* 3 (May), 219–243.

Courchene, T. J., and Shapiro, H. T. 1964. "The Demand for Money: A Note from the Time Series." *Journal of Political Economy,* 42 (October), 498–503.

Crouch, R. L. 1971. "Tobin vs. Keynes on Liquidity Preference." *The Review of Economics and Statistics,* 53 (November), 368–371.

Cuthbertson, K. 1991. "Modelling the Demand for Money." in C. J. Green and D. T. Llewellyn (eds.), *Surveys in Monetary Economics,* vol. 1. Oxford: Basil Blackwell for the Money Study Group.

Cuthbertson, K., and Taylor, M. P. 1990. "Money Demand, Expectations and the Forward Looking Model." *Journal of Policy Modeling,* 12 (Summer), 289–316.

Deaver, J. V. 1970. "The Chilean Inflation and the Demand for Money," in D. Meiselman (ed.), *Varieties of Monetary Experience.* Chicago: University of Chicago Press.

DeLeeuw, F. 1965. *The Demand for Money, Speed of Adjustment, Interest Rates and Wealth* (Staff Economic Studies, Board of Governors of the Federal Reserve System). Washington, D.C.

Dickey, D. A.; Jansen, D. W.; and Thornton, D. C., 1991. "A Primer on Cointegration with an Application to Money and Income." *FRB of St. Louis Review,* 73 (March-April), 58–78.

Diewert, W. E. 1974. "Intertemporal Consumer Theory and the Demand for Durables." *Econometrica,* 42 (May), 497–516.

Diz, A. C. 1970. "Money and Prices in Argentina, 1935–62," in D. Meiselman (ed.), *Varieties of Monetary Experience.* Chicago: University of Chicago Press.

Dotsey, M. 1988. "The Demand for Currency in the United States." *Journal of Money, Credit and Banking,* 20 (February), 22–40.

Dowd, K. 1990. "The Value of Time and the Transactions Demand for Money." *Journal of Money, Credit and Banking,* 22 (February), 51–64.

Dutton, D. S. 1971. "The Demand for Money and the Price Level." *Journal of Political Economy,* 79 (September-October), 1161–1170.

Dutton, D. S., and Gramm, W. P. 1973. "Transactions Costs, the Wage Rate, and the Demand for Money." *American Economic Review,* 63 (September), 652–665.

Eden, B. 1976. "On the Specification of the Demand for Money: The Real Rate of Return versus the Rate of Inflation." *Journal of Political Economy,* 84 (December), 1353–1360.

Edgeworth, F. Y. 1888. "The Mathematical Theory of Banking." *Journal of the Royal Statistical Society,* 51, 113–127.

Eisner, R. 1971. "Non-linear Estimates of the Liquidity Trap." *Econometrica,* 39 (September), 861–864.

Entzler, J.; Johnson, L.; and Paulus, J. 1976. "Some Problems of Money Demand." *Brookings Papers on Economic Activity,* 1, 261–280.

Faig, M. 1989. "Seasonal Fluctuations and the Demand for Money." *Quarterly Journal of Economics,* 104 (November), 847–861.

Fase, M. M. G., and Kure, J. B. 1975. "The Demand for Money in Thirteen European and Non-European Countries: A Tabular Survey." *Kredit und Kapital,* 3, 410–419.

Feige, E, 1964. *The Demand for Liquid Assets: A Temporal Cross-Section Analysis.* Englewood Cliffs, N.J.: Prentice-Hall.

――――. 1967. "Expectations and Adjustments in the Monetary Sector." *American Economic Review,* 57 (May), 462–473.

――――. 1974. "Alternative Temporal Cross-Section Specifications of the Demand for Demand Deposits," in H. G. Johnson and A. R. Nobay (eds.), *Issues in Monetary Economics.* London: Oxford University Press.

Feige, E., and Pearce, D. K. 1976. "Substitutability Between Money and Near Monies: A Survey of the Time Series Evidence" (SSRI Workshop Series 7617). University of Wisconsin (mimeo).

Fisher, D. 1968. "The Demand for Money in Britain: Quarterly Results 1951 to 1967." *Manchester School,* 36 (December) 329–344.

Fisher, I. 1911. *The Purchasing Power of Money.* New York: Macmillan.

Freedman, C. 1983. "Financial Innovation in Canada: Causes and Consequences." *American Economic Review,* 73 (May, Papers and Proceedings), 101–106.

Frenkel, J. 1977. "The Forward Exchange Rate, Expectations and the Demand for Money: The German Hyperinflation." *American Economic Review,* 67 (September), 653–670.

Fried, J. 1973. "Money, Exchange and Growth." *Western Economic Journal,* 11 (September), 285–301.

Fried, J., and Howitt, P. W. 1983. "The Effects of Inflation on Real Interest Rates." *American Economic Review,* 73 (December), 968–980.

Friedman, B. M. 1978. "Crowding Out or Crowding In? The Economic Consequences of Financing Government Deficits." *Brookings Papers on Economic Activity,* 3, 593–641.

Friedman, M. 1956. "The Quantity Theory of Money, A Restatement," in M. Friedman (ed.), *Studies in the Quantity Theory of Money.* Chicago: University of Chicago Press.

――――. 1959. "The Demand for Money—Some Theoretical and Empirical Results." *Journal of Political Economy,* 67 (June), 327–351.

――――. 1960. *A Program for Monetary Stability.* New York: Fordham University Press.

――――. 1966. "Interest Rates and the Demand for Money." *Journal of Law and Economics,* 9 (October), 71–85.

――――. 1969. "The Optimum Quantity of Money," in *The Optimum Quantity of Money.* London: Macmillan.

――――. 1977. "Time Perspective in Demand for Money." *Scandinavian Journal of Economics,* 79, 397–416.

Friedman, M., and Schwartz, A. J. 1970. *The Monetary Statistics of the United States: Estimates, Sources, Methods.* New York: Columbia University Press for the NBER.

――――. 1982. *Monetary Trends in the United States and the United Kingdom.* Chicago: University of Chicago Press for the NBER.

Frowen, S. F., and Arestis, P. 1976. "Some Investigations of Demand and Supply Functions for Money in the Federal Republic of Germany, 1965–74." *Weltwirtschaftliches Archiv,* 112, 136–164.

Gandolfi, A. E., and Lothian, J. R. 1983. "International Price Behaviour and the Demand for Money." *Economic Inquiry,* 21 (July), 295–311.

Gandolfo, G., and Padoan, P. C. 1984. *A Disequilibrium Model of Real and Financial Accumulation in an Open Economy.* Berlin: Springer.

Garcia, G., and Pak, S. 1979. "Some Clues in the Case of the Missing Money." *American Economic Review,* 69 (May, Papers and Proceedings), 330–334.

Gilbert, J. C. 1953. "The Demand for Money: The Development of an Economic Concept." *Journal of Political Economy,* 61 (April), 144–159.

Goldfeld, S. M. 1973. "The Demand for Money Revisited." *Brookings Papers on Economic Activity,* 3, 577–638.

———. 1976. "The Case of the Missing Money." *Brookings Papers on Economic Activity,* 3, 683–730.

Goldman, S. M. 1974. "Flexibility and the Demand for Money." *Journal of Economic Theory,* 9 (October), 203–222.

Goodfriend, M. 1985. "Reinterpreting Money Demand Regressions," in K. Brunner and A. H. Meltzer (eds.), *Understanding Monetary Regimes* (Carnegie-Rochester Conference Series, vol. 22). Amsterdam; North-Holland.

Goodhart, C. E. A. 1982. "Disequilibrium Money—A Note." Bank of England (mimeo).

Gordon, R. J. 1983. "The 1981–82 Velocity Decline: A Structural Shift in Income or Money Demand?" in FRB San Francisco, *Monetary Targeting and Velocity.*

———. 1984. "The Short-Run Demand for Money—A Reconsideration." *Journal of Money, Credit and Banking,* 16 (February), 403–434.

Gray, M. R., and Parkin, J. M. 1973. "Portfolio Diversification as Optimal Precautionary Behaviour," in M. Morishima et al., *Theories of Demand, Real and Monetary.* London: Oxford University Press.

Gray, M. R.; Ward R. J.; and Zis, G. 1976. "World Demand for Money," in J. M. Parkin and G. Zis (eds.), *Inflation in the World Economy.* Manchester: University of Manchester Press.

Gregory, A. W., and McAleer, M. 1981. "Simultaneity and the Demand for Money in Canada: Comments and Extensions." *Canadian Journal of Economics,* 14 (August), 488–496.

Grice, J., and Bennett, A. 1984. "Wealth and the Demand for £M3 in the United Kingdom 1963–1978." *Manchester School,* 52 (September), 239–270.

Hafer, R. W. 1982. "The Stability of the Short-Run Demand for Money Function 1920–1939." FRB of St. Louis Research Paper 82-009.

Hafer, R. W., and Hein, S. E. 1979. "Evidence on the Temporal Stability of the Demand for Money Relationship in the United States." *FRB of St. Louis Review,* 61 (December), 3–14.

Hafer, R. W., and Jansen, D. W. 1991. "The Demand for Money in the United

States: Evidence from Cointegration Tests." *Journal of Money, Credit and Banking,* 23 (May) 155–168.

Hamburger, M. J. 1966. "The Demand for Money by Households, Money Substitutes and Monetary Policy." *Journal of Political Economy,* 74 (December), 600–623.

———. 1977a. "The Demand for Money in an Open Economy: Germany and the United Kingdom." *Journal of Monetary Economics,* 3 (January), 25–40.

———. 1977b. "The Behavior of the Money Stock: Is There a Puzzle?" *Journal of Monetary Economics,* 3 (July), 265–288.

———. 1983. "Recent Velocity Behavior, The Demand for Money and Monetary Policy," in FRB San Francisco, *Monetary Targeting and Velocity.*

Harberger, A. C. 1963. "The Dynamics of Inflation in Chile," in C. F. Christ et al., *Measurement in Economics: Essays in Mathematical Economics and Econometrics in Memory of Yehuda Grunfeld.* Stanford, Calif.: Stanford University Press.

Heller, H. R., and Khan, M. 1979. "The Demand for Money and the Term Structure of Interest Rates." *Journal of Political Economy,* 87 (February), 109–129.

Hendry, D, F., and Ericsson, N. R. 1983. "Assertion Without Empirical Basis: An Empirical Appraisal of Friedman and Schwartz' Monetary Trends in the . . . United Kingdom," in Bank of England Panel of Academic Consultants, *Monetary Trends in the United Kingdom* (Panel Paper 22).

———. 1991a. "An Econometric Analysis of U.K. Money Demand in *Monetary Trends . . .* by Milton Friedman and Anna J. Schwartz." *American Economic Review,* 81 (February) 8–38.

———. 1991b. "Modelling the Demand for Narrow Money in the United Kingdom and the United States." *European Economic Review,* 35 (May), 833–881.

Hendry, D. F., and Mizon, G. 1978. "Serial Correlation as a Convenient Simplification, Not a Nuisance, A Comment on a Study of the Demand for Money by the Bank of England." *Economic Journal,* 88 (September), 549–563.

Hicks, J. R., 1935. "A Suggestion for Simplifying the Theory of Money." *Economica,* 2 (February), 1–19.

Hu, T. W. 1971. "Hyperinflation and the Dynamics of the Demand for Money in China, 1945–1949." *Journal of Political Economy,* 79 (January-February), 186–195.

Hynes, A. 1967. "The Demand for Money and Monetary Adjustments in Chile." *Review of Economic Studies,* 34 (July)), 285–294.

Jacobs, R. L. 1975. "A Difficulty with Monetarist Models of Hyper-inflation." *Economic Inquiry,* 13 (September), 332–360.

Johnson, H. G. 1963. "Notes on the Theory of Transactions Demand for Cash." *Indian Journal of Economics,* 44 (172), part 1 (July), 1–11.

———. 1969. "Inside Money, Outside Money, Income Wealth and Welfare in

Monetary Theory," *Journal of Money, Credit and Banking,* 1 (February), 30–45.

Johnston, J. 1972. *Econometric Methods.* New York: McGraw-Hill.

Jonson, P. D. 1976a. "Money and Economic Activity in the Open Economy: The United Kingdom 1880–1970." *Journal of Political Economy,* 84 (September-October), 979–1012.

———. 1976b. "Money Prices and Output: An Integrative Essay." *Kredit und Kapital,* 4, 499–518.

Jonson, P. D.; Moses, E.; and Wymer, C. 1976. "A Minimal Model of the Australian Economy." Reserve Bank of Australia Discussion Paper 7601. Also in *Conference in Applied Economic Research.* Sydney: Reserve Bank of Australia, 1977.

Judd, J., and Scadding, J. 1982a. "The Search for a Stable Money Demand Function: A Survey of the Post-1973 Literature." *Journal of Economic Literature,* 20 (September), 993–1023.

———. 1982b. "Financial Change and Monetary Targeting in the United States," in *Interest-Rate Deregulation and Monetary Policy,* Asilomar Conference. San Francisco: Federal Reserve Bank of San Francisco.

Kanniainen, V., and Tarkka, J. 1983. "The Demand for Money: Microfoundations for the Shock Absorption Approach." Bank of Finland (mimeo).

Karni, E. 1972. "A Note on the Transactions Money Demand and the Term Structure of Interest Rates." Ohio State University, Division for Economic Research, Report 7232.

———. 1974. "The Value of Time and the Demand for Money." *Journal of Money, Credit and Banking,* 6 (February), 45–64.

Kavanagh, N. J., and Walters, A. A. 1966. "The Demand for Money in the United Kingdom 1877–1961: Preliminary Findings." *Bulletin of the Oxford University Institute of Economics and Statistics,* 28 (May), 93–116.

Keynes, J. M. 1923. *A Tract on Monetary Reform.* London: Macmillan.

———. 1930. *A Treatise on Money.* London and New York: Macmillan.

———. 1936. *The General Theory of Employment, Interest, and Money.* London and New York: Macmillan.

Khan, M. 1973. "A Note on the Secular Behaviour of Velocity within the Context of the Inventory Theoretic Model of the Demand for Money." *Manchester School,* 51 (June), 207–213.

———. 1974. "The Stability of the Demand for Money Function in the U.S. 1901–1965." *Journal of Political Economy,* 82 (November-December), 1205–1220.

Khoury, M., and Myhrman, J. 1975. "Econometric Analysis of the Demand for Money in Sweden: 1909–1968." University of Stockholm (mimeo).

Khusro, A. M. 1952. "An Investigation of Liquidity Preference." *Yorkshire Bulletin of Economic and Social Research,* 4 (January), 1–20.

Klein, B. 1974a. "The Competitive Supply of Money." *Journal of Money, Credit and Banking,* 6 (November), 423–454.

———. 1974b. "Competitive Interest Payments on Bank Deposits and the

Long-Run Demand for Money." *American Economic Review,* 64 (December), 931–949.

———. 1975. "Our New Monetary Standard: The Measurement and Effects of Price Uncertainty 1880–1973." *Economic Inquiry,* 13 (December), 461–484.

———. 1977. "The Demand for Quality Adjusted Cash Balances: Price Uncertainty in the U.S. Demand for Money Function." *Journal of Political Economy,* 85 (November), 691–716.

Kliman, M. L., and Oksanen, E. H. 1973. "The Keynesian Demand for Money Function: A Comment." *Journal of Money, Credit and Banking,* 5 (February), 215–220.

Klovland, J. T. 1983. "The Demand for Money in Secular Perspective: The Case of Norway 1867–1980." *European Economic Review,* 22 (July), 193–218.

Knoester, A. 1979. "Theoretical Principles of the Buffer Mechanism, Monetary Quasi-Equilibrium and Its Spillover Effects." Erasmus University, Rotterdam.

Kohli, U. R. 1981. "Permanent Income in the Consumption and the Demand for Money Functions." *Journal of Monetary Economics,* 7 (March), 227–238.

Kostas, P., and Khouja, M. W. 1969. "The Keynesian Demand for Money Function: Another Look and Some Additional Evidence." *Journal of Money, Credit and Banking,* 1 (November), 765–777.

Koyck, L. M. 1954. *Distributed Lags and Investment Analysis.* Amsterdam: North-Holland.

Laidler, D. 1966a. "Some Evidence on the Demand for Money." *Journal of Political Economy,* 74 (February), 55–68.

———. 1966b. "The Rate of Interest and the Demand for Money—Some Empirical Evidence." *Journal of Political Economy,* 74 (December), 545–555.

———. 1969. "The Definition of Money: Theoretical and Empirical Problems." *Journal of Money, Credit and Banking,* 1 (August), 508–525.

———. 1971. "The Influence of Money on Economic Activity: A Survey of Some Current Problems," in G. Clayton, J. C. Gilbert, and R. Sedgwick (eds.), *Monetary Theory and Policy in the 1970s.* London: Oxford University Press.

———. 1980. "The Demand for Money in the United States—Yet Again," in K. Brunner and A. H. Meltzer (eds), *On the State of Macroeconomics* (Carnegie-Rochester Conference Series in Public Policy, vol. 12). Amsterdam: North-Holland.

———. 1982. *Monetarist Perspectives.* Deddington: Philip Allan; Cambridge, Mass.: Harvard University Press.

———. 1984. "The Buffer Stock Notion in Monetary Economics." *Conference Proceedings, Supplement to the Economic Journal,* 94 (March) 17–34.

———. 1990. *Taking Money Seriously.* (Hemel Hempstead: Philip Allan; Cambridge, Mass.: MIT Press.

Laidler, D., and Bentley B. 1983. "A Small Macro-Model of the Post-War United States." *Manchester School* 51 (Dec) 317–340.

Laidler, D., and Estrin, S. 1989. *Introduction to Microeconomics,* 3rd ed. Hemel Hempstead: Philip Allan.

Laidler, D., and Parkin, J. M. 1970. "The Demand for Money in the United Kingdom 1956–1967: Preliminary Estimates." *Manchester School,* 38 (September), 187–208.

———. 1975. "Inflation—A Survey." *Economic Journal,* 85 (December), 741–809.

Lane, T. D. 1990. "Costly Portfolio Adjustment and the Short-Run Demand for Money." *Economic Inquiry,* 28 (July), 466–487.

Latané, H. A. 1954. "Cash Balances and the Interest Rate—A Pragmatic Approach." *Review of Economics and Statistics,* 36 (November), 456–460.

Lee, T. H. 1967. "Alternative Interest Rates and the Demand for Money: The Empirical Evidence." *American Economic Review,* 57 (December), 1168–1181.

———. 1969. "Alternative Interest Rates and the Demand for Money—Reply." *American Economic Review,* 59 (June), 412–417.

Leponiemi, A. 1966. *On the Demand and Supply of Money: The Evidence from the Quarterly Time Series in the United States, in the United Kingdom and Finland.* Helsinki: Finnish Economic Association.

Lerner, E. 1956. "Inflation in the Confederacy 1861–1865," in M. Friedman (ed.), *Studies in the Quantity Theory of Money.* Chicago: University of Chicago Press.

Lewis, M. 1978. "Interest Rates and Monetary Velocity in Australia and the United States." *Economic Record,* 54 (April), 111–126.

Lieberman, C. 1980. "The Long Run and Short Run Demand for Money, Revisited." *Journal of Money, Credit and Banking,* 12 (February), 43–57.

Lothian, J.; Darby, M.; and Tindall, M. 1990. "Buffer Stock Models of the Demand for Money and the Conduct of Monetary Policy." *Journal of Policy Modeling,* 12 (Summer), 325–346.

Lucas, R. E., Jr. 1973. "Some International Evidence on Output Inflation Trade-Offs." *American Economic Review,* 63 (June), 326–334.

———. 1976. "Econometric Policy Evaluation," in K. Brunner and A. H. Meltzer (eds.). *The Phillips Curve and the Labor Market* (Carnegie-Rochester Conference Series, vol. 1). Amsterdam: North-Holland.

———. 1988. "Money Demand in the United States: A Quantitative Review," in K. Brunner and B. T. McCallum (eds.), *Money, Cycles and Exchange Rates: Essays in Honor of Allan H. Meltzer* (Carnegie-Rochester Conference Series, vol. 29) Amsterdam, North-Holland.

MacDonald, R., and Taylor, M. P. 1991. "A Stable U.S. Money Demand Function 1874–1970." Washington, D.C.: IMF (mimeo).

Macesich, G. 1970. "Supply and Demand for Money in Canada," in D. Meiselman (ed.), *Varieties of Monetary Experience.* Chicago: University of Chicago Press.

MacKinnon, J. G., and Milbourne, R. D. 1988. "Are Money Demand Equations Really Price Equations on Their Heads?" *Journal of Applied Econometrics,* 3, 295–305.

Mankiw, G., and Summers, L. 1986. "Money Demand and the Effects of Fiscal Policies." *Journal of Money, Credit and Banking,* 23 (November), 415–429.

Marty, A. 1961. "Gurley and Shaw on Money in a Theory of Finance." *Journal of Political Economy,* 69 (February), 56–62.

Mason, W. 1976. "The Empirical Definition of Money: A Critique," *Economic Inquiry,* 14 (December), 525–538.

Matthews, R. C. O. 1963. "Expenditure Plans and the Uncertainty Motive for Holding Money." *Journal of Political Economy,* 71 (June), 201–218.

McCallum, B. T. 1983. "The Role of Overlapping Generations Models in Monetary Economics," in K. Brunner and A. H. Meltzer (eds.), *Money, Monetary Policy and Financial Institutions* (Carnegie-Rochester Conference Series, vol. 18.) Amsterdam: North-Holland.

————. 1989. *Monetary Economics Theory and Policy.* New York: Macmillan.

McCallum, B. T., and Goodfriend, M. S. 1987. "Demand for Money: Theoretical Studies," in J. Eatwell, M. Millgate, and P. Newman (eds.). *The New Palgrave: A Dictionary of Economics.* London: Macmillan.

Melitz, J. 1976. "Inflationary Expectations and the French Demand for Money 1959-1970." *Manchester School,* 44 (March), 17–41.

Meltzer, A. H. 1963. "The Demand for Money: The Evidence from the Time Series." *Journal of Political Economy,* 71 (June), 219–246.

Meyer, P. A., and Neri, J. A. 1975. "A Keynes-Friedman Money Demand Function." *American Economic Review,* 65 (September), 610–623.

Michaelson, J. B. 1973. *The Term Structure of Interest Rates.* New York and London: Intext.

Michener, R. 1987. "Fixed Exchange Rates and the Quantity Theory in Colonial America," in K. Brunner and A. H. Meltzer (eds.), *Empirical Studies of Velocity, Real Exchange Rates, Unemployment and Productivity* (Carnegie-Rochester Conference Series, vol 27. Amsterdam: North-Holland.

Milbourne, R. D.; Buckholtz, P.; and Wasan, M. T. 1983. "A Theoretical Derivation of the Functional Form of Short-Run Money Holdings." *Review of Economics Studies,* 50 (July), 531–542.

Miller, S. M. 1991. "Monetary Dynamics: An Application of Cointegration and Error Correction Modeling." *Journal of Money, Credit and Banking.* 23 (May), 139–154.

Motley, B. 1983. "Dynamic Adjustment in Money Demand." FRB San Francisco (mimeo).

Mussa, M. 1975. "Adaptive and Regressive Expectations in a Rational Model of the Inflationary Process." *Journal of Monetary Economics,* 1 (October), 423–442.

Muth, J. R. 1961. "Rational Expectations and the Theory of Price Movements." *Econometrica,* 29 (July), 313–335.

Namba, S. 1983. "The Stability of the Demand for Money and the Choice of

Financial Intermediate Targets—An Empirical Study on the Monetary Aspects of Japan." Tokyo, Bank of Japan (mimeo).

Niehans, J., and Schelbert-Syfrig, H. 1966. "Simultaneous Determination of Interest and Prices in Switzerland by a Two-Market Model for Money and Bonds." *Econometrica,* 34 (April), 408–413.

Orr, D. 1970. *Cash Management and the Demand for Money.* New York and London: Praeger.

Parkin, J. M., and Bade, R. 1984. *Modern Macroeconomics.* Oxford: Philip Allan.

Patinkin, D. 1965. *Money, Interest and Prices,* 2d ed. New York: Harper-Collins.

———. 1969. "The Chicago Tradition, The Quantity Theory, and Friedman." *Journal of Money, Credit and Banking,* 1 (February), 46–70.

Perlman, M. 1970. "International Differences in Liquid Asset Portfolios," in D. Meiselman (ed.), *Varieties of Monetary Experience.* Chicago: University of Chicago Press.

Pesek, B. P., and Saving, T. R. 1967. *Money, Wealth and Economic Theory.* New York: Macmillan.

Philips, L. 1978. "The Demand for Leisure and Money." *Econometrica,* 46 (September) 1025–1043.

Pifer, H. W. 1969. "A Nonlinear, Maximum Likelihood Estimate of the Liquidity Trap." *Econometrica,* 37 (April), 324–332.

Pigou, A. C. 1917. "The Value of Money." *Quarterly Journal of Economics,* 37 (November), 38–65.

Poloz, S. 1980. "Simultaneity and the Demand for Money in Canada." *Canadian Journal of Economics,* 13 (August), 402–420.

———. 1982. "The Demand for Money in a Multicurrency World." Ph.D. dissertation, University of Western Ontario.

Porter, R. D., and Mauskopf, E. 1978. "Cash Management and the Recent Shift in the Demand for Demand Deposits." Board of Governors of the Federal Reserve System (unpublished).

Rasche, R. H. 1987. "M_1, Velocity and Interest Rates: Do Stable Relationships Exist?" in K. Brunner and A. H. Meltzer (eds.), *Empirical Studies of Velocity, Real Exchange Rates, Unemployment and Productivity* (Carnegie-Rochester Conference Series, vol. 27). Amsterdam: North-Holland.

———. 1990. "Equilibrium Income and Interest Elasticities of the Demand for M_1 in Japan." *Bank of Japan Monetary and Economic Studies,* 8 (September), 31–58.

Rose, A. K. 1985. "An Alternative Approach to the American Demand for Money." *Journal of Money, Credit and Banking,* 17 (November), 439–455.

Samuelson, P. A. 1958. "An Exact Consumption Loan Model of Interest With or Without the Social Contrivance of Money." *Journal of Political Economy,* 66 (December), 467–482.

Santomero, A. M., and Seater, J. J. 1981. "Partial Adjustment and the

Demand for Money." *American Economic Review,* 71 (September), 566–578.

Sargent, T. J. 1986. *Rational Expectations and Inflation.* New York: Harper-Collins.

Sargent, T. J., and Wallace, N. 1982. "The Real Bills Doctrine Versus the Quantity Theory: A Reconsideration." *Journal of Political Economy,* 90 (December), 1212–1236.

Saving, T. 1971. "Transactions Cost and the Demand for Money." *American Economic Review,* 61 (June), 407–420.

Selden, R. 1956. "Monetary Velocity in the United States," in M. Friedman (ed.), *Studies in the Quantity Theory of Money.* Chicago: University Chicago Press.

Shapiro, A. A. 1973. "Inflation, Lags, and the Demand for Money." *International Economic Review,* 14 (February), 81–96.

Siklos, P. L. 1989. "The End of the Hungarian Hyper-inflation of 1945–1946." *Journal of Money, Credit and Banking,* 21 (May), 135–147.

——— . 1991. "Income Velocity and Institutional Change: Some New Time Series Evidence. 1870–1986." Wilfrid Laurier University (mimeo).

Slovin, M. B., and Sushka, M. E. 1983. "Money, Interest Rates and Risk." *Journal of Monetary Economics,* 12 (September), 475–482.

Smith, B. 1985a. "American Colonial Monetary Regimes: The Failure of the Quantity Theory and Some Evidence in Favour of an Alternative View." *Canadian Journal of Economics,* 18 (August), 531–565.

——— . 1985b. "Some Colonial Evidence on Two Theories of Money: Maryland and the Carolinas." *Journal of Political Economy,* 93 (December), 1178–1211.

Spinelli, F. 1980. "The Demand for Money in the Italian Economy 1867–1965." *Journal of Monetary Economics,* 6 (January), 83–104.

Spitzer, J. J. 1976. "The Demand for Money, the Liquidity Trap and Functional Forms." *International Economic Review,* 17 (February), 220–227.

Starleaf, D. 1970. "The Specification of Money Demand-Supply Models Which Involve the Use of Distributed Lags." *Journal of Finance,* 25 (June), 743–760.

Starleaf, D., and Reimer, R. 1967. "The Keynesian Demand Function for Money: Some Statistical Tests." *Journal of Finance,* 22 (March), 71–76.

Startz, R. 1979. "Implicit Interest on Demand Deposits." *Journal of Monetary Economics,* 5 (October), 515–534.

Sumner, M. 1990a. "Leakages from the Money Demand Function." University of Sussex (mimeo).

——— . 1990b. "Demand for Money in the U.K.: Breadth, Scale and Seasonality." University of Sussex (mimeo).

Teigen, R. 1965. "Demand and Supply Functions for Money in the United States." *Econometrica,* 32 (October), 477–509.

——— . 1971. "The Demand for Money in Norway 1959–1969." *Statokonomisk Tidsskrift,* 3, 65–99.

Tobin, J. 1947. "Liquidity Preference and Monetary Policy." *Review of Economics and Statistics,* 29 (May), 124–131.

———. 1956. "The Interest Elasticity of Transactions Demand for Cash." *Review of Economics and Statistics,* 38 (August), 241–247.

———. 1958. "Liquidity Preference as Behavior Towards Risk." *Review of Economic Studies,* 25 (February), 65–86.

Tucker, D. 1971. "Macroeconomic Models and the Demand for Money Under Market Disequilibrium." *Journal of Money, Credit and Banking,* 3 (February), 57–83.

Vogel, R. C. 1974. "The Dynamics of Inflation in Latin America, 1950–1969." *American Economic Review,* 64 (March), 102–114.

Wallace, N. 1988. "A Suggestion for Oversimplifying the Theory of Money." *Conference Papers,* supplement to *Economic Journal,* 98 (March), 25–36.

Walters, A. A. 1977. "The Demand for Money: The Dynamic Properties of the Multiplier." *Journal of Political Economy,* 75 (January-February), 293–298.

Weinrobe, Maurice D. 1972. "A Simple Model of the Precautionary Demand for Money." *Southern Economic Journal,* 39 (July), 11–18.

Whalen, E. L. 1966. "A Rationalisation of the Precautionary Demand for Cash." *Quarterly Journal of Economics,* 80 (May), 314–324.

Wicksell, K. 1898. *Interest and Prices.* Trans. R. F. Kahn. London: Royal Economic Society, 1936.

Working, E. 1927. "What Do Statistical Demand Curves Show?" Reprinted in G. J. Stigler, and K. E. Boulding (eds.), *Readings in Price Theory.* London: Allen and Unwin, 1953.

Yoshida, T. 1990. "On the Stability of the Japanese Money Demand Function—Estimation Results Using the Error Correction Model." *Bank of Japan Monetary and Economic Studies,* 8 (January), 1–48.

Yoshida, T., and Rasche, R. 1990. "The M_2 Demand in Japan: Shifted and Unstable?" *Bank of Japan Monetary and Economic Studies,* 8 (September), 9–30.

Index